BLACK WEALTH

BLACK WEALTH

Your Road to Small Business Success

ROBERT L. WALLACE

JOHN WILEY & SONS, INC.
New York • Chichester • Weinheim • Brisbane • Singapore • Toronto

This book is printed on acid-free paper. ♾

Published by John Wiley & Sons, Inc.

Published simultaneously in Canada.

First published by Duncan & Duncan, Inc.

ISBN: 0-471-38053-9

Printed in the United States of America.

10 9 8 7 6 5 4 3 2 1

This book is dedicated to my Lord and Savior Jesus Christ.
Without Him, I would never have experienced the joy of being
raised by outstanding parents—Irene, Daniel, and Leon.
Nor would I ever have experienced the true and wonderful love
that I have found in my lovely bride of more than 23 years, Carolyn,
and our five outstanding children,
Robert, Joshua, Collin, Jordan, and Taylor Irene.

Praise God from whom all blessings flow!

Contents

Introduction

Like many others in my generation, I've come to the conclusion that, as we enter a new millennium, the most critical issue facing people of color in America is economic empowerment, or economic justice, as some have coined it. Until we as a nation address this economic quagmire all the symptoms that we typically associate with the impoverished residents of our urban centers (i.e., crime, drugs, fratricide, hopelessness) will persist for yet another one hundred years.

Our economic dilemma troubled me further when I matriculated at the Amos Tuck School of Business at Dartmouth College in 1982. My studies at Dartmouth further exposed the widening gap between black and white Americans. However, as I began exploring solutions to this dilemma I was encouraged by the possibility that entrepreneurship, the accelerated formation of viable businesses in the community, could close the gap. At that point, I began a journey that some said I would never finish. Beginning as a research project, I sought to construct the blueprint for minority and female entrepreneurial success. I have always felt that entrepreneurial success could and should be modeled. I reasoned that if I could identify a large enough group of successful minority and female entrepreneurs and then study their business experiences over a long enough time horizon, I could develop a model of business and entrepreneurial success that could be used by emerging, embryonic, and established minority and female entrepreneurs.

My hypothesis further concluded that if this success model could be effectively constructed, the same model could later be used as a basis for developing training programs, entrepreneurship curricula, audiotapes, videotapes, CD-ROM software, and web-based training particulars. Since the inception of my research, my firm has begun converting the findings of the study into many creative and functional products and services, including training curricula, seminars, training tapes, and web-based training modules. As a matter of fact, our new company, EntreTeach.com, specializes in providing web-based training for minority and female entrepreneurs.

Since the first publication of my book in 1993, I have been interviewed on a host of television, radio, and cable TV programs. My viewpoints on entrepreneurship and economic development have been quoted in the *Wall Street Journal*, on ABC News, BET, and other media. I have lectured at many prestigious colleges and universities across the United States and my book is being used as an entrepreneurship textbook at schools of business throughout the nation. I have addressed groups as diverse as local chambers of commerce, minority business societies, corporate executives, schoolteachers, government workers, politicians, woman entrepreneur societies, and community organizations in most major cities.

Currently I spend from one-third to one-half of my time on the road lecturing and providing workshops and seminars. The mass exposure and rich interaction with people from all over America and other parts of the world have resulted in the formation and refocusing of my views and have shaped my current recommendations on economic development strategies. These new strategies are based on the premise that the only vehicle available for minorities and females to obtain economic freedom and economic parity in America is the entrepreneurship vehicle.

One of the cornerstones of my views on minority entrepreneurship is that it must be viewed simply as a means to an end. The end that the minority and female community should be trying to realize is the accumulation of power. Power, plainly defined, is simply the ability to achieve purpose. While the African American community has labored in building its overall power structure, it is the accumulation of economic power that has especially eluded the community. In my opinion, economic power can be summarized as the accumulation of:

- Land, labor, capital
- Intelligence
- Open access to markets

No matter how we define it, power is the only thing that matters in America or in any other society, particularly a society based upon the economic principles of capitalism. Consequently, if you have no power in America then you are invisible. When you become invisible, you become a nonperson and to all intents and purposes you cease to exist.

When you cease to exist, social and economic policies of the society in which you live begin to reflect your invisibility. Incidents like the Rodney King beating, the waving of the Confederate flag in South Carolina's capital, and the attacks on affirmative action reflect a flagrant disregard for those fighting to be recognized. Unfortunately, social freedom without economic undergirding is like building your house on sand instead of rock. When the strong rains and high tide come crashing into your house, it will be unable to withstand the constant pounding of these relentless forces. Without sufficient undergirding the house will eventually collapse and its members will be scattered across the vast ocean.

Recently, our figurative house as a group has been beaten upon and its foundation compromised. The conservative movement, which has historically been an enemy of minority and female rights, has been emboldened by a recent string of successful skirmishes whose intent is to completely dismantle all governmental efforts to assist minorities and females in their transition into the economic mainstream of America. Most notably was the passing of Proposition 209 in the state of California. This proposition, rather than remedying what's wrong with the affirmative action programs that exist, had the dubious effect of abolishing affirmative action completely. Since Proposition 209, other states have begun to follow California's lead. Even more disturbing attacks on minority and female business programs continue to be launched unabated.

Not only are minorities and females under siege from the legislative maneuvers of those in the conservative movement, but information is also coming forward that suggests that some corporations are solidifying the proverbial glass ceiling—purposely impeding the progress and advancement of blacks and other minorities. The nation was shocked when it learned that senior executives with Texaco Inc. bantered comfortably among themselves, plotting the destruction of documents demanded in a highly visible discrimination case and berating the firm's minority employees with racial epithets. We can only speculate on what effect this type of racism has had on the development and implementation of key corporate policies that would dramatically impact the thousands of Texaco employees across the nation.

There are obviously many more disheartening examples of the

racism, bigotry, and ignorance that confront minorities and females on a daily basis, but my premise is simply that until blacks and other minorities complete the construction of their power base or the triad of power as outlined in Chapter 3 of this book, they will continue to face these hostilities and injustices with even greater frequency.

Early in the book I introduce the concept of the triad of power. In my analysis the triad consists of three integral lattices: ethnic rooting, political power, and economic power. I suggest that throughout the 1950s, 1960s, and 1970s, blacks and other minorities were able to build the ethnic rooting component of the triad with a great deal of success. Likewise, the political power component of the power triad was successfully constructed largely due to the 1965 Voting Rights Act. As a result of this far-reaching legislation, the number of minority elected officials, from congresspeople to city council people, have increased significantly in the 30 plus years since the inception of this law. However, blacks and other minorities have failed to sufficiently build the economic power component of the triad and consequently find themselves in a weakened position of power and at the mercy of the more powerful. After seven years of lecturing on the subject of minority economic empowerment and after hundreds of speeches, workshops, and seminars, I am still convinced that the only way to finish the development of the economic power component is through the rebirth of entrepreneurship within the minority community.

However, the focus of our entrepreneurial efforts should not be primarily to create jobs for our community, even though that is important. Instead our focus needs to be the accumulation of wealth—Black Wealth. In my assessment wealth can be defined as:

$$\text{Wealth} = \frac{M \times T \times I}{R}$$

where:

M = material resources
T = technology
I = intelligence
R = degree or level of resistance

As blacks and other minorities become more successful at creating wealth in America it will become easier for the group to implement "Blackconomics." Blackconomics is simply the control of production, distribution, and consumption of goods and services by blacks and other minorities in such a way that there is equitable sharing of economic and social opportunities among *all* Americans. Expanding entrepreneurship and wealth creation make the practice of "Blackconomics" possible.

But if one accepts the premise that entrepreneurship and wealth creation is key to the building of an economic power base for the community and ultimately to creating a formidable power base for the community to stand on, the question becomes: How do we build this entrepreneurial base rapidly and effectively? The answer that I provide in this book and in my workshops is a simple one. It is based upon an approach that suggests that if we can identify a group of successful minority and female entrepreneurs, study their habits over a significant period of time, isolate the critical skills and strategies that are employed by this select group, then we can develop an entrepreneurial success model or blueprint that can be emulated by those who desire to achieve similar outcomes in their business lives. The impact of such an approach is that once the data have been captured and the modeling is complete, the information can be packaged into many different products and can be disseminated to the public via numerous communication media, such as our new Internet portal, EntreTeach.com.

The entrepreneurship success model that you will read about in later chapters of this book is based upon the **Wallace 4 Quadrant Model for Entrepreneurial Success**. I developed this model during my 10-year study of successful minority and female entrepreneurs. I initiated this study during my tenure as a graduate student at the Tuck School of Business at Dartmouth College. The model states that there are four critical areas that an entrepreneur must focus on each day to incease his or her probability of long-term entrepreneurial success. These quadrants are:

1. Know thy self (maximizing one's ability and capacity to do work and to perform tasks).
2. Know thy plan (developing a bridge to close the gap between the present and some future entrepreneurial event).
3. Know thy universe (maintaining harmony between strategy and the constraints and guidelines of the universe). This quadrant has been expanded upon in my third book, *Soul Food: The 52 Principles of Success for Minority and Female Entrepreneurs* (Perseus Books, 2000).
4. Know thy resources and make them thine own (leveraging the successes and failures of those who have gone before you).

The failure of an entrepreneur to address and build upon these four areas every single day can and often does lead to the ultimate failure of the business enterprise.

Integrated into my analysis of black and minority entrepreneurship is the use of case studies of some of the minority and female entrepreneurs that were used in my research. These case studies are sprinkled throughout the chapters to present to you the human side of entrepreneurship. It is my hope that maybe you'll be able to relate to one or all of these brave, bold pioneers.

As our nation and the world face a new millennium, we must recognize that there is also a dawning of a new movement within the world order. This movement, unlike the movements of the 1950s and 1960s, which focused on more political and social changes, is an economic equality movement. I believe that this movement will elevate the status of African, Asian, Caribbean, and Latin economies to that of Western economies. This movement will provide unparalleled opportunities to those who are prepared. As each of us faces the challenges that such a movement will present, let us always remember the words spoken by Malcolm X more than a quarter century ago:

> The old order must be completely destroyed and replaced with new political and economic systems that allow blacks and whites to share power equally. . . . We never can win freedom, justice, and equality until we are doing something for ourselves.

Let us work diligently and passionately to realize economic justice through entrepreneurship. God bless us all.

Robert L. Wallace
President & CEO
The BiTH Group, Inc.
and
EntreTeach.com

BLACK WEALTH

1

Economic Overview of the Black Community: Why the African American Community Needs Black Entrepreneurs—Now!

One of the reasons this book has been written is to support and stimulate the rapid development of business formation within the African American community. Many of the small corner stores located within many black and minority communities are owned and operated by people who live outside the community. Once again, as before, neighborhood dollars are being removed from circulation within the community and are finding their way into other local economies.

In reviewing this situation, it becomes painfully obvious that the basic problem facing the black community is that it has failed to exercise its inherent power to control and direct its economic destiny.

BLACK POLITICAL POWER—HAS IT HELPED BLACKS ECONOMICALLY?

Certainly no one can argue that blacks have won significant political rights in the past 40 years, which has greatly empowered the African American political machine. The changes in the political power structure of the black community are sometimes manifested in the number of American cities that are currently managed by black chief executives. As shown in Exhibit 1.1, many of America's major urban centers are being managed by African American mayors.

Exhibit 1.1 Black Mayors of Major Cities

Cities	Rank by Population	1998 Census Figures	African American Mayor
Houston	4	1,786,691	Lee P. Brown
Dallas	9	1,075,894	Ron Kirk
Detroit	10	970,196	Dennis W. Archer
San Francisco	12	745,774	Willie L. Brown Jr.
Philadelphia	5	1,436,000	John Street

Source: U.S. Bureau of the Census.

Even in cities where blacks do not enjoy a substantial numbers advantage, more and more whites are finding it more comfortable to vote for black politicians and to view them in leadership roles. Norm Rice, mayor of Seattle, Washington, and Michael White, mayor of Cleveland, Ohio, are proof that the racial politics of the past can be defeated. Even in cities not managed by someone of color, blacks and other minorities in those urban centers often wield a sizable amount of political power.

Unfortunately, these outstanding political gains are overshadowed by statistics that show African Americans lagging far behind white Americans in terms of housing, education, and economic status.

The increased racial intolerance visible today is dwarfed when compared to the lack of economic inclusiveness of African Americans in the workplace. A review of the economic status of the African American work force also may serve to spotlight the challenges facing African Americans. Of the nation's 34.2 million black people (12.8 percent of the population), 13.9 million participate in the nation's work force. Of these 13.9 million people in the work force, 29.2 percent work in blue-collar jobs and almost one out of every four labor in service occupations. This ratio in service jobs is double that of whites in the same fields. Among the 48.7 percent who are white collar workers, only 34 percent of black males have the designation "professional, technical, manager, or administrator" compared to 44 percent for white males.

Although opportunities for advancement of blacks within the lower-paying jobs are few, among the top executive ranks the chances for advancement are almost nonexistent. In one of Korn/Ferry's ongoing executive surveys, they surveyed 1,700 senior executives across the United States who earned six figures per year. Of those executives, only three (less than 1 percent) were black. In a Chicago study of 13,000 managers with the rank of department head or higher, only 117 (again, less than 1 percent) were black.

These statistics confirm what minorities and females have known all along. There exists a glass ceiling for women and minorities in corporate America, above which they are prevented from moving, no matter how talented they are. Even those who make it to executive heights are usually placed in highly visible jobs, such as human resources and public relations, but are restricted from entering positions that lead to powerful, top-level responsibilities.

THE TRIAD OF POWER

Why, with all the great victories won during the 1960s, has the African American community's economic prosperity been so delayed on all fronts? Can racism be used to justify all of the economic and social problems that still confront this community in such a big way? Clearly racism is a factor, but how much of a factor? I submit that there are other factors that at least deserve some special attention.

The biggest factor is that the African American community has not yet completed the essential triad of power. This triad consists of ethnic rooting (pride), political power (prowess), and economic power. Yes, while blacks have been successful at rebuilding their culture to the point of being proud of their African heritage and the contributions their ancestors have made to the world, as well as the impressive political clout amassed, their performance at completing the third leg of the triad, that is, economic empowerment, has been less than impressive.

Malcolm X, a man whose vision was probably too intense for his time, summarized the economic challenge that looms in front of the African American community when he said:

> The man who tosses worms in the river isn't necessarily a friend of the fish. All the fish who took him for friend, who think the worm's got no hook in it, usually end up in the frying pan.

In deep disgust, Malcolm would later comment, "I watched brothers entwining themselves in the economic clutches of the white man, who went home every night with another bag of money drained from the ghetto."

Malcolm realized, long before most other leaders of his time, that the key to social and economic parity and the accumulation of power was the achievement of economic self-reliance. He viewed prosperity as the ultimate equalizer. As a member of the Black Muslims, economic empowerment became the heart of his message to African Americans. He knew that economic self-reliance would supply not only jobs and security, but also badly needed self-esteem and respect from the overall community.

When blacks complained about the slums they were forced to live in, Malcolm would scold them bitterly for their slavelike dependence on white America. He, like many of us today, felt that the need to develop businesses within the black community was of an urgent nature. Like mainstream America, he saw the ownership of property, whether that property was land or business, as a necessary requirement for any real freedom or independence. Malcolm's vision was to see blacks turn their neighborhoods into bustling centers of economic activity and prosperity.

ECONOMIC PERFORMANCE OF AFRICAN AMERICANS

Since Malcolm conveyed this strategy, the vision for economic self-reliance has been somewhat dimmed. The following pages provide a factual look at the current economic condition of African Americans and confirm the seriousness of the matter.

At the writing of this book, America is celebrating the longest period of continuous growth in its history. Starting in March 1991 and having reached beyond 107 months of expansion, we have surpassed the record set between 1961 and 1969, at the height of the Vietnam War. The phenomenal expansion of the "go-go" 1990s has erased the deficit (first time since 1969), reduced unemployment to record lows (below 5½ percent), and raised the real gross domestic product by more than a third. What is even more amazing about this gangbuster economy is that it shows no signs of slowing down and losing steam.

While blacks and other minorities have not fared as well as others in the booming 1990s, some progress has been realized. To begin with, according to the Census Bureau the number of Americans living below the poverty level decreased dramatically from a high of 10.5 percent in 1991 to 8.5 percent in 1998. Black unemployment has dropped from 12 percent to 7 percent for black women and 14 percent to 7 percent for black men. Black teenagers, who are consistently among the chronically unemployed, saw their unemployment rate drop from 36 percent to 28 percent. Home ownership among blacks and Hispanics is up, currently hitting 46.7 percent and 45.5 percent respectively.

Despite the encouraging improvements, the fact is that the economic parity gap between black and white America still remains. This gap is clearly visible when the following economic barometers are reviewed:

1. Unemployment
2. Mean net worth
3. Per capita income
4. Median family income
5. Persons below poverty level (as percent of group)
6. Persons below poverty level (number of people)

Unemployment

The U.S. Department of Labor's Bureau of Labor Statistics reveals, as shown in Exhibit 1.2, that the unemployment rate in the black community was 8.9 percent in 1998 while the rate for whites was 3.9 percent. For black teenagers the unemployment rate until recently, often hovered between 30 percent and 40 percent. Traditionally, the black unemployment rate has fluctuated between 1.5 and 5.3 times that of whites.

Mean Net Worth

Basically, net worth is the result of summing up all of your assets minus your liabilities. In other words, if you were to sell everything you owned,

Exhibit 1.2 Unemployment Rates (1998)

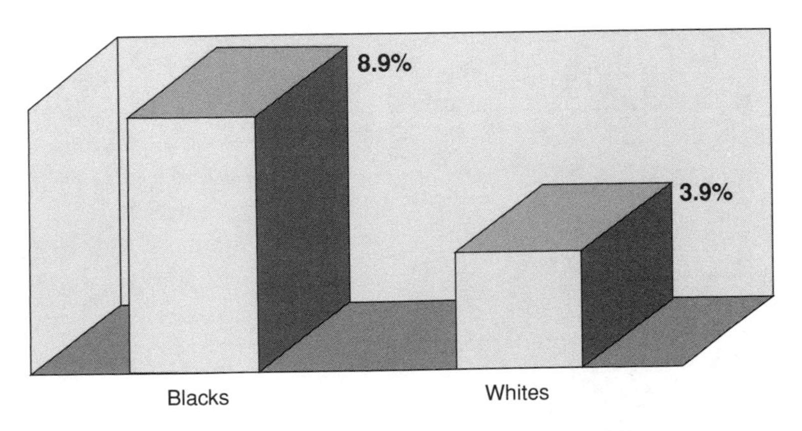

Source: U.S. Census Bureau Statistical Abstract of the United States: 1999.

obtained the cash from this sale, then use the cash to pay off all of your bills, whatever is left would be your net worth (somewhat depressing, huh?). Mean net worth is the average net worth for all members of that particular group. Most people build net worth by putting a portion of their earnings obtained from their jobs into investments and savings accounts. Over a period of time these assets appreciate. Consequently, there is a strong correlation between income and net worth.

According to the U.S. Department of Commerce, in 1993 (the latest data available at this time, as shown in Exhibit 1.3) the mean net worth of black Americans was approximately one-fifth that of whites. In 1989 the mean net worth of blacks was one-fourth that of whites.

One of the participants of this study put it best when he said that our community is basically in a sharecropping economic mode. Some African Americans live from paycheck to paycheck. If that paycheck was taken away, the little net worth available would be eroded rapidly, plunging the community further into poverty.

Per Capita Income

Per capita income is calculated by dividing the total aggregate income by the total number of people in the target population. Basically it is the amount of income per person, for every man, woman, and child. Per capita income includes the income of all individuals, whereas family income includes the income of related persons living in households. Ac-

Exhibit 1.3 Mean Net Worth (1993)

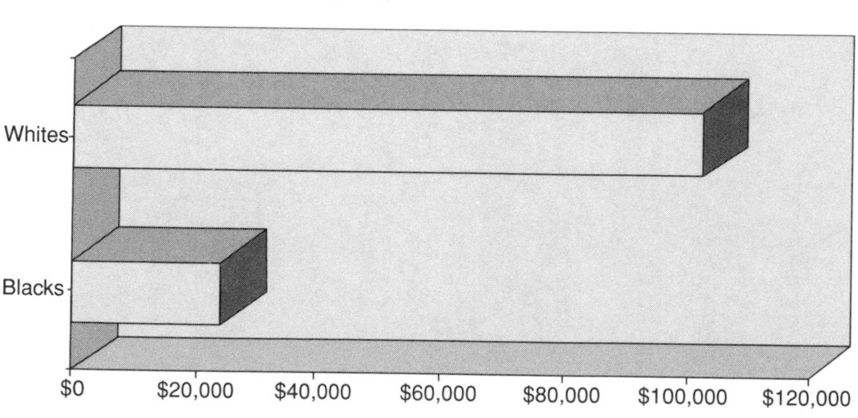

Source: U.S. Dept. of Commerce.

cording to the U.S. Department of Commerce, Bureau of the Census, the recent report (as of Sept. 1998) on money, income, and poverty status in the United States reveals the following per capita income results for the three major groupings:

All races	$19,241
White	$20,425
Black	$12,351
Hispanic	$10,773

Exhibit 1.4 shows that in 1997 blacks continued to lag behind whites by $8,074 per person per year. Another way of stating these data is that every black family of four must earn more than $32,296 more per year for blacks to achieve economic parity with whites. This gap is even more difficult to close given that there are typically two wage earners in each family.

Median Family Income

The median income is an income level in which half of the households earn less than the median and the other half earn more than that income. The median family income is important because within the American

Exhibit 1.4 Per Capita Income (1997)

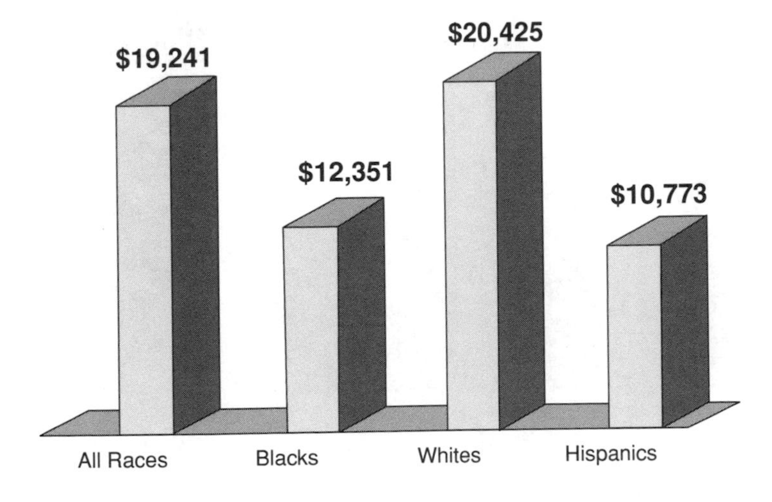

Source: U.S. Bureau of the Census.

society, the family unit remains the cornerstone of societal structure. Thus, economic information on the family unit often is a more realistic indicator of group performance. In 1997, as shown by Exhibit 1.5, the median family incomes of the four major groups were as follows:

Blacks	$25,050
Whites	$38,972
Hispanics	$26,628
Asians, Pacific Islanders	$45,249
All races	$37,005

These data indicate that the median family income for black families is 64.3 percent that of whites. However, when a comparison is made between median family incomes for married couples (two parents in the home), blacks fare much better in comparison to whites. In fact, the median family income of blacks increases to 87 percent that of whites in this comparison. For married couples the median family income is as follows:

Whites	$52,098
Blacks	$45,372
Hispanics	$33,914

Exhibit 1.5 Median Family Income (1997)

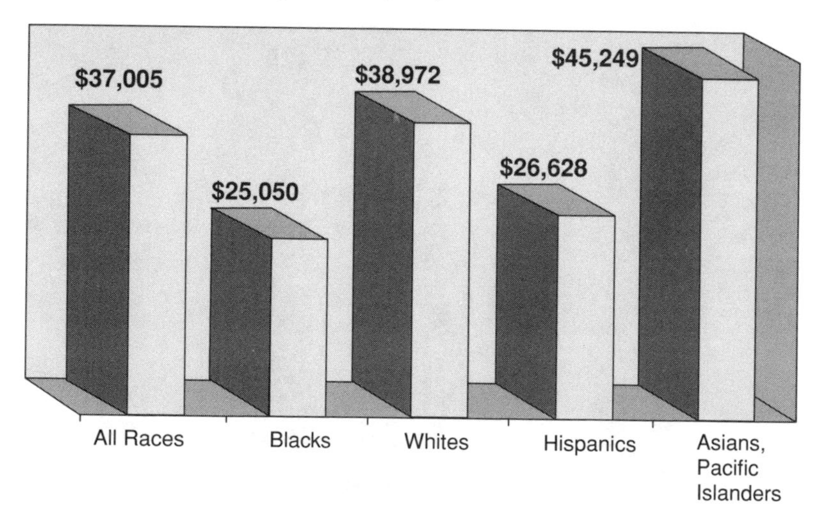

Source: U.S. Bureau of the Census.

Exhibit 1.6 Percentage of Groups below Poverty Level (1997)

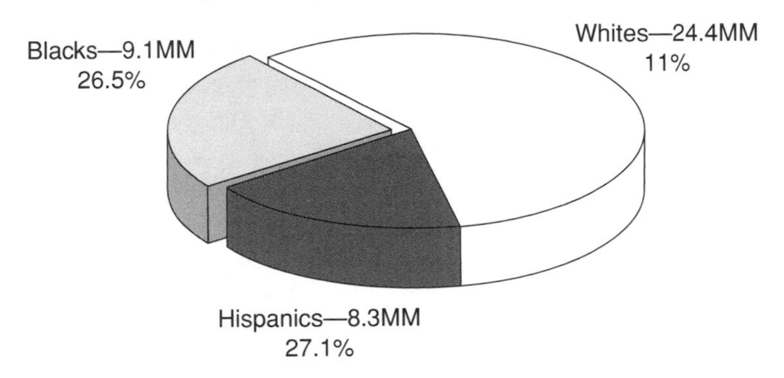

Source: U.S. Bureau of the Census.

Persons below Poverty Level (As Percent of Group)

The poverty definition used here is adopted for official government use by the Office of Management and Budget and consists of a set of income thresholds that vary by family size and composition. Families or individuals with incomes below their appropriate thresholds are classified as below the poverty level. The poverty thresholds are updated every year to reflect changes in the Consumer Price Index.

As depicted by Exhibit 1.6 and Exhibit 1.7, blacks have consistently absorbed a disproportionate share of the poverty in this country. In 1980, 13 percent of all Americans lived below the poverty level; during the next

Exhibit 1.7 Number of Persons below Poverty Level (1997)

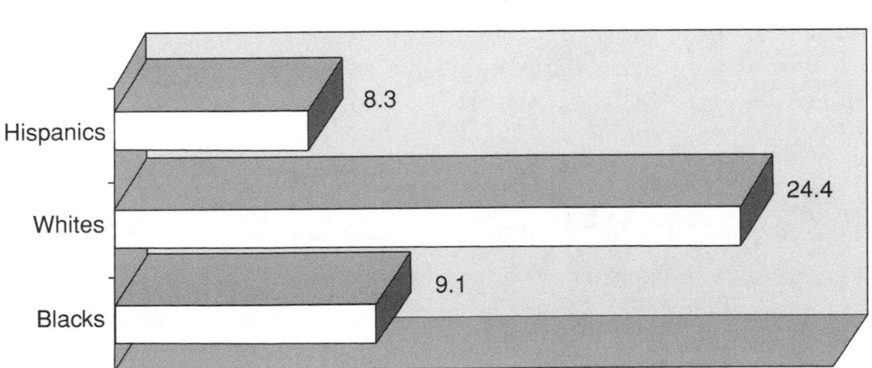

Source: U.S. Bureau of the Census.

eight years, the percentage peaked at 15 percent during 1982, dropped to 10.5 percent in 1991 and even lower to 8.5 percent in 1998. During this same period, the percentage of blacks living under the poverty level peaked at 35.6 percent during 1982 and ended around 30.7 percent in 1989. In 1997, 11 percent of whites lived below poverty level, while the percentages for blacks and Hispanics were 26.5 percent and 27.1 percent, respectively.

Persons below Poverty Level (Number of People)

One of the fallacies that some people like to perpetuate is that blacks and other minorities are the groups who soak up the social programs paid for with tax dollars. As shown in Exhibit 1.7, this is not the case. In 1980, just as President Reagan was taking over the Executive Office, there were close to 30 million Americans living below the poverty level. Almost two-thirds of those people were white, while blacks and Hispanics made up a much smaller proportion. During the eight years of the Reagan administration, the number of people living below the poverty level increased to close to 35 million people, with all groups sharing in the increase. The total number of people living in poverty in 1997 by group were as follows:

Whites	24,396,000
Blacks	9,116,000
Hispanics	8,308,000

Income of Households—Aggregate

Exhibit 1.8 illustrates the aggregate total of incomes from the preceding three groups. These figures are compiled by multiplying all households by the amount of income they generated in 1997. Whites, due to their greater numbers, had an aggregate income of approximately $4.5 trillion per year, while blacks had an aggregate income of approximately $427 billion per year. Hispanics generated approximately $331 billion during the same period of time.

WHAT DOES IT ALL MEAN?

As you can see from the summary of economic statistics, the African American community faces a monumental challenge in realizing economic parity with mainstream America. Although some progress has been made, there still exists a significant economic parity gap between blacks and whites and, in certain instances, between blacks and other

Exhibit 1.8 Aggregate Incomes (1997)

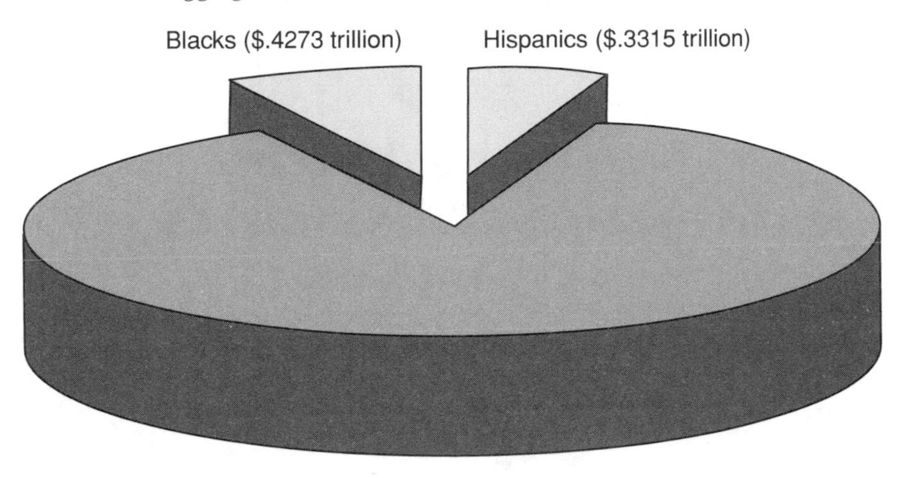

Source: U.S. Bureau of the Census.

minority groups. If the African American economy were to be isolated, it would become obvious that economic justice has not been realized within the black community, and urgent measures must be taken to rectify the situation. It is because of this urgency that the role of African American entrepreneurs takes on a new and pivotal role in the community's survival and future development.

2

Status of African American Businesses

I hope there are no doubts in anyone's mind of the critical role that African American entrepreneurs will play in the survival of the black community. As we move into the 2000s and the twenty-first century, black entrepreneurs will share an even greater burden to enhance the well-being of all Americans, especially Americans of African descent.

If black entrepreneurs are to assume this burden, it makes sense to understand their strengths and weaknesses. Consequently, a thorough analysis of the building of economic power through the rapid formation of business enterprises should begin with the current status of African American businesses within the United States. Only after we've documented where we are and where we'd like to be can we begin to construct a workable strategy for focusing our resources intelligently to accomplish the economic power of which we speak.

They say that opinions are like hearts—everyone has one. I certainly do have mine, particularly when it comes to evaluating the current status of black businesses. In my opinion, the condition of black businesses is that at best they're surviving. Although we have seen significant growth in the number of businesses started, the depth and breadth of these new players tends to be somewhat limited.

Currently, 89.6 percent of all African American businesses are sole proprietorships, which is good for the individual but doesn't provide much leverage for the African American community. According to a survey by the U.S. Commerce Department's Census Bureau (the most recent data available), the number of African American business firms in the United States increased from 424,000 in 1987 to 620,912 in 1992. This equates to a 46.4 percent increase during a five-year period.

For minorities in general, according to the March 8, 1999, edition of *USA Today*, 14 percent of U.S. businesses are owned by blacks and other minorities. The percentages of businesses owned by minorities in key industries are:

Industry	Percent Businesses Owned by Minorities
Transportation	21 percent
Services	16 percent
Construction	15 percent
Manufacturing	14 percent

As shown by Exhibit 2.1, while the number of black firms was increasing, so was the total number of firms. All U.S. firms rose 22 percent,

Exhibit 2.1 U.S. Firms

	1992		1987	
	Black-Owned Firms*	All Firms	Black-Owned Firms*	All Firms
a) # Business firms	620,912	16,696,000	424,000	13,700,000
b) % Total	3.7%	100%	3%	100%
c) Receipts	$32.2 billion	$10,962 billion	$19.8 billion	$1,994.8 billion
d) % Total	0.3%	100%	1%	100%
e) Receipts per firm	$51,935	$656,564	$47,000	$146,000
f) % Firms in service	53.4%	47.3%	49.4%	43.4%
g) % Firms in retail	14.0%	15.1% (est.)	15.6%	16.4%
h) % Firms in construction	7.0%	10.7%	8.7%	12.1%
i) % Firms in transportation and public utilities	7.9%	4.1%	8.7%	4.3%
j) % Firms in finance, insurance, real estate	6.6%	12.5%	6.4%	9.0%
k) % Firms in manufacturing	1.7%	2.7%	1.9%	3.2%
l) % Firms in agricultural services, forestry, fishing, and mining	1.7%	4.5%	1.8%	3.5%
m) % Firms in wholesale	1.2%	2.1% (est.)	1.3%	3.2%

*Total number of black-owned firms does not include C corporations.
Source: U.S. Bureau of the Census, Commerce Department.

from 13.7 million to 16.7 million during the same time period. These 620,912 businesses constitute 3.7 percent of the total U.S. business base. Concurrently, these 620,912 businesses generated $32.2 billion in annual revenues, which comprises less than 1 percent of the nation's total receipts.

COMPARISON TO MAINSTREAM FIRMS

Also as shown in Exhibit 2.1, the percentage of the nation's firms owned by African Americans grew to 3.7 percent of total businesses from 1987 to 1992 (according to the most recent data available) and generated less than 1 percent of total receipts for those years. Receipts per firm averaged $51,935 for black-owned firms, compared with $656,564 for all U.S. firms. Approximately 10.4 percent of all black-owned firms had paid employees. The number of firms that employed people numbered 64,478. The same firms produced $22.6 billion of sales and receipts in 1992, which comprises 70.2 percent of total receipts for black-owned firms.

INDUSTRY GROUPS

As indicated by Exhibit 2.2, the black-owned firms in the industry group with the largest dollar volume of receipts in 1992 were miscellaneous retail operations. Health care services was the second largest industry group in terms of dollar volume of receipts. More than one-half of all dollar volume receipts generated by black-owned businesses were generated in miscellaneous retail, automotive dealers and service stations,

Exhibit 2.2 Industry Groups

Ten Industry Groups with Largest Dollar Volume of Receipts	Dollar Volume of Receipts ($ billions)
a) Automotive dealers and service stations	2.4
b) Business services	2.4
c) Health care services	2.9
d) Special trade contractors	1.5
e) Miscellaneous retail	7.0
f) Eating and drinking places	1.8
g) Trucking and warehousing	1.3
h) Food stores	1.0
i) Personal services	1.5
j) Wholesale trade, nondurable goods	1.8
Total dollar volume of receipts	23.6

Source: U.S. Bureau of the Census, Commerce Department.

business services, health care services, wholesale trade, and eating and drinking places industry groups.

METROPOLITAN AREA BREAKDOWN

The top 10 metropolitan areas with the largest number of black-owned firms accounted for 36 percent of the national total for all black-owned businesses and 36 percent of gross receipts. It is interesting to note that of the top ten areas, eight had black mayors at one time and have a sizable African American population. Are these examples of political leverage's being used to promote and support black enterprises? What do you think? The top 10 metropolitan areas are shown in Exhibit 2.3.

WHERE DO WE GO FROM HERE?

Although I applaud the fact that the number of black-owned businesses has increased by 46.4 percent from 1987 to 1992, the fact remains that 89.6 percent of all black-owned businesses are sole proprietorships and that black-owned businesses as a whole make up only 3.7 percent of total U.S. firms. As I mentioned earlier, these same firms generate less than 1 percent of the total receipts of U.S. businesses. Although the community is adding economic and entrepreneurship development to the top of its national agenda, the fact remains that our current pace will not rapidly lead

Exhibit 2.3 Top Ten Metropolitan Areas

Metropolitan Area	Revenue ($ billions)	Number of Black-Owned Businesses*
1) New York	1.2	28,063
2) Los Angeles-Long Beach	1.3	23,932
3) Washington, D.C.	1.0	23,046
4) Chicago	0.9	15,374
5) Houston	0.4	12,989
6) Atlanta	0.7	11,804
7) Philadelphia	0.6	10,249
8) Detroit	0.5	9,853
9) Baltimore	0.3	8,593
10) Dallas	0.2	7,857

*The Bureau of the Census included only individual proprietorships, partnerships, and subchapter S corporations in its total count of black-owned firms. C corporations were not included.
Source: U.S. Bureau of the Census, Commerce Department.

to the community's realizing any substantial benefit in terms of the number of jobs created and the creation of wealth.

Some will ask: Well, how many black-owned businesses should there be to achieve economic parity? What percent of the total receipts generated by America's businesses should black-owned businesses contribute? What should be the makeup of black-owned businesses in the various industry groups and across legal structures (i.e., corporations, partnerships, sole proprietorships) to provide a foundation for further economic development? These are all very good questions. Honestly, your answer is as good as mine. However, we need to start somewhere. As an initial target, we should have representation in the number of businesses and in total receipts that are commensurate with our percentage of the population. Currently, African Americans constitute 12.8 percent of the population. Therefore, it makes sense that 12.8 percent of total businesses be owned by African Americans and that this same group, on average, generate 12.8 percent of the total receipts.

3

The Creation of Wealth-Building Power within the African American Community

With all this talk about power, one might rightly ask: What is power and how is it defined? There are some who assume that our numbers and supposed political clout directly translate into power. If you view power in these terms, then it would be correct to conclude that because of our numbers, African Americans do exert significant power, particularly in our urban centers. However, as we learned from the experiences of black South Africans, a majority in numbers does not always equate equitable power sharing. Let's try to develop this concept of power sharing a bit further.

POWER STRUCTURE: WHAT IS IT?

Dr. Martin Luther King, Jr. once said that power is simply the ability to achieve purpose. For our discussion of purposes let's define power as the ability to have a direct impact on one's destiny or the ability to effect change. Although it is easy to define power, it requires a more thorough explanation to understand it and why it is essential to the survival of all ethnic groups in a capitalistic society. I believe it is much more accurate to view power in terms of a multidimensional structure. As shown by Exhibit 3.1, there are various components or members of the power structure.

Exhibit 3.1 Power Structure Components

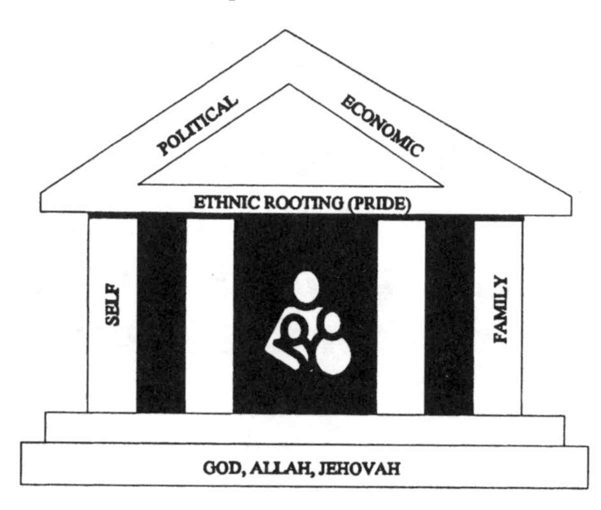

Analogous to this depiction is the civil engineering involved in designing and constructing a high-rise building. Before any walls are raised or roofs attached, the foundation of the building must be properly designed and constructed so that it can support the weight of the structure and help fortify it from the internal stresses and external natural forces that will inevitably act upon the structure. Next, the walls are put up to support the roof and help translate the stresses from the roof to the foundation and to provide lateral support. The later stages of construction require that the structure, up to that point, is strong enough to allow the roofing component to be laid in place and fastened to protect the internal occupants and solidify the building's structural integrity.

Before any ethnic group can demand its rightful share of power in our society, like constructing a high-rise building, it must first ensure that all components of the structure are in place and able to share their portions of the load. Every element of the structure must meet the specifications that are defined for it or ultimately the entire structure will fail. It is an all-or-nothing arrangement.

If the analogy of the power structure that is proposed in this book were translated into individual or group terms, it might be depicted with the major components (power segments) as explained below:

God (spiritual)
Self (education)
Family
Ethnic pride/power
Political power
Economic power (economic justice)

I reiterate that if one of these segments is weakened, the entire structure becomes severely weakened.

Let's try to analyze the status of black America's existing power base as it relates to the power model developed in Exhibit 3.1. The most critical component of the power structure is God (i.e., Allah, Jehovah, the Almighty, etc.). Without the God element, the group may prosper in the short term, but will ultimately self-destruct and lose its direction. No one can question the rich, spiritually uplifting influence that God and spirituality has had on the black community. Faith in God is and always has been the glue that has held the African American community intact during the dark and sometimes uncertain centuries. It should come as no surprise that the civil rights movement in America was initiated, planned, orchestrated, and implemented from the pulpits of black America's churches.

Of course, some people will assume the opposite position, which suggests that the black community's reliance on religion and spirituality is what continues to hold the black community back. Some will ask the logical question: If God is our supposed foundation, then why did He allow our people to be stolen from Africa, lost during the middle passage, and persecuted under the American system of justice? Although this is a fair question, and while I love God, I'm not qualified to speak for Him. I don't know the answer. What I do know is that it is a major miracle that despite these impediments black Americans are 34 million strong in America. Despite centuries of oppression African Americans' relationship with eternal God is the major reason for the group's survival. African American parents and grandparents believed that God was on their side, which provided them the moral high ground necessary to fight long, hard, and bitter battles. Whether one views the glass as half empty or half full, it is clear that spirituality runs thick within the black community, and despite the many challenges, faith in God remains the rudder of its collective ship.

Just as God is the foundation of the complete model defined in Exhibit 3.1, *self* is the basic element of the family unit. Self is important because unless each individual is strong enough to carry his or her own weight, the family unit and everything else will suffer. The strengthening of self requires that as individuals, we fortify our physical selves, our intellectual selves, and our spiritual selves.

Like mainstream Americans, black Americans have become better informed about their health and the importance of proper diet and exercise. The baby boom generation is especially interested in how it looks and how well it ages. This helps explain the booming diet and health club industries. Although the United States as a whole continues to fight alcohol and drug epidemics across the nation, people (blacks included) are taking their physical bodies more seriously than ever before.

Intellectually and spiritually, despite formidable obstacles, blacks continue to advance and prosper. Although the number of African Americans attending college has been on the decline in recent years, many young black people continue to successfully prepare themselves to assume leadership roles in the society. In the 2000s and beyond, we will continue to see more young black lawyers, engineers, doctors, and other professionals than ever before. Besides formal education, many young blacks are beginning to *teach themselves* about their ancestors' contributions to the world and what their own roles should be in today's environment.

This desire for intellectual stimulation is manifested in many black youths' embracing the teachings of Malcolm X. These once-maligned teachings of Malcolm X are now being studied with great vigor and enthusiasm by today's young people. This generation understands there are differences between blacks and whites and that it is not necessary to feel inferior or to be uncomfortable with that fact. Although some blacks once hated the color of their skin, there is now joy in its individuality and uniqueness. The teachings of Malcolm X and other black leaders helped to orchestrate this change.

To continue developing the power structure model beyond God and self it is necessary to leverage these two elements to promote strong and cohesive *family units.* No other component of the black community has been more maligned by the media and scholars of this country than the black family. These critics often point to the supposed breakdown of family values, the abuse of lethal drugs, the spreading of fatal diseases resulting from irresponsible and licentious behavior, households that are managed by single mothers, rampaging gangs of youths who appear to have no guidance, out of control welfare dependency, and skyrocketing numbers of teen pregnancies, and they conclude that all is lost for the black family.

Although these are indeed difficult challenges that must be addressed, these conditions are by no means unique to African Americans and are in fact common to many of the ethnic groups who made their way from the underclass to the upper class. Even as European Americans began migrating to the cities near the turn of the twentieth century, their living conditions mirrored those of today's poor black urban dwellers. Consequently, it is my belief that because the obstacles we face are common to any other group of people making the transition from the lower economic class to the middle class, the black community's overall family structure remains solid.

The fourth component of the power structure model is built upon the God foundation and undergirded by self and family. This fourth element is *ethnic rooting* or *ethnic pride.* Let no one fool you into thinking that this aspect of the power structure is insignificant. Having pride in one's heritage, culture, physical appearance, and overall contribution to society is necessary for survival in a competitive world. Unlike with most other ethnic groups, it took a major civil rights movement to galvanize the black community into one loud, angry voice that forever changed the way America looked at its citizens of color. The pride and direction generated from this movement solidified black America's realization that their destiny was connected to that of their brothers and sisters throughout the world—that somehow all blacks from the diaspora have a binding connection.

The long and difficult civil rights struggle reaped numerous benefits for the black community, particularly in the areas of ethnic pride. No longer were African Americans ashamed of their kinky hair. They started wearing Afros to accentuate it. No longer were they ashamed of their dark skin. "I'm black and I'm proud" became the battle cry for the younger constituency of the movement. It made blacks more comfortable with themselves and their contributions to the world in the fields of science, mathematics, engineering, health, agriculture, and every other aspect of civilization. This new-found ethnic pride soon spilled over into the political battlefield as the 1960s progressed.

The *political power* component of the power structure has been an overwhelming success for black Americans. This element of the structure is important because it allows blacks to help set the national agenda and enhances their ability to dictate what the distribution of the country's resources will be. Political power assures that blacks and any ethnic group enjoy an equitable share of the pie. Without this aspect of the structure, even noble and well-meaning deeds will be doomed to failure.

To chronicle the acquisition of political power by blacks is indeed a case study in perseverance and courage. With the passage of the 1965 Voting Rights Act, with its focus on the South, most legal barriers to full political participation by blacks were removed. For example, three years after its passage, black voter registration in the state of Mississippi, a state then rampant with violence and racial injustice, increased from 6.7 percent to 60 percent. The new legislation opened the door for many of the disenfranchised voters to cast their votes—many for the first time in their lives.

This groundswell of political activity led to the election of new black political leaders at every level of government. White politicians, who once had the luxury of totally ignoring the black electorate, now were forced to court the black vote just as they had the white vote. Issues that concerned African Americans moved up on the politicians' priority lists and onto the national agenda. Once on the agenda, these issues were often dealt with with a certain degree of urgency and seriousness. With the African American's increase in numbers, the political landscape has been permanently changed. Blacks now manage many of the country's strategic urban centers.

Of the top 15 largest cities in America, five are managed by black mayors and the number seems to be growing rapidly. An African American, Douglas Wilder, was elected governor of a southern state, for the first time since Reconstruction. In 1992 the state of Illinois elected Carol Moseley-Braun the first black woman to the U.S. Senate. In the same year, black Americans overwhelmingly supported Governor Bill Clinton and in record numbers helped him defeat President George Bush and defeat Senator Dole in 1996. Vice President Al Gore and Governor Bush will be the likely candidates in 2000. Either way blacks will play a critical role in the outcome of this key election. Although there are some who would like to turn the political clock back on blacks, the community's political achievements to date cannot be denied.

However, what has been denied is the African American's quest to share economic power in the American society. There were many who assumed that once political power was achieved, economic power would automatically follow. How wrong they were. It is impossible to overstate the importance of black economic power. It is one of the most important elements of the power structure model because without it, the community relinquishes some control of its economic destiny. Until this economic power component is strengthened, the entire power structure for black Americans will remain weak and tenuous. Thus, the remaining sections speak to the process of seizing economic power.

SEIZING ECONOMIC POWER

Seizing economic power will not be as easy as it sounds. Naturally, questions will be asked: How do you seize economic power? How do you know when you have it? To begin with, what is meant by *seizing economic power*? Three criteria are as follows:

1. Close the economic parity gap between blacks and whites.
2. Accumulate significant wealth that is pervasive and lasting.
3. Control commerce and industry within the African American community and increase the circulation rate of dollars within the black community.

CLOSING THE ECONOMIC PARITY GAP BETWEEN BLACKS AND WHITES

At first glance, the idea of closing the economic parity gap between black and white Americans in a reasonable time frame may seem quite formidable. However, the fact of the matter is, we already have the ability to completely erase the parity gap by using the resources within our own community. Consider the following:

1. As shown in Exhibit 3.2, let's assume for this exercise that each year the African American community earns approximately $500 billion. (I realize this is different from the census figure, but I believe the real number is greater than what the census data indicate.) Of the total amount earned, on average the black community spends only 6.6 percent or $33 billion/year in African American-owned businesses. Consequently, the amount of dollars that run through our hands and into the hands of nonblack enterprises without even circulating through the community once is about $467 billion.

2. As mentioned earlier, the per capita income as of September 1998 (the most recent data available) was $12,351 for blacks and $20,425 for whites. The difference in per capita income is $8,074. This says that if we are to achieve economic parity using per capita income as a yardstick, then every black man, woman, and child would have to earn

Exhibit 3.2 Black Annual Revenue

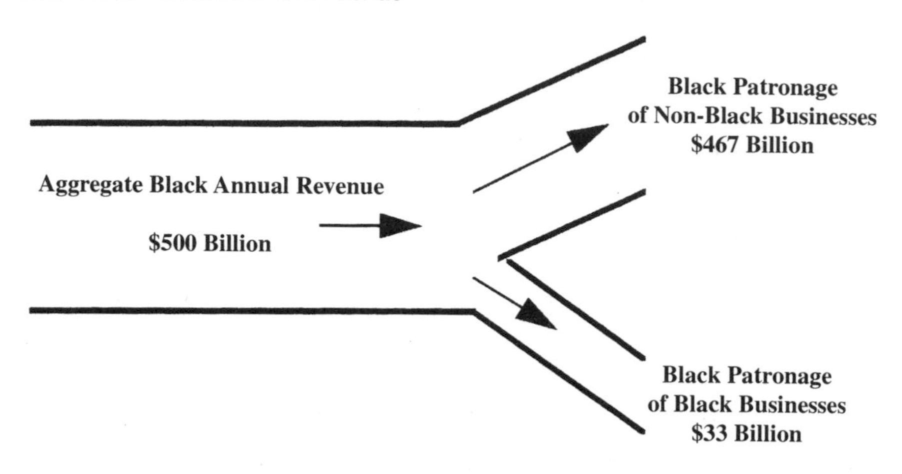

$8,074 more per year than what is earned now. For a family of four that works out to be $32,296 per family per year.

3. There are approximately 34.8 million African Americans living in the United States, based on the 1999 census update.

Now, in Exhibit 3.3, let's take a look at what would happen to the parity gap if we spent larger percentages of our dollars in black-owned businesses. Look at what could happen if African Americans allowed their dollars to turn over in their community just a few times instead of less than once. In an ideal world, the information in Exhibit 3.3 would be quite plausible. However, reality suggests that the realization of this decrease in the gap would be impacted by the flaws in the following assumptions:

1. The additional dollars spent with an African American business will not equate dollar for dollar into additional income for the owner or his or her workers. Obviously, a portion of the additional funds would be used to cover business expenses and the tax expense.

2. All employees working for African American-owned businesses may not be of African descent; thus additional funds would be diverted outside the community.

3. Any additional dollars spent in black businesses may serve only to make rich blacks richer without the dollars being widely dispersed among the black population, thus reducing any positive impact

Exhibit 3.3 Estimated Changes in Per Capita Income Gap between Blacks and Whites

Available Black Consumer Dollars Not Spent in Black Businesses	% Consumer Dollars to Be Spent in Black Businesses (estimated)	Current Per Capita Income Gap between Blacks and Whites	New Per Capita Income Gap between Blacks and Whites (with Increased Patronage of Black Businesses)
$467 billion	50% ($233 billion)	$8,074	$1,246 (Lower than Per Capita Income for Whites)
$467 billion	69% ($322 billion)	$8,074	$1,348 (Higher than Per Capita Income for Whites)
$467 billion	90% ($420 billion)	$8,074	$4,215 (Higher than Per Capita Income for Whites)

that the shift of funds into minority businesses might have on the overall community.

Aside from the assumptions made, the example above is used to illustrate a point. Basically, there is a tremendous amount that blacks can do on their own to gain economic parity, without any additional inflow from mainstream America. The critical point to remember here is that the power of the African American dollar should not be underestimated; rather, it should be leveraged as much as possible.

HOW TO ACCUMULATE WEALTH AND CONTROL COMMERCE: FOUR OPTIONS

As mentioned earlier, the two other requirements for seizing economic power are to accumulate wealth and to reclaim control of our local economies. The options at our disposal to achieve any one of these goals is pursuit of one or a combination of the following:

1. Excel in the private sector (e.g., work for IBM, Procter & Gamble, DuPont, NBA, NFL, etc.).
2. Excel in the public sector (e.g., work for the federal or local governments).
3. Capitalize on sin and suffering (e.g., sell drugs, alcohol, and get-rich-quick schemes).
4. Stimulate the formation of business development within the community.

Option #1: Excel in the Private Sector

Probably the first frontier that was attacked during the height of the civil rights movement was the entry of blacks and other minorities into America's corporate ranks. For years, women and minorities were denied access to this potentially lucrative environment because of their gender and skin color. With the introduction of affirmative action programs throughout corporate America, the very groups that were once denied the opportunity to participate in the board rooms were suddenly invited in as equal players. Consequently, during the late 1960s, 1970s, and 1980s we saw a large influx of women and minorities into the good old boy networks across the country. Or so we thought.

Although the civil rights movement opened the door for women and minorities, some would argue that the opportunities that were hoped for have never really materialized. A year-long study of the employment and promotion practices of nine Fortune 500 companies, conducted by the United States Department of Labor and released during the summer of 1991, concluded that glass ceilings do exist and that the ceiling is lower for minorities than for women. The Labor Department's study was based on surveys of businesses, a review of nine Fortune 500 companies, as well as detailed independent research and discussions with representatives from management, women's groups, business and labor, and civil rights groups.

The report uncovered some startling, but not surprising, facts. Among them was the fact that only 16.9 percent of the 31,184 managers at the nine firms surveyed were female and only 6.6 percent were minorities. The study also found that most women and minorities who were in management were working in areas such as research, administration, and human resources. Of the 4,491 executive level managers (defined as assistant vice presidents and above), only 6.6 percent were women and 2.6 percent were minorities. The report further concluded that companies need to do a better job of monitoring women and minorities for access to advancement opportunities, improve the monitoring of compensation policies and perquisites, and improve recordkeeping of affirmative action efforts.

Even for those who are able to break the glass ceiling, most people still live from paycheck to paycheck. Although we can live comfortable lives working in the private sector, chances are it will take a long time to accumulate enough cash to have a significant impact on the overall community or even to close the economic parity gap. Even as progress for minorities and females is being made through promotions and career advancements, the upper echelons of corporate America remain mostly male and mostly white.

Even if you are one of the few lucky ones who makes her or his way up, the current flurry of corporate acquisitions and mergers makes you especially vulnerable. People are no longer guaranteed lifetime employment. Therefore, even if you're a top performer, you could still very well become a victim of the reshaping of corporate America. Furthermore, when corporations slim down, typically the people in control of that task have a tendency to keep people who look, act, and think like them and "right size" those who have the misfortune of being different from themselves.

To compound this inequity even further, women and minorities can no longer depend on the Supreme Court or other parts of the federal government to protect their rights. There was a time when minorities who were unfairly treated in the corporate environment had the option of using federal legislation to review the situation and decide on corrective actions.

Unfortunately, President George Bush didn't see it that way. With the stroke of a pen, he vetoed the Civil Rights Act of 1990. This act was not about quotas as the Bush administration tried to convey. Instead, it was about economic justice in the workplace, which had long been denied to people of color. The law would have ensured only that those who continue to be victimized by the legacy of racism within the hallowed halls of corporate America would have the means to redress their grievances. A much watered-down version of the act was ultimately signed into law by the president. Consequently, with no pressure from the federal government or the federal courts (which I don't foresee changing any time soon), except for human decency and a commitment to fair play, the corporate decision makers have no other incentives to be fair. Therefore, women and minorities will continue to assume a disproportional share of the cutbacks and may have fewer opportunities to advance.

One of the other fallacies of the corporate dream is that after giving some company 40 to 50 years of our lives, the company will then take good care of us in our twilight years. My father thought that. Don't get me wrong—my father was a great man whom I loved and respected. However, he didn't make it very far in school. I believe he completed the seventh grade before he left school to work and help support his family. For more than 50 years, he slaved in the private sector at various blue collar jobs. Each morning he left at 4:30 A.M. to catch his bus and returned home hours after sunset. It didn't matter what the weather was; he religiously put in his 12- to 16-hour days, never complaining and never missing a day.

Even when he got up in age and could hardly walk due to arthritis and other ailments, he continued to make that daily trek until one day his employer told him that they no longer needed his services and asked him to retire. Not having a job hit my father like a hammer. He started freaking out. He shaved his head, ran away from home, became very irritable, and began to question his value to his family and to the general society. Unfortunately until that point, he had always measured his self-worth by the job that he was performing and how much money he was making. I wonder how many of us measure ourselves the same way? My father recently died with little money in his pocket, in spite of his more than one-half century of dedicated labor to someone else.

Option #2: Excel in the Public Sector

One area of the country that is supposedly recession proof is the Baltimore-Washington, D.C., Metropolitan Area. This area includes Washington, D.C., Baltimore, and the surrounding areas of northern Virginia and southern Maryland. The reason it is supposed to be recession proof is that the economy there is heavily fueled by the activity of the federal government. Theoretically, even in times of recession, the wheels of government continue to turn, fueled by our tax dollars and driven by the direction of Congress and the executive branch. Unlike for the federal government, working for municipalities is not considered recession proof because the city's revenue streams are not as certain as the federal government's, and cities often trim their services in order to balance their budgets.

Yet like the private sector, working in the public sector can be treacherous and uncertain. The highly political and intricate bureaucracies that drive these organizations tend not to reward their most talented people. Creativity, drive, and outstanding performance are rarely rewarded. Instead, those who have the right political connections and who socialize with the right people generally move ahead and are awarded the lucrative opportunities. Besides, these public sector jobs do not pay exceptionally well, unless you're at certain GSA levels. Therefore, it becomes increasingly difficult to accumulate significant wealth in a reasonable period of time. Thus, the impact on the overall community is minimal.

Option #3: Capitalize on Sin and Suffering

Every major city in America is facing enormous challenges in battling increased drug trafficking and the violent crime that tends to follow the drug flow. It has been noted that many of these drug dealers, at least on the street level, are minority youth. It should be no surprise then that 50 percent of the murder victims in America are black. Now, most people abhor the selling and use of drugs within the community, but let's put this issue into some sort of perspective.

With few exceptions, every ethnic group that migrated to the American cities during the turn of the past century established their initial economic base in some form of illegal enterprise. During the Prohibition Era, many of the Irish, Italian, and Jewish mafia created and conducted illegal bootlegging operations across the United States and Canada. Some groups even developed intricate prostitution, loan sharking, and drug rings in order to capitalize on America's flirtation with sin and pleasure. Having accumulated significant cash through these illegal operations, these various groups were then able to launder these huge amounts of cash and use them to develop legitimate businesses within and external to their own ethnic communities.

Clearly, while I could never condone these types of criminal activity, I certainly understand the lure of easy money. If I'm poor and uneducated the criminal option looks even more attractive. Unless someone has moral, legal, or ethical values that serve to prohibit him or her from engaging in these enterprises, they become attractive business opportunities. Very few business opportunities exist today where an untrained, uneducated person can accumulate so much cash so quickly. This person can generate significant cash flow without having to consume capital in plant and equipment, utilities, medical plans, or burdensome salary and administrative costs. Besides, the return on investment for these types of enterprises is phenomenal.

Of course, there are two problems with taking this entrepreneurial route. First, you will probably never get to enjoy the money. You will either die young or you will waste your life in prison. Second, these drugs are destroying our future—our young people. These two factors alone make this option highly undesirable.

Option #4: Accelerate Business Formation within the Community

Without a doubt, the best way for us to accumulate wealth quickly and increase the circulation rate of our dollars within our community is through the rapid formation of businesses within that community. To accomplish this, we must start directing a greater number of our young people through the entrepreneurship channel. This will benefit not only the African American community, but the overall American community.

As the United States struggles to remain competitive in an increasingly competitive global economy, America will have to rely more and more on the segment of the population that has historically been left out (women and minorities). The Department of Labor projects that the workforce will increase by 17 million workers between 1998 and 2008. This equates to a 12.3 percent change with an annual growth rate of 1.2 percent. The median age of the workforce is 41. Also, by the year 2008 the labor force will have the following characteristics.

Group	Percent of Labor Force	Annual Growth Rate
Whites	69.2	.9
Hispanics	12.7	3.2
Blacks	12.4	1.8
Asians	5.7	40.3
Women	47.5	1.4
Men	52.5	.9

Although this new majority is great in numbers, it will be the least prepared and most poorly trained. Unless these groups are provided the skills that will give them the ability to contribute and to make a good living honestly, these young people ultimately will take to the streets and become a lifelong burden to society.

Although estimates vary, most experts agree that as much as one-fourth of the United States workforce (approximately 28 million Americans) do not have a firm enough grasp on mathematics, reading, and writing skills to perform basic job tasks. Business leaders are concerned that as the world becomes increasingly competitive the American workforce will not be sufficiently trained to meet this global challenge. American corporations currently spend a significant amount of corporate resources each year teaching their employees the basic skills that they should have learned while in grade school.

Many fear the problem will be further compounded by significant changes in the makeup of the worker population. In years past, as the labor force grew rapidly due to the influx of the baby boom generation, corporations could take their pick of the best employees. Now, however, the next generation of workers is decisively smaller with a much different gender and color breakdown.

Will white, male-run corporations commit to train and prepare these new people of color and women? What will be the vehicle for training these young, bright, but untested people? The federal government? Maybe. The federal government's move away from government support programs is alarming though.

Although the total burden cannot and should not be left solely with the African American entrepreneurs, I believe it is reasonable to assume that a portion of this responsibility will reside with black business leaders.

Recently, an MIT researcher, David Birch, estimated that 80 percent of all new jobs are created by small and medium-sized businesses. These businesses will transcend all geographic and industrial boundaries. If this is true, then we need to make sure that we are represented adequately in those new business developments so that African Americans have a fair shot at these new opportunities.

Certainly, our quest for economic equality in the 2000s and beyond will best be realized through the creation of wealth through accelerated business formation within the African American community.

4

Preparing Yourself for Starting Your Own Business

BE HONEST WITH YOURSELF. WHY DO YOU WANT TO DO THIS?

After my graduation from business school, my wife, Carolyn, and I agonized over what our next adventure should be. I was fortunate to have many attractive job opportunities with reputable corporations at new and exciting locations around the country. However, after careful review, we decided to relocate to our home town of Baltimore, Maryland. As it turned out, coming home was a real blessing.

First, I could spend more time with my family and friends. Also, my parents were getting older, and my father's health was beginning to fail. Being home afforded me the opportunity at last to spend some special time with Mom and Dad. Second, at the risk of sounding corny, I had always dreamed of coming back home and making a contribution to my community. Maybe I could mentor the kids in my old neighborhood and keep them from going astray. Unfortunately, there is a tremendous amount of talent that we're losing to crime and drugs every day. Third, my interest in building business enterprises within the African American community was stimulated by my experiences at Dartmouth, and what better location to get started than the Baltimore-Washington corridor? With Baltimore being managed by a progressive white mayor and Washington, D.C. by an astute black mayor and the region's large and active black middle class, it seemed an ideal place to put down business roots.

As Carolyn and I started to reacquaint ourselves with our family, old friends, and all the changes that had taken place, I soon realized that I was not the only one who had a strong interest in developing the business infrastructure within the African American community. What a pleasant surprise!

With all of these potential business partners, I thought my mission of building coalitions and formulating partnerships would be easy. My excitement quickly turned to dismay when I found that many of these people were not really serious about pursuing viable business opportunities. Further investigation revealed that many of them naively thought they could quickly start a business, accumulate significant wealth, and retire on a private Caribbean island at the ripe old age of 30. Their lack of commitment, planning, and genuine understanding of the nuances of business formation was somewhat disturbing.

Business people are always asked: "Why did you go into business?" Based on the subjects of this study, I find that there is no one clear-cut response to this question. People go into business for as many reasons as there are different types of entrepreneurs. Although the stories of Microsoft's Bill Gates, AOL's Steve Case, and Time Warner's Gerry Levin are well documented in today's press, the good fortune and success that they enjoyed are quite rare. It will probably be another 10 to 20 years before another William Gates mesmerizes the business community. But then again, maybe not. It certainly is conceivable that you could be the next William Gates, but if you're not, don't be dismayed. There is still lots of money out here to be made by mere mortals.

Although most people are motivated by the idea of making large sums of money quickly, there are a few who want to start their businesses just for the challenge of it. Some people have very strong egos and feel that if anyone can be successful in business it certainly must be they. They shudder at the thought of working tirelessly for someone for 50 years only to be given a gold watch and then led off to pasture until their Maker calls them home. Their convictions and commitment remind them daily that they have all the smarts, ideas, and energy to make their dreams a reality. These people simply want the satisfaction of being able to say: "I did it!"

One group within the community who will be challenged by the building of enterprises is a group I've called the *emerging entrepreneurs.* This group of professionals can be found in corporations, the federal government, or in various types of consulting firms. They're biding their time and patiently waiting for the right opportunities before they make their moves. At the proper moments, they will emerge onto the business scene and make names for themselves.

These emerging entrepreneurs are motivated to participate in the creation of successful business enterprises that benefit the community because they understand the correlation between strong economic development and social and economic parity in our society. They learned the Golden Rule of American economics a long time ago, which says: He Who Owns the Gold, Rules.

Unfortunately, many people still don't understand the correlation between money and power and, quite frankly, don't care. As a matter of fact, some entrepreneurs started their ventures out of sheer necessity. As revealed by my study at Dartmouth, some of the business owners started their businesses because they needed another way to provide for their families. Due to circumstances outside their control, entrepreneurship was the most logical and visible option for them at the time. They were not seeking wealth and fame. Their only desire was to make an honest and decent living. Having spent some time with these reluctant entrepreneurs, I often have difficulty mustering up much sympathy for those unemployed people who drown themselves in self-pity. Anyway, believe it or not, the reluctant entrepreneur does exist.

Starting a business out of necessity is quite plausible and may even be noble, but there are folks out there who actually desire to be entrepreneurs because it is the hip thing to do. During the go-go decades of the 1980s and 1990s, it became popular to start your own business or at least to say that you wanted to start one. You don't believe me? All right. I suggest that you conduct your own survey and use your family and friends as a sampling group.

I would bet my firstborn that if you were to ask them to articulate their long-term professional goals, embedded somewhere in the babbling would be the words "start my own business." It has been my experience that about 90 percent of the people you poll will say this. Let's face it, the 1980s and 1990s were the decades of the entrepreneurs. We're still bombarded daily with stories of entrepreneurs—their successes and failures. Internet start-ups and small technology companies absorbed the lion's share of the $45 billion venture capital spent in 1999. Why do you think people like Donald Trump are constantly in the news? People like to hear and read about what old Donald is up to because he's rich and successful.

Unfortunately, most people in your casual survey may lack a clear understanding of business and the business savvy necessary to make a venture successful. Most will be without a sound plan or strategy that would allow them to set those dreams loose on the world. For them, the idea of owning a business is just a thought that languishes on the thresholds of their imaginations. One of the purposes of this book is to reveal the reality of going into business to people who may not be closely in touch with this critical economic development component.

The point of this discussion is to convey to you the importance of understanding why you want to go into business. The source of your motivation is just as important to your long-term success as the quality of your idea or the persuasiveness of your business plan. Your reason for pursuing a venture ultimately will help to dictate which markets you attack. Going into business because it's the hip or slick thing to do is not slick; it is sick. Be careful. Going into business for the wrong reason could actually ruin your life.

INTERNAL SUCCESS ACTUALIZATION

Internal success actualization is defined as the situation in which the would-be entrepreneur has completed the steps necessary to prepare herself or himself for the rigors of various business endeavors. The ability to achieve these internal success requirements is basically within the control of the individual and is often independent of external events or forces. This pyramid of internal success requirements is shown in Exhibit 4.1.

Exhibit 4.1 Internal Success Actualization

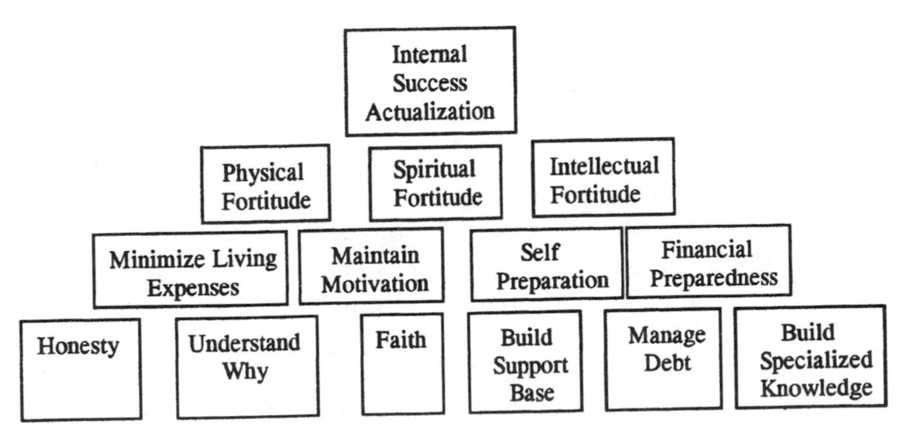

GETTING YOUR LIFE TOGETHER

After having assessed your reasons for going into business carefully, the next step is to get your house in order. A house that is not in order cannot and will not stand. You have to be strong if you're to have any chance of making this journey successfully. Your checklist for getting your house in order should at least include the following set of tasks:

- Building your spiritual fortitude
- Facing the enemy within and defeating him
- Building your physical fortitude
- Self-preparation
- Learning how to stay motivated
- Obtaining specialized knowledge in appropriate areas
- Preparing yourself financially
- Establishing a strong support base
- Taking the leap of faith and starting a business despite the odds

BUILD YOUR SPIRITUAL FORTITUDE

With few exceptions, the entrepreneurs profiled successfully established a high level of spiritual fortitude in their life. Spiritual fortitude is expressed when the entrepreneur masters the factors he can control but then depends on God to manage those factors that he cannot control. No matter how you perceive your God, you will need His power to guide you through the tough times, to sustain you when you're in the valley, and to humble you after you've scaled the mountain tops. There is power in knowing your God. Use this power to your advantage.

The second most important aspect of getting your house in order is loving and drawing close to your family. The majority of the entrepreneurs in the case studies did not enjoy the luxury of having family members who were familiar with the business environment. Consequently, the families were unable to assist them with specific business matters. However, what the families lacked in understanding the business was more than compensated for in the amount of love and support they showered on the struggling entrepreneurs. In most situations, the entrepreneurs' spouses contributed the lion's share of the love and support.

One's spouse is especially important when you're starting a business. A good man or woman beside you can often mean the difference between success and failure. Most of the entrepreneurs interviewed had strong spouses who strengthened them when they grew weak and motivated them when they became discouraged. Although I espouse the institution of marriage, if matrimony is not in your plans, then make sure that you have a mate who will support you, love you, and share in your successes and your failures. Money or success is no fun unless you have someone you love with whom to share it.

However, whatever you do, don't try to start a business when your love life is on the rocks. There exists only a finite amount of energy with which you're blessed. If the majority of this energy is consumed finding, courting, and nurturing multiple love relationships, then what energy is left to build an enterprise? In his book *The Art of Loving,* Erich Fromm states, "The deepest need of man is the need to overcome his separateness, to leave the prison of his aloneness. The absolute failure to achieve this aim means insanity." Many businesses have been built and prospered due to the love of a mate. Seek this love, capture it, and then harness it to do great things for you.

FACE THE ENEMY WITHIN AND DEFEAT IT

A strong argument could be built to suggest that African Americans have been the most oppressed ethnic group in the history of this country. Yet in spite of all the damage external oppressors have inflicted upon blacks, I submit that the most vicious oppressor is the one that lives on top of our shoulders. The system in which we live has been so effective at attacking our self-esteem that it has made some of us believe that we cannot be successful entrepreneurs. Our society has left us with such an inferiority complex that we are often afraid to make mistakes or even to engage in business transactions. Some fear that white America will ridicule us and use the experience to confirm their often quoted thoughts about our supposed inferiority.

Before you can seriously entertain the idea of becoming an entrepreneur, you must first confront the enemy within you and defeat it. Successful minority entrepreneurs have become experts at battling the enemy within and bringing it to its knees. I'm convinced that one of the most compelling reasons that African Americans are not better represented in the entrepreneurial ranks is because they think they cannot be successful. As a man thinketh, so is he. Never be afraid to fail. Take every opportunity to engage. Vince Lombardi summed it up best when he said, "Success is not in never falling, but in rising every time you fall."

BUILD YOUR PHYSICAL FORTITUDE

Physical and mental fitness would appear to be an obvious attribute of maintaining the order of one's house, but too often it is overlooked by anxious and impatient would-be entrepreneurs. Ralph Waldo Emerson once said, "The first wealth is health." One of the Hispanic members of this study shared a story with me about his young bride and how it took her some time to accept the importance of exercise and good health.

As young newlyweds, they argued excessively about the amount of time he spent at the gym working out. Like most other young brides, she felt that her new husband should be spending more time with her and less time at the gym or health club. What she failed to realize at the time was that getting exercise for him was not a luxury but in fact a necessity! These brief interludes at the gym allowed him to release his stress, clear his mind, and remain focused on the business. This Hispanic brother rationalized that in order to function efficiently, his body needed a good workout just as it needed food, water, and love.

Exercise is a part of our well-being. Any of you who are athletes or former ones can probably attest to the existence of a "natural high" experienced after a good workout. Numerous studies have shown that when your body is in this state, you are sharper and much more alert. This high produces significantly more creativity, and there appears to be a higher level of consciousness. Those of us who are physically unfit tend to lack energy, drive, perseverance, and endurance. With few exceptions, every entrepreneur I interviewed looked healthy, vibrant, trim, and in shape. Many confessed to having some type of regular workout routine—from aerobic classes to a daily walk around the local park.

EDUCATE YOURSELF

Before any business can be successful, its owner or leader must prepare himself or herself to handle the multiple situations that can arise. We've already talked about getting close to your God and about building up your support base. Now, let's talk about building you up!

When I took the entrepreneurship course while attending the Amos Tuck School of Business, I had a unique opportunity to break bread with a few venture capitalists who were evaluating our business projects. Having strong entrepreneurial ambitions myself, I wanted to pin these folks down on how they evaluate a business deal. One day, I thought, I'll be financing my business, so now is a good time to better understand how the venture capitalist business works.

Prior to my meeting with these venture capitalists, I had always assumed that these guys experienced orgasms from studying slick spreadsheets and rosy cash flow projections. However, I was terribly wrong. For the most part, the most important criteria used in evaluating a deal were the people behind the deal. One venture capitalist with whom I became friends often said, "I don't bet on the horse; I bet on the jockey!"

My friends and former business partners, Eliot Powell and Jerome Sanders of SDGG Holding Company, often reminded me of this fact as we made the rounds on Wall Street in our attempt to put together financing packages for our acquisitions. It may be difficult to believe, but the majority of venture capitalists focus on the people, and not on just the ideas or business plan. They clearly are more concerned with the education, work experience, integrity, and realism of the management team than with cash flow projections.

One venture capitalist went on to say that integrity and honesty ranked highest on his list. In other words, having a willingness to face the facts, admit when you're wrong, and accept the advice of others is critical. The road to entrepreneurial success is full of sharp turns and steep inclines. It takes an extremely confident person to tolerate this uncertainty, admit mistakes, and at the same time, keep traveling down the road. This same self-confidence is what forces the soon-to-be entrepreneurs to say good-bye to their prestigious positions in corporate America—health plans, profit sharing, and everything else. This blew me away! I had misunderstood completely the makeup of typical venture capitalists and what their hot buttons were. This experience confirmed my present belief about the importance of building yourself up. But how does one build himself or herself up?

First, let me get something off my chest. There was a time when I felt that in order to be a successful entrepreneur, you first had to go to a "good" school and earn a respected degree. Well, I'm not so sure that I totally agree with that philosophy any longer. Although some of the subjects of these case studies had impressive academic credentials, the majority had humble academic beginnings. To their credit, many of the participants in the study had gone back to college to obtain degrees after starting their businesses. However, there were also some who were very successful with no college degrees at all! (Although in the new economy I believe a college education is essential.)

There are some who suggest that having a respected degree from a top-tier school is the worst thing that an aspiring entrepreneur can do. The theory goes that these schools turn out highly paid bureaucrats instead of thirsty entrepreneurs. I must say that there may be some truth to this theory, although that trend is shifting to small businesses and start-ups.

I'm reminded of a conversation I had with a young entrepreneur who had started a plastics injection business in Michigan. This young man had impeccable academic credentials—a B.S. in engineering and an M.B.A. from Harvard. He shared with me that before he attended B-School he had contemplated going into a number of different businesses—from opening a barber shop to starting his own engineering company. At that time, he hadn't learned all the latest and greatest in spreadsheets, cash flow analyses, market strategies, net present values, and so forth. Consequently, although he was a "dumb engineer," he would not hesitate to pursue a deal purely based on rough financial projections and gut level feelings.

Unfortunately, after earning his M.B.A. from Harvard, he soon realized that every deal that came across his desk had to be taken through a number of algorithms that looked at projected business growth, market analyses, cash flow projections, and other criteria that he was taught in business school to analyze before he'd make a move. In essence, he had become what I've termed M.B.A. spooked. This term means that you analyze a deal so thoroughly that you eventually convince yourself that the risks are too high for you to proceed with the idea.

It doesn't matter how sweet a deal is, if you analyze it long and hard enough you can always find reasons it won't work. Instead, you need to focus on the reasons it will work! Although I don't condone blind pursuit of business deals, most successful entrepreneurs agree that it is possible to overanalyze a deal. For all of you hotshot M.B.A.s out there, don't let yourself become M.B.A. spooked.

There is another side to this prestigious education theory. If you're a minority person, having the proper academic credentials as feathers in your cap will help your cause. Unfortunately, there still remain some business leaders in positions of power who will listen only to black entrepreneurs if they come to the table with certain credentials. One of the business owners in the study said, "If you want your kids to be entrepreneurs, don't send them to Ivy League schools. This type of school will only turn them into highly paid corporate Dobermans." Although most would agree that our young people do face the risk of being blinded by the corporate glitter, having certain credentials will make it easier for them to get through the door and at a minimum be listened to.

You are probably asking yourself how much education is needed before venturing out on your own. At the risk of sounding contradictory, it is suggested that you obtain as much as you can as quickly as you can. The point I made previously is that you don't want your education to blind you. The Lord gave us all natural mechanisms that assist us in making good and logical decisions. Don't ignore those natural mechanisms (insight, gut level feeling, hunch, dream, etc.) and totally rely on technical tools and analytical methods. As long as you can remain committed to an idea and plan, you should get training from a good school and obtain the best business skills that you can acquire. If you already know what business you'd like to get into, try obtaining a degree in that area. Specialized knowledge is critical to success.

Build up as many potent weapons in your personal arsenal as possible. An M.B.A. from a prestigious university is a good weapon to have. Another benefit the M.B.A. gives you is that it strengthens your self-confidence. One of the most debilitating problems that our community faces is a shortage of confidence. If you are told and shown enough times that you can't compete pretty soon your subconscious mind, if not your conscious mind, will believe it.

STAY MOTIVATED

Staying motivated will be one of the most difficult things for you to do during your quest to get started. People's interest or intensity of purpose in a project usually follows the normal distribution curve. When people first start their ventures they're extremely excited and full of energy as shown by the steep incline in the early stages of the project. Over time though, as the burdens and problems of making their ventures realities confront them, their energy and excitement start to wane.

As shown by the schematic in Exhibit 4.2, at some point in time their interest peaks and then falls dramatically. Your interest curve is especially vulnerable if you're one of those people trying to start a business while remaining a full-time employee for someone else. It will be almost impossible to do both jobs well. Also with the pressures of a mortgage, a demanding spouse, civic responsibilities, child rearing, and the usual problems of life, you could become severely stressed.

This additional stress caused by your attempt to get your business off the ground will generally result in frustration, anxiety, and

Exhibit 4.2 Excitement Points

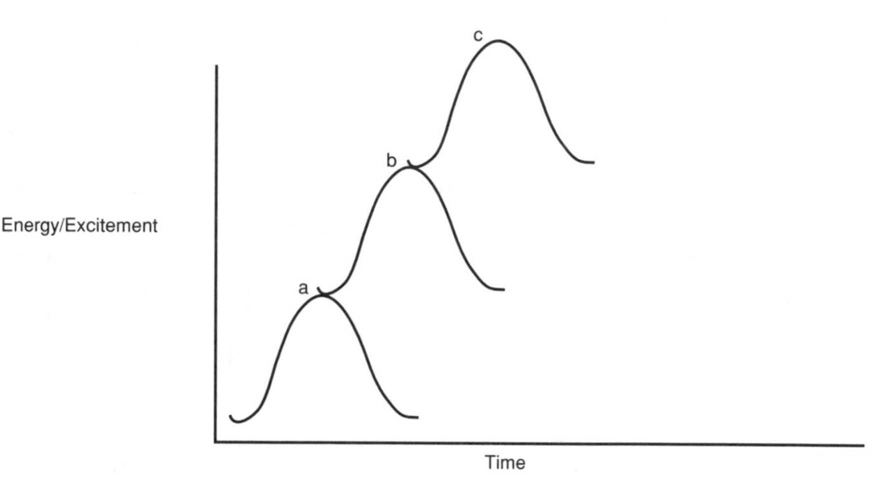

disillusionment. It is during these times that it becomes essential for you to inject *excitement points* into your efforts. African American entrepreneurs who excel understand the importance of these excitement points. The excitement points a, b, and c shown in Exhibit 4.2 serve to generate for you a new interest curve to take over when your prior one peaks.

Excitement points are unique to the individual. Whatever excites you to the point at which you become refocused, recommitted, and passionate about achieving your goal is considered an excitement point. These excitement points could include buying a new sports car, joining a new organization of entrepreneurs, benefiting from divine intervention via a dream or a real life experience, talking quietly with your God, receiving a vision, or reading an outstanding book. The idea here is that you need to understand what excites you to the point that it forces you to occasionally regenerate your interest curves and inject those excitement events into your life on a regular basis.

OBTAIN SPECIALIZED KNOWLEDGE IN APPROPRIATE AREAS

To prepare yourself for future entrepreneurial action, I'd be remiss if I failed to mention the need to develop specialized knowledge in some area. If you looked at the successful entrepreneurs in our society, you would find that the majority started their empires by providing a needed product or service; or, they possessed the creativity to produce brilliant ideas that could be sold easily for profit. One effective way to gain this knowledge is to pursue a job in an area in which you would like one day to start a business.

The results of the study of the alumni of Dartmouth's Minority Business Executive Program reveal that there is a strong correlation between the industry entrepreneurs worked in prior to starting their businesses and the type of firms they ultimately start. Christopher Williams of Williams Financial Services, Inc., spent many years working on Wall Street and learning his trade in the financial services industry, before launching his highly successful Wall Street firm.

Walter Hill, co-founder of ECS Technologies, a systems integration and value-added reseller for IBM in the Baltimore-Washington area, initially worked for Westinghouse Electric Corporation for close to 10 years before starting his firm. While he was employed by Westinghouse, one of his main responsibilities was to acquire many of the essential electronic components and computer systems used in the manufacture of radar systems. While in that capacity, he learned the technical details of the components, made contacts with key vendors in the industry, and began to develop an appreciation for the opportunities in this field. When he and his partner, Eillen Dorsey, left their jobs to start their business, they both brought with them a clear set of marketable skills, valuable customer contacts, sufficient technical competence, and market insight.

Clearly, if you have a good idea about which industry you'd like to compete in, try to obtain a job in that industry. By allowing someone else to pay the cost of training you, you minimize your investment in training once you start your business, thus reducing your initial capital requirements.

PREPARE YOURSELF FINANCIALLY

Not a day passes that I don't discuss with someone somewhere the idea of starting a small business. Many of my cohorts in the information technology and Internet industry have dreams of building their own businesses but few have taken the initiative to make the dream a reality. Probably the biggest excuse that I hear is that they lack the proper funds needed to adequately capitalize the business. Indeed, this is probably the biggest stumbling block of most small and aspiring business owners. However, this obstacle is no excuse for not working on your plan.

This issue of lack of funds certainly didn't stop many of corporate America's most successful CEOs. Do many of you get your taxes filed by H&R Block? Well, consider the fact that Henry Block and his brother Richard started preparing tax forms for clients around 1954. The initial financing came from a $5,000 loan from one of their family members. The rest of the funding came from internally generated funds, thanks to the many customers who swarmed over Henry and his brother for tax assistance. H&R Block is now a major online brokerage firm serving its clients over the Internet. Speaking of the Internet, look at all the new Internet companies (and Internet millionaires). Yahoo! was started by college students. The company's market value is now in the billions.

Wait! Don't start thinking that all of the success stories are in the Internet and computer technology industries because that's not the case. Consider for a moment Ms. Leone Ackerly. Ms. Ackerly purchased a few cleaning supplies in 1973 and began cleaning houses. The initial supplies cost her less than $10 but she was able to parlay this idea into a nationwide franchise called Mini-Maid International of Marietta, Georgia.

You do not always need a significant amount of cash to start your business. In fact, too much cash might be harmful! Experts say that an abundance of cash tempts people to start enterprises that are bigger and more complex than they can handle. Mr. Geoffrey Kessler, a small business consultant based in Los Angeles, said that starting out with little money makes an initial flop easier to recover from. "It's like riding a bicycle on the sidewalk; if you fall down, you can keep trying until you get it right. But if you start out on the freeway, there's no room for mistakes." Mr. Kessler has also observed that business owners working with little capital are forced to be more innovative when considering several solutions to a problem.

Don't worry. I'm not trying to kid myself. I realize that even with minimal capitalization requirements, we're expected to provide some cash to help fund the enterprise. Unfortunately, for many of us, coming up with even a few thousand dollars to bring life to a worthy venture is a formidable task. Based on the information I've compiled, I have some suggestions that may help to alleviate this problem.

Manage Debt and Accumulate Cash

This concept may sound simplistic, but the first thing you need to do is evaluate your present financial situation. The evaluation can be completed by yourself or a financial planner. In my household, I run the operation like it was a business. Although I consider myself the president, my wife, Carolyn, is actually the chief executive officer (my boss).

I think my wife is amused by how seriously I take my role but she lets me have my little kicks anyway. Just as in a business, my role in Wallace Family, Inc. is to maintain the financial posture of the entity, respect and take care of its workers (my wife and kids), and turn a profit for the shareholders (accumulate capital for college educations, exotic vacations, and lucrative business ventures). As president of your family business, you need to understand the resources your family has at its disposal and the results achieved by their use. The type of information needed to effectively leverage the assets may include:

- Operating information
- Management accounting information
- Financial accounting information

Believe it or not, a considerable amount of information is required to conduct the day-to-day operations of the home. Expenses have to be met, amounts owed must be known, up-to-date status on asset base must be maintained, and the well-being of your loved ones must be constantly monitored. To assist me in carrying out this task, I often rely on the management accounting skills I obtained while attending business school. For those M.B.A.s reading this, you may recall that management accounting information is used to control, coordinate, and plan our family's finances.

Controlling the finances of a family is not an easy task, as many of you can probably attest. One entrepreneur who owned a small manufacturing company in New England shared the story about his lovely wife, who did many things well, but who left their checking account in ruins! He jokingly recalled that his wife was one of those people who writes a million checks and consistently forgets to make the entries in the checking log. Consequently, when he was evaluating their financial position at any point in time, his records might indicate that he had more cash in the bank than he really had. After she had done this enough times, they decided to put a system in place that alerts her when she makes that mistake and encourages her to act in a way that is consistent with the family's overall goals and objectives. Their system sometimes acts as an attention getter, signaling when problems that require investigation and possibly action exist.

Just as important as control is coordination. Clearly, every component of a household must work in unison to achieve its objectives. This implies that communication between the various members (you and your spouse) must be open and frank. If I, for example, come up with new guidelines and objectives, they must be communicated to my wife; otherwise her actions may be detrimental to the achievement of our goal. Someone in your household must take responsibility for this role and become semifanatical about making it work. Household bills must be scrutinized continually and innovative ways developed to minimize them.

Coordination without planning is useless. Planning is the process of deciding what action should be taken in the future. One important form of planning is called budgeting (sound familiar?). Budgeting is the process of planning the overall activity of your household for a specified period of time. Most people budget on a monthly basis. My wife and I integrate the various needs of all members of the family, such that all assets are effectively leveraged. Planning often involves making difficult decisions, such as: Do I really want to go into business? Am I willing to make the sacrifices necessary for the business to succeed once it has started? Do I really need to get this Mercedes-Benz now?

Usually the process of maintaining operating information on your household finances through control, coordination, and planning positions you well in dealing with outside financial institutions. If you've ever borrowed money from any financial house, you know what I mean. As far as your financial condition is concerned, every aspect of your financial posture is reviewed. Just as potential stockholders of a corporation need certain information about a company to help them decide if they want to invest, most banks want similar information about you!

Prepare a Personal Financial Statement

Even before you decide what business to pursue, your first step is to construct your personal financial statement. In most situations, a financial statement serves two purposes. The first purpose is to provide you a clear and honest picture of your financial status and to help you pinpoint any financial weaknesses you may want to strengthen before approaching potential investors. The second purpose is that it is usually required when negotiating with investors, business brokers, or potential sellers.

Typically, your financial statement should be broken into two major parts: a balance sheet composed of your assets and liabilities, which shows your net worth, and an income-expense statement, which gives a picture of your cash flow. Some statements also include information about you, your family, and your past credit performance. You should state (if it's true) that you've never been through bankruptcy court and have no suits or judgments against you. In the business and science sections of most libraries, you will find examples of how a personal financial statement should be structured.

In general, the bank or other lender wants information that will show that your financial position is sound, and that there is a high probability that the loan will be repaid when it comes due. The more successful you are at controlling your expenses, increasing your asset base, and enhancing your net worth, the better positioned you'll be to launch your venture.

Minimize Living Expenses

People who were raised in lower income environments usually have difficulty when it comes to minimizing their living expenses. To be honest about it, this phenomenon is prevalent among anyone who has not had an opportunity to benefit from America's wealth. Usually, when the only contact you've had with the niceties of American life is through television or the pages of a magazine, the first chance you get to splurge, you do so. This phenomenon is not unique to one race. It includes poor white people as well as poor people of color. People in this group find it exceedingly difficult to postpone the good life until the struggling venture has paid off significant dividends. They want the good life now!

Why does this tend to be the case? Clearly, there are numerous reasons. To start, a large number of minority Americans were probably raised in environments where everyone struggled daily to survive and very few enjoyed the conveniences and pleasures that many of their mainstream counterparts took for granted.

One of my fraternity brothers, who started his own software business, recalled his days growing up in the inner city of Chicago. There were times when his family went for long periods without heat or running water. Even when the water was on, the system could not deliver enough hot water to satisfy the needs of his large family. Boiling water, pouring it into a basin, and washing from that basin was their primary method of bathing. Showers were unheard of in his neighborhood during that time.

This young man escaped the projects when he attended a predominantly white high school, where he lettered in three sports. To him, the best part of participating in sports was the fact that he got a chance to get a hot shower each day. The rest of the guys took hot showers for granted, but not this grateful young man. For him, it was an emotional event because he was not used to this luxury and found out that he really enjoyed it! Today, this young man will not even look at a house unless it has lots of showers.

This person's experience is a good example of how some of us overcompensate for what we lacked as children. The point is that when you're forced to live in a way that prevents you from enjoying many of the privileges that most Americans take for granted, you'll go right out and recreate that object or experience that you've desired for so long the first opportunity that you get.

Another reason that struggling people have difficulty minimizing living expenses is because of their need to convince the world that they have more than they really do. Have you ever noticed how some rich people fanatically try to downplay their wealth (at least some of them). They often wear the same old jeans and button-down oxford shirt day after day. They seem to place very little emphasis on the clothes they wear, often preferring to be seen in well-worn garments. Some even prefer to drive around in old, outdated automobiles that most of us would hate to be seen in. Usually, contrary to what they would have you believe, these people may have vast holdings of real estate and other assets and enjoy a very high standard of living invisible to the public eye.

The subjects of this study have made it crystal clear that, if you want to get into business, there is no getting around the fact that you have to accumulate some cash for starting capital. Most agree that the way to do that is to cut expenses as much as possible by minimizing your standard of living. However, if you're committed, your sacrifices today will pay big dividends for you tomorrow.

This idea of postponing the good life reminds me of a story told to me by one of the small business owners from southern California interviewed for this study. The individual told me of one of his childhood friends who had the philosophy that since you don't know what's going to happen to you tomorrow, you should really live it up today. "Why save for tomorrow when there is no guarantee that you'll be living tomorrow?" this young man was often heard saying.

As fate would have it, this man lived for a long time, but in his latter years was forced to struggle daily to meet his basic human needs. Many people in our community espouse this type of philosophy—in my opinion, too many. No, the future is not promised, but there comes a time when you just have to believe in your longevity and plan for the future.

ESTABLISH A STRONG SUPPORT BASE

This section on self-development and self-preparation for your upcoming entrepreneurial venture is one of the most important. Here I address the importance of surrounding yourself with trustworthy and intelligent people as you strive to create and build your enterprises.

In his book titled, *Think and Grow Rich,* Napoleon Hill discusses in great detail the benefits of surrounding yourself with great minds. Dr. Dennis Kimbro, author of *Think and Grow Rich: A Black Choice,* touches upon this same concept. Mr. Hill labels this group a mastermind group and delineates the criteria for choosing members. He explains that there are two characteristics of the mastermind principle, one of which is economic in nature and the other is psychic. From an economic standpoint, the benefits are quite obvious.

When you surround yourself with brilliant minds, you have a unique coordination of knowledge, spirit, effort, and direction that works in harmony to help achieve some common goal or objective. Although the psychic component of the mastermind principle is more difficult to appreciate, it is nevertheless a powerful part of this pair. Mr. Hill later suggests that whenever two strong and sincere minds come together for a common cause, there exists a part of the human energy element that is spiritual and that those spiritual energies somehow go through some form of metamorphosis that in essence creates a third mind. Every single minority business owner in this study in some way or another had a group of advisers with whom they confided for ideas and support.

Not only must you surround yourself with good minds, you must also associate yourself with other aspiring and accomplished entrepreneurs. There is no doubt that you are a product and a reflection of your environment. If you are consistently around solid professionals whose goal in life is to climb the corporate ladder and be a corporate executive, then there is a good probability that you'll assume the same ambitions and desires. If your running buddies are into drugs and alcohol, then you'll probably start doing drugs and indulging in excessive drinking.

However, when you're constantly around aspiring or established businesspeople, a synergy is created and you become a part of it. You will start thinking like a businessperson, looking like a businessperson, and even believing that you are already a business owner. Each level of excitement catapults you to another, until your vision of business ownership becomes reality. In most cases, just the fact that you have a personal relationship with an existing business owner removes much of the mystery usually associated with being an entrepreneur, causing you to take the attitude that *if she can do it, so can I!*

Once you've gotten your brain trust group together, which I hope will consist of intelligent, trustworthy, conscientious entrepreneurs and soon-to-be entrepreneurs, you then need to weed out all of your dead-end relationships and sever the connections. Why is this important? The answer is simple. When you start putting your plans together for your venture and ultimately start it, you will need all the time and support that you can get!

There are only so many hours in a day and days in a week, and you'll need all of them to accomplish your goals while maintaining your sanity. You don't need to waste your precious time with folks who are insincere, selfish, weak minded, and lacking direction and drive. Learn quickly how to identify and isolate these relationships and move quickly to terminate them.

While you're severing dead relationships, whatever you do, strengthen the good ones that you have. The people in your life who are important to you and whom you love should be told that. Tell them how much you love them and how important they are in your life. Whether it is your wife, husband, father, mother, brother, sister, or pal, they need to know how much they mean to you. Nearly every person in this study articulated this critical fact at some point. Many of them reiterated the fact that when you go into business, your family and friends go in with you. You'll need their love and support, so work to strengthen those relationships now, before you start.

TAKING THE LEAP OF FAITH AND STARTING A BUSINESS DESPITE THE ODDS

I realize that I've just taken you through an enormous amount of information in my attempt to make sense of the detailed information collected from the participants of my study. I trust that the previous chapters have encouraged you enough that you're excited about starting your venture in spite of the odds.

In discussing entrepreneurship with minorities and females, the most difficult part of getting into business is determining what type of business one wants. Naturally, there are many options. There is consulting, which requires very little capitalization; manufacturing, which requires high capitalization; Internet start-ups, which are easy to start and expensive to capitalize; or other businesses in between. You will have to take your best guess, given the information you have, and choose an area. Even if it turns out to be the wrong choice, you'll be that much closer to finding the right option for you.

CASE STUDY

This case study shows how first generation entrepreneurs are faring and the issues they face in transitioning their businesses into the new economy. Mr. Chavis is a Native American.

EARL CHAVIS

Founder, Chavis Tool & Company
Lamar, South Carolina

"There Is No Time for On-the-Job Training"

It has often been said that going into business with someone is like getting married. Like marriage, it requires that all people involved maintain a certain amount of trust and commitment among themselves. When the trust factor breaks down, then all parties involved need to reevaluate whether they should continue with a venture or not.

Early in 1976, Earl Chavis, CEO of Chavis Tool & Company, was confronted with this very dilemma. A few years earlier, Earl, bristling with confidence and optimism, left Rockwell International to form his own machine tool company in South Carolina. At the time, Earl was very low on cash, but had a surplus of experience, credentials, and creative ideas. One day while in church, Earl started a conversation with one of the church members concerning the company that Earl was contemplating starting. To Earl's surprise, the other man appeared very excited about the deal and even suggested that maybe he could help provide some of the financing. Earl could not believe his ears. His prayers had been answered, or so he thought.

After further discussions with the man and determining that he was quite serious, Earl and his new acquaintance decided to create a partnership in which each man controlled 50 percent of the stock. The initial agreement between the two was that Earl would not have to put up much capital to start the company, but would instead contribute his leadership and expertise.

Initially, the arrangement between the two men was like a match made in heaven. The two got together and developed a strong business plan identifying their markets, equipment needs, and what type of building they would need to house all of the equipment. After more detailed discussions with their advisors, they decided to rent a 6,000-square-foot warehouse and to contract with an equipment leasing company to lease the necessary machinery.

From dealing with the leasing company, Earl soon learned an important lesson. That is, if you have a strong financial statement, you can borrow money as often as you like and as much as you like. In financing equipment acquisitions, it became apparent to him that you could actually acquire equipment without having to put any cash down. Because Earl's partner had millions of dollars in personal net worth, he had no difficulty getting the banks to loan the team money. The fact that the partner was white and well connected in the small South Carolina town didn't weaken their position, either.

By the end of the first year of operation, Earl's small business was doing about $250,000 in sales and was on the verge of experiencing exponential growth in the coming year due to the anticipated award of lucrative government contracts. Unfortunately, huge cash requirements are also a companion of rapid growth and Earl realized the company would need a quick cash injection to handle the additional business. At that time, Earl's partner was handling the company finances so whenever there was a cash requirement, his partner was the one to write the checks. When the firm ran low on cash, the partner would write checks from his own personal accounts—or so he was leading Earl to believe.

As the new contracts began filtering in, Earl started noticing that the customers were taking an unusually long time to pay their bills. This situation lasted for a few months before Earl became really concerned and started making calls to his friends in those companies. What he heard made him sick to his stomach. As it turned out, the companies were promptly paying their bills as they had agreed. The problem was that instead of depositing the checks into the corporate accounts, Earl's partner was depositing the funds into his personal account.

Earl was infuriated and later sought to bankrupt the firm so that he could bring an end to this business relationship as quickly and effortlessly as possible. Earl's partner denied any wrongdoing and insisted that the company continue on its present course. Earl refused and, after finishing the contracts that he had agreed to complete, ended up liquidating the firm's assets. He called in the leasing company to take back the leased equipment and sold the building. Due to some outstanding debt that the firm was saddled with, Earl walked away from the liquidation debt free but penniless. Earl recalls:

> When I liquidated my business, the only income I had was from my unemployment insurance. I went from earning $25,000 per year down to a fraction of that amount. The difficulty of my dilemma was further complicated because I had four kids who were still in school. After swallowing

a little pride, I forced myself to apply for food stamps (I got $300 worth for $15) and used my unemployment income to feed my family and pay my mortgage. My family and I lived like this for about a year. I had nothing.

Earl was obviously very hurt by this fiasco. He felt cheated and violated. But as time passed, he began to realize that he had learned a tremendous amount from this experience. To his credit, he had started a business without investing a dime of his own money and had acquired brand new equipment to build his products. The experience had taught him that it was possible to start a business with very little of his money and still make it work.

STARTING OVER AGAIN

Undaunted by his most recent setback, Earl resolved to start his business again but this time he would do it his way—the right way. He began this time by studying programs that were available to help start minority firms. He contacted the Small Business Administration (SBA), identified the specific programs, and arranged numerous face-to-face meetings with the representatives of the SBA to determine if and how they could help him. Unlike many of his counterparts at that time, Earl refused to rely completely on the SBA. While he was negotiating with them, he continued to pursue other options he had on the outside.

One lesson Earl had learned from his previous experience was that in order for him to make a product, he didn't have to do all the manufacturing himself. He could use subcontractors to build a portion of the product and then he could provide the finishing touches. Rough calculations on the merits of subcontracting convinced him that he could in fact make money this way instead of doing everything himself.

This second time around, Earl also reconsidered how he would purchase his equipment and manufacturing space. Instead of buying brand new equipment Earl opted to buy used equipment at a significant discount. He was able to fix up the equipment himself at very little cost to his new company. For $1,000, Earl was able to buy all the equipment he would need initially, even though he had to borrow the money from his brother-in-law because he was still broke. Earl was just as creative in his search for a building to house the equipment. He happened to know a friend in his lodge who had a vacant building available and convinced his friend to rent him the building for $25 per month. Once Earl began making money, he would pay the monthly rent at a level that was more realistic.

LEVERAGING POLITICAL CONNECTIONS

While Earl continued to build his business from the ground up, he also began building a strong working relationship with the SBA. Although he hadn't been successful in obtaining funding yet, he had completed all the paperwork and had met with most of the officials running the agency. After a period of time, Earl became frustrated and disillusioned with the SBA and its ability to help him. About this time, Earl heard about an SBA conference that was being held at Benedict College in South Carolina, which Senator Ernest Hollins would attend.

The intent of the conference was to convey to all the small businesses in South Carolina that the SBA was sponsoring some very creative programs to stimulate small business activity in the state. Earl decided to attend the conference. To dramatize his frustration, he brought along all the paperwork that he had completed for the SBA before he could get any help. Earl tells the story:

> So I stood up with a stack of papers this high under my arm and I stood out in the middle of the hallway. There were no whites in there, other than government officials. The majority of the people there were black. We don't have many Native Americans left in South Carolina. I said, "Senator, you said I have to do this and this and this and then the Small Business Administration would take over. Right?"
>
> "That's exactly right!" he said.
>
> I dropped the stack of papers on the floor and said, "Senator, do you see all these papers I just dropped on the floor? This is all the paperwork I've completed for the SBA. I have done everything you've said that I need to do and I still haven't gotten much help."
>
> The senator turned around and looked at the guy who was the director of the Small Business Administration and said, "What's the matter with you people? This man has done everything he was supposed to do and you haven't done anything yet?" Senator Hollins then turned back to me and instructed me to call the SBA office on Tuesday, and if they hadn't done anything by the following Monday, he would intervene. I thanked the senator, quickly picked up my papers off the floor and quietly left the room.

After Earl's encounter with Senator Hollins, things started to happen very quickly at the SBA. The following Monday morning the SBA called Earl in for a meeting and helped him draw up the paperwork for a $50,000 loan. In June 1976, 18 months after he had applied, Earl finally received a check for $50,000, which he used as working capital to acquire inventory, pay utilities, and repair old equipment.

As the business began to expand, Earl's capital requirements also began to spiral upward. Early in 1980, Earl was awarded a Department of Defense contract to produce gun barrels. The contract was worth close to $1,000,000. Unable to meet this contract with funds on hand, Earl was forced to borrow $300,000 from a local bank that was guaranteed by the SBA. The $300,000 was going only to buy the raw materials and the tooling. Earl's firm was forced to meet any other expenses. Shortly thereafter, Earl was forced to borrow another $100,000 from the same community bank. This time the funds were used for operating capital. Unfortunately for Earl, inflation took off about the same time he floated the additional debt and for some time he was saddled with high interest rates, diminishing his ability to service the debt.

DEFINING THE CUSTOMER SET

After making the additional loans, Earl turned his attention to firming up his customer base. Although much of his business was coming from the federal government, he did have some success generating customers from the private sector as well. A few of his private customers included General Electric, Cummins Engines, and Southeastern Steel Company. Earl claims that his success in attracting business from private companies was a combination of contacts, timing, and luck. As he explains:

> Once someone is in a key position with a company, while they may have to move, chances are they will continue in the same line of work. After you've been around for a while and you've worked at various companies, you begin to know all the people in your profession. The fact that you see them socially and at various professional forums helps you keep track of their whereabouts. Consequently, everyone knew that I had been a technical director at Rockwell and A. B. Dick. After convincing potential customers of my ability to perform the task at hand, I usually was awarded the work.

DEFINING THE CORRECT BUSINESS STRATEGY

Chavis Tool & Company has been in business for more than 20 years. The sales volume generated usually falls under $10 million per year. Earl has taken the business to a critical point, and he must now decide what his next step will be:

> At my age, the question of what I'm going to do for growth is a difficult one. Regardless of what strategy we follow, there are a few things that we

> must do. First, we must upgrade all our equipment to realize efficiency benefits. We are in the process of doing that. It is estimated that we'll spend somewhere between a half million to a million dollars in capital equipment improvement over the next few years. Now for us to elevate our shop to the point where we can consistently generate sales above the $5 million mark, we will have to invest in advanced equipment and new automation technologies. Right now, we are diversified. We can go in any direction at any time that we choose. We have many options.

Currently, Earl is purposely running the plant far below capacity. He is currently servicing a heavy debt load and doesn't have the capital to run the operation at full capacity. Part of his short-term strategy is to reduce his debt to more manageable levels before he initiates his next growth spurt. He also would like to reevaluate alternative funding strategies and debt financing, and possibly to factor his receivables.

Earl has four children—two boys and two girls. However, only one of his children is actively involved in running the business. Earl manages basically all the administrative functions, including financing, purchasing, office managing, buying, selling, and marketing.

Because Earl is over 60 years of age, he often debates whether he should commit the resources to move the business to the next level or should just turn over the reins to his son and take early retirement. He has already estimated that he would need to invest at least $500,000 in new equipment to have any chance of meeting his growth goals. The problem he faces is that he may have to put up more collateral than he's willing to commit in order to satisfy the banks. Earl is visibly concerned about investing for this growth and then having the bottom fall out. He cautions:

> A business owner has to be careful. Let's assume that you've used every asset you own as collateral to acquire loans. As you continue to grow and expand you will probably find that you'll need additional funding. But what will you use for collateral? How are you going to get more money? What are you going to use to get money? That's what you have to watch out for—growth, fast growth.

BORN TO BE PROUD

It is a major accomplishment that Earl has accumulated and achieved so much in his lifetime, based on his impoverished childhood. Born into the Cheraw Lumbee tribe in a small rural area of North Carolina, Earl was one of 12 children. He is proud of his Native American roots and is quick to remind people that Native Americans of the Cheraw Lumbee tribe were once part of the great Tuscarora nation. This nation, which originated in what is now North Carolina, later populated the areas that are now called New York and Ontario, Canada.

Like many of the other men of this nation, Earl's father was a farmer and performed sharecropping services for many of the rich, white landowners. All of the children were expected to help out on the farm, including Earl. However, Earl had bigger ambitions and often dreamed of going off to college. Thanks to his mother, Earl was given that chance. Even though she was illiterate, she understood the value of education and did all she could to ensure that her son would have it. She often reminded him that without education he couldn't do anything.

Responding to his mother's wishes, after completing his tour of duty in the Navy, Earl was able to attend college and earn his degree. With the Navy and college behind him, Earl married his Greek sweetheart and began his career. During his long and illustrious career, Earl worked for companies such as Western Electric, A. B. Dick, and Rockwell in various engineering, R&D, and management positions.

ADVICE TO YOUNG ENTREPRENEURS

Earl is quick to caution all young entrepreneurs to be sure to go into a business they know something about unless they are going into business with someone who has knowledge in the area:

> There is no time for on-the-job training. You have to know what you are supposed to do before you go out. If you are in school and you do not know what you want to do, take some business administration courses. A sound business background provides you many options for pursuing business. An individual with good business training and a good business mind can be very beneficial to a business. For example, if one is an engineer, he could probably do the technical, administrative, and possibly the managerial work. One person fulfills more than one functional role.

Although most small businesses experience cash flow problems, Earl suggests that if you're going to have cash flow problems, it's better to experience them early in the venture instead of later. He's found that if you're smart, it's easier to survive when they hit you early versus the later years. Earl adds:

> Throughout the booming 1980s, many businesses failed. In my opinion, the primary reason they folded was because the people were not familiar

> with and didn't know how to function under severe cash flow constraints. Too many have been taught to go to the bank and get whatever money they need to solve the particular problem. In the 1980s, the rules changed. You couldn't go to the banks to get the money because they wouldn't give it to you! You had to learn how to run your business with less cash. I think as we move into the 2000s people will be a little more conservative and cash conscious.

The fact that Chavis Tool & Company is a minority firm has not helped or harmed the company, according to Earl. To his chagrin, some of his local competitors believe that because his is a minority firm, his business gets better opportunities than theirs. Earl's response to this prevailing sentiment is "bull crap."

> I was given nothing! The minority status only helps you if it is used in the manner it was designed to be used. If you try to use it in some other form or if you try to circumvent it in some other way, you are dead. You are going to have all kinds of problems. Although the federal government has the 8(a) program for disadvantaged businesses and although I've participated in the program since 1977, I have not received a significant amount of business at this point. Unfortunately, the only time the public hears about the 8(a) program is when it's being abused. You've seen a competitor all over the news. Those people stole millions of dollars. They abused the system and now it is costing me and other minority business owners. I have to pay for their greed.

Earl further cautions young businesspeople to maintain a low profile and some degree of humility. If you maintain a high profile, this means there are more people who can take shots at you. Earl recommends that if you need that type of attention, let someone else do it for you. If what you're doing is that spectacular, then it will only be a matter of time before the public begins to notice.

Earl advises young entrepreneurs to remember that while they're building their businesses, they should do something for themselves and their families. In spite of difficult times, Earl was able to buy a farm in South Carolina and a beachfront home for the summer. Earl will soon have the farm, his plant, his beach home, and his primary home paid off.

CASE STUDY

This case study illustrates the challenges of a partnership as well as how to use government initiatives to help grow your business. Ms. Dorsey and Mr. Hill are African American.

WALTER W. HILL JR. and EILLEN E. DORSEY

Founders, ECS Technologies
Baltimore, Maryland

"We Need to Be Able to Effectively Network"

From the front window of the ECS offices, the bright new headquarters of the National Association for the Advancement of Colored People (NAACP) can be seen clearly. The city of Baltimore, with its African American mayor, Kurt Schmoke, and its sizable African American population, has become a mecca for minority-based organizations who want to relocate to an area that is economically attractive and yet sensitive to the issues that confront the African American community.

So it was fitting that ECS sat there, a hub of activity, under the shadow of the nation's oldest civil rights organization. As I waited in the small but nicely furnished offices of ECS for Walter Hill Jr., one of the company's two founders, I wondered how it was possible for him and his partner, Eillen, to generate so much business from such a small office with only a handful of employees. As I soon learned, this dynamic duo had a knack for taking very little and turning it into something sizable and valuable, through courage, creativity, and hard work. This ability to leverage meager resources into long-term gain served both people well as they cut their business teeth in corporate America and prepared themselves to move into the entrepreneurial ranks.

LEARNING FROM CORPORATE EXPERIENCE

Walter, better known as Billy to his family and friends, decided after college that he wanted to work for the largest private employer in the state of Maryland—Westinghouse Electric Corporation. Although he was overqualified for the position, he accepted a job as a buyer. Billy did not find the job especially difficult. As a result, he was able to get quick promotions and additional responsibility at a young age. For his first three years, his role was an entry-level buyer. Later, he was promoted to a contract specialist position and excelled at this role for two years before he was moved to the next level as a senior subcontract specialist.

Having obtained this level by the time he was 26 years old, Billy had set a new precedent and had surpassed the majority of his peers. Even though Hill had shown that he had the skills, business savvy, and boldness to be successful at Westinghouse, there were still many people who were in positions of power who just weren't ready for a 26-year-old hotshot manager who happened to be black.

Eillen, Billy's partner, a salesperson for a company that distributed electronic components, was facing similar issues, and was poised to make the conversion from employee to employer at the same time Hill was. No stranger to hard work and perseverance, Eillen was raised in Harford County, Maryland, the youngest of eight children. Her parents, Walter and Louvina Blackston, although members of a generation of black Americans that was harshly oppressed legally and systematically, taught their eight children that if they dreamed long and hard enough and if they were committed to their dream, they could defeat racism and ignorance and turn their dreams into reality. This message rang loud and clear in Eillen's mind as she matured into a young woman and began making her mark in the business world. As she and Hill began to forge their business alliance, Eillen's business experience in the electronic components business proved invaluable in allowing ECS to get off to a strong start. Eillen fondly recalls the genesis of ECS:

> Walter and I developed a personal friendship during the early 1970s. During this period, we were both encouraged by the number of minority firms that were sprouting up in the Baltimore-Washington corridor to take advantage of the lucrative contracting opportunities with the federal government. To our chagrin, we later learned that some of these firms were only fronts for majority firms. Walter and I both felt that if we made the commitment to go into business that we would become a true minority firm and dedicate ourselves to providing high-quality products at competitive prices.

Billy's commitment to starting a business peaked at about the same time that Eillen's did. Although still an employee of Westinghouse, Billy recalls with a mischievous grin:

> I guess I was consciously planning my exit because I realized that every corporation producing machinery of any type had to buy some electrical components to complete the manufacturing of the product. I knew that many of these businesses were interested in doing business with minority firms and felt that an opportunity existed for Eillen and me to help meet this need. Public law 95507 indicates any company purchasing or having a

> federal contract from the federal government totaling $500,000 or more is requested to do business with minority companies.

Hill quit with the promise from his boss that if he failed he could always get his old job back. He would later say, "I realized what was being procured out there and figured let the best salesman win."

THE BIRTH OF ECS

Although ECS Technologies has made the strategic transition from electrical components distributor to computer systems integrator, the company's original charter was to sell electronic components to major manufacturers of electronic-based products from stereo systems to intricate Department of Defense radar systems. While a buyer at Westinghouse, Billy had made the extra effort to develop his potential client base. Eillen also had developed measures to solidify her customer base prior to her departure from Technico, and between the two of them, they wisely built the backlog of their business before opening the doors of ECS. Billy adds:

> Eillen was working for a similar company which was fronting a minority company and she had grown tired of that company. The managers asked Eillen if she were interested in buying the company. She called me because we had an excellent business relationship and had become friends. We decided not to buy that company but to start our own. We got our first order in the day we opened our doors. This was a result of the relationship.

In 1979, with orders from Westinghouse, Bendix, and Boeing, the company started out at a brisk pace. Hill thinks it was easier for his company initially because the business they chose to start was familiar to them. Both he and his partner had experience in purchasing, sales, and customer service. They kept in close contact with their clients and built a strong foundation upon which future business opportunities could be developed.

GROWTH

ECS opened their one office suite in Towson, Maryland. Very quickly they realized they needed more space and added three additional suites until they decided to move to a new location. They needed docking facilities and relocated to a larger office with docking space. The company thinks that the new location was exceptional because it put them in closer contact with some of their largest customers.

When Billy and Eillen first started out, they had white accountants and white lawyers. Now that they are doing well, they have black accountants and black lawyers who understand the plight of minorities. Billy feels that minority professionals can usually add more value to situations because of their sensitivity to the challenges facing minority businesspeople.

Buoyed by their earlier marketing successes, Billy and Eillen did something that is rarely accomplished in any new venture—they made a profit the first month! The year remained profitable for them as they paid themselves $15,000 apiece and ended up spending only $500/month for the small office space they occupied. Because both of their spouses worked at full-time jobs, Billy and his partner were able to divert more of the company's funds into new marketing efforts, hiring additional employees and acquiring more office and warehouse space.

LIVING FOR THE CITY

Hill's humble beginnings would have provided little warning of his future success. Born into a lower-middle-class family in south Baltimore, he emerged from an environment that had little material wealth, but actively encouraged hard work. Billy, however, was never content with having little and always wanted more. "I wanted; that's what drove me," he says.

Hill's parents were proud people. His father worked for the federal government for most of his career, and his mom was a custodian in the Baltimore City Public Schools. Billy has appreciated the importance of working ever since his elementary school days. Ironically, it even appeared that work might prevent him from attending college, but when he presented this option to his father, it was sternly rebuked. As Hill later added, "My father told me okay, don't go to college, but don't ever ask me for anything else in life. I applied to college right away."

At his father's urging, Billy attended the University of Maryland at College Park. Although extremely bright, he had a difficult time academically while in college. Despite the difficulties, Hill continued with his studies and ultimately graduated from the University of Maryland in 1973. While still at Westinghouse, Hill earned his Master of Business Administration from Morgan State University in 1976 before he started the business. He liked going to a black university and feels he not only obtained good business contacts, but a great education as well.

Both Billy and Eillen maintain close ties with the contacts they generated during their matriculation at colleges in Maryland. Eillen attended Catonsville and Essex Community colleges. The team amassed a network of cohorts that reaches from the marble halls of corporate America to the gray corridors of the local municipal governments. They both stress the importance of leveraging relationships in building one's business.

NO MISTAKES

Eillen and Billy both echo a common complaint made by black businesspeople across America: Black businesspeople are not allowed to make mistakes. One mistake with the wrong company and the wrong buyer at the wrong time could ruin a company's chances for generating any further business at that account. That same mistake could ruin your chances for contracts within that entire city or geographic area. One way to rectify this situation is to have more minority buyers. People like to buy from people they know and can relate to. Billy feels there aren't many black buyers currently and is emphatic about the importance of having more minority buyers in the major corporations. Billy adds:

> If there were more minority buyers in corporate America, there would be a much greater probability that minority businesses would get their fair share of the pie. Black buyers can relate to black businesspeople and I believe there is a sincere desire to help one another. Black businesspeople have first to get into the company, then give them a good price, deliver on time, and minimize errors. You can't afford to make mistakes. It's not acceptable. White contractors may mess up, but we don't have that luxury.

FINANCING

Due to the nature of their business, Hill and his partner required very little up-front capitalization to get their distributor business off the ground. Both Hill and his partner initially contributed $5,000 to ECS's capitalization. The additional funds came from a $35,000 loan they secured by using the equity in both their homes as collateral. The fact that they had already won a contract also helped with the acquisition of the loan. This situation was quite a rarity for a small start-up minority business.

In 1982, responding to additional cash requirements caused by increased business, ECS went out to secure additional financing. Because each of the partners had enough personal collateral, the banks were a lot more flexible than they would have been and ended up giving them a $200,000 line of credit.

Despite these early successes, Billy is quick to point out that his company has had its share of financial difficulties. Overconfident by the company's early successes, Billy and Eillen began to aggressively expand their sales force in anticipation of aggressive sales growth. Unfortunately, about the time they made these expenditures, they experienced a dramatic drop in orders and business activity in general. Although this was a difficult time, it taught Billy and his partner one important lesson:

> One of the things you need to do is borrow money when you don't need it. If you establish these financial channels before you actually need them, then the money will be available to you when you do need cash. It's a classic lesson I learned. I know that blacks have difficulty getting loans and the one thing that would help is if they had black friends at the bank. We need to be able to effectively network if we are to get a decent business loan. Unfortunately, blacks don't want to be loan officers. They want to be vice presidents instead. The result is that we don't have many friends in those key financial positions.

DIFFICULTIES

Hill concedes that his business has not been that tough on him, but occasionally he looks at his corporate friends, who still work nine-to-five days, who still go on nice, regularly scheduled vacations, and who work regular hours with an almost guaranteed paycheck and wishes he were back there. Many of these people, he suggests, take these benefits for granted. He often reminds his peers:

> I've got to be the accountant, check with the lawyer, be customer service, and work overtime—no time off, no vacation. My partner and I split up the responsibilities though and she usually does what she likes and I do what I like. Luckily, our skill sets complement one another. If I had to do it again though, I would.

REPRESENTING MINORITIES

Even with the difficulties, Hill concedes he would never quit. It is clear that Billy gets a high from the work that he does. He approaches his business responsibilities with a missionary zeal:

> I represent black Americans and there just aren't many of us out there working in our own businesses and succeeding. I have to be there for them, be a role model. Besides, the challenge is important to me as well.

Eillen shares Billy's zest for the business and the new direction in which ECS is moving. During 1992, ECS began a strategic initiative to diversify its business even more by building new business units. The company is aggressively building its technical and marketing staff and is well positioned to capitalize on the fast-growing areas of LAN/WAN design and implementation, UNIX support services, telecommunications, systems integration, and other computer services. With an air of quiet confidence, Eillen Dorsey, the president of ECS, summarizes the firm's strategy for the future:

> We will always give the customer the best possible service that we can—consistently. While we strive to grow, we are also taking measures to ensure that the growth is controlled. As we leverage ourselves through various teaming arrangements with other firms, we will work diligently to keep communication lines open between our business partners and our employees. The lifeblood of our business is our employees, and we must constantly remind them that they have a major impact on the success of our business. They must always strive to conduct themselves professionally and commit themselves to excellence.

Excellence is what got ECS to this point and excellence is what will take them to the next level of success.

CASE STUDY

Aathome Pediatrics Nursing Team represents a growing trend of business opportunities in the home healthcare field. Also, Ms. Peters' experience in selling her business to a large conglomerate is revealing. Ms. Peters is a West Indian American.

LOIS PETERS

President and Founder, Aathome Pediatrics Nursing Team
Clarksville, Maryland

"Once Again, She Prayed for Guidance"

Lois Peters could accurately be described as energy in a dress! Her high-pitched voice, electrifying smile, and spirited eyes beam power. Femininity is hardly lost as her compact body and close-cropped hair appear in a doorway and emancipate the room of all pretenses. As she settles comfortably in her chair Lois smooths her yellow cotton dress. She looks about the room, and the color of ripe mango flutters in the scarf that is loosely draped about her neck. She has a presence that is captivating. Clearly she is at home anywhere, as comfortable in the company of royalty as she is at home with the aged throwaways that no one wants. As her story unfolds, it is clear that Lois has not always been as comfortable with herself. On the contrary, comfort was a wayward friend as she was growing up in Jamaica.

Born in Mandeville, Jamaica, Lois describes herself as a second-generation Seventh Day Adventist. The foundation of her family existence is built upon a powerful faith in the God whom she serves. "We had little and often prayed for the basic necessities." The eldest of three children, Lois has memories of playing with the children of the missionary family for whom her mother worked. Unwilling to leave her child alone, Lois' mother often took her curious daughter to work with her where Lois played with the missionary children. She remembers that when her parent's employers came home, her mother would quickly hide her. Bidding her to sit quietly in a back room lest the missionaries discover that their children had befriended the native girl, Lois would play alone daydreaming about one day becoming a nurse in a prestigious hospital. Her dream would one day become a reality.

Recognizing her potential to become an outstanding nurse, Lois' parents focused on making sure that their daughter got a good education. In addition to the formal education, her mother pursued a strategy that would further her children's success. Lois recalls:

> She constantly reinforced the positives about us. If we did something good she would tell the neighbors, the church members, and the entire family, always within our hearing. On the other hand, she never repeated negative stories or told of our mistakes. Those were buried at the bottom of the sea, never to surface again.

Her mother became astute at building her children's self-esteem and at planting the seeds of hope and service that would one day sprout up and provide comfort to the sick throughout the world.

In 1969 Lois came to America to complete her education. After graduating from high school in Boston she enrolled at Atlantic Union College where she completed her associate's degree in nursing. The degree that normally took two years to complete took Lois four years. She was determined to be successful and decidedly moved beyond each barrier that was set in her way. She recalls an example of the types of barriers that she encountered, which involved the head nurse, who evaluated Lois in the clinical portion of the Nursing Fundamentals course:

> "Well, you are not going to pass this course," the teacher assured her, even before that course was finished.
>
> "But why?" Lois questioned, knowing that she had sufficiently completed all of the tasks assigned for the course.
>
> "I've overheard you talking to the others," the nurse returned. "I've heard you say, Turn on the pipe when you referred to the faucet. I also heard you refer to a box of milk instead of a carton of milk. You are in America now and you will have to learn to use the proper terms in order to be a nurse here." Although heartbroken, Lois was unwavering in her determination to continue.

In 1975 Lois finally graduated, and began her professional career as a nurse in the Intensive Care Unit (ICU) at New England Memorial Hospital. She had interned in that hospital and had established a reputation as a hard worker. Lois flourished as an ICU nurse. She loved her work and liked to stay busy. When there were nurse shortages in other areas of the hospital, Lois eagerly volunteered to float to the other units to help. Her willingness to help others and to do whatever she could to care for the patients quickly built her skill base and she became proficient in most areas of nursing. This experience would serve Lois well later in her career, but her exciting work assignment was about to change.

Like the obstacles that had dogged Lois throughout her schooling issues occasionally surfaced and served to slow her professional progress. After her first child was born, Lois returned from a maternity leave to discover that she had been reassigned out of the ICU. She thought nothing of the reassignment as nurses were commonly reassigned when returning from an extended leave. It was several months later when she applied to fill a new vacancy in the ICU that she learned that one of the nurses had specifically asked that Lois be reassigned out of the ICU. The nurse had cited that she and her peers did not believe that the ICU was the appropriate place for a black nurse to work. As the supervisor explained why Lois had been reassigned upon her return, the words stung like a thousand bees. Lois was wounded, not only because of the unfairness of the situation but also because apparently the one nurse that she had considered to be a best friend had led the charge in filing the complaint. "I ran home and screamed and screamed and screamed," she recalled.

The next day she went back to work and acted as if nothing had ever happened. Hospital management apologized for the incident and offered Lois her choice of work assignments anywhere in the hospital. Holding no resentment, Lois continued to care for patients throughout the hospital and showered them with love and attention, just as she always had.

Lois eventually left Boston and moved to the Washington, D.C., area with her husband Leroy. Once settled in the district, she learned of a new Seventh Day Adventist hospital that was opening nearby. Responding to an ad in the paper, she applied for a supervisor's position at the new Shady Grove Adventist Hospital. When she called to inquire about the position, a brief interview was held over the phone. Upon learning that Lois held only an associate's degree, the Director of Resource Nurses politely informed Lois that the supervisory position required a bachelor's degree, and that Lois would not qualify.

Apparently, soon after the phone call, the director went out to lunch, thoughtlessly leaving the scrap of paper with Lois' name and phone number on her desk. Looking for an update on the status of the hiring process, the Vice President of Nursing came into the vacated office. While there she noticed Lois Peters' name scribbled on a piece of paper so she waited for the director to return from lunch:

> "Oh," she began, as the surprised director entered her office with a doggie bag in her hand. "So you are going to hire Lois Peters as the hospital night supervisor. That's great!" she exclaimed.
>
> A little bewildered by the apparent misunderstanding, the director hurried to explain. "No, I've hired another woman to fill the supervisor's role. I spoke to Lois Peters, but she doesn't have a B.S. degree. I told her that she did not qualify for the position."
>
> Obviously disappointed to hear this, the vice president responded crossly, "Well, you need to hire Lois."
>
> The director explained, "But I've already hired someone else to fill the position."

> "Well, I suggest that you unhire her," her boss replied quite firmly. "Lois Peters can be the night supervisor and you can make whoever you have hired the assistant."
>
> The director made a call to Lois offering her the position as night supervisor for the hospital. Lois was confused by the reversal of the job offer that occurred within the span of a few hours. Later she understood when she learned that the Vice President of Nursing at Shady Grove was the same woman who had been V.P. of Nursing at New England Memorial Hospital during the incident in which Lois had been barred from working in the ICU. Lois had handled the adversity in such a professional and Christian way that the woman had never forgotten her. She knew Lois Peters and she knew exactly what she was getting by hiring her.

The week the new hospital opened, Lois made a name for herself. In charge of the hospital for the eleven to seven shift, it was Lois' job to set resource priorities. One evening she found herself with all four of the beds in the small ICU filled, when the emergency room received a call that there had been a serious automobile accident and the helicopter was transporting one of the victims to Shady Grove. The ER nurses were on the phone trying to reach the dispatcher to direct him to transport the patient to another hospital several miles away. Evaluating the seriousness of the situation, Lois intervened:

> "No, don't send that patient away," she said, realizing that the reputation of the new hospital was being determined. "We are closer and can give him the best care." She made arrangements to cover the ICU, telling them to call her if they needed her. Carrying a pager, she went to the ER herself to care for the accident victim. In the morning she explained what had happened to the director, who assured her that she had done the right thing. As Lois put on her coat and prepared to leave for home, she overheard the director recounting the story to her boss. The V.P. of Nursing gently tugged the director's arm and quietly boasted, "Now do you see why we hired her?"

Lois' compassion and tireless work became legendary. The patients and staff alike loved her. Everyone wanted Lois to be a part of their team. Things seemed wonderful but then the bottom fell out.

Lois became seriously ill and was unable to work for several months. During that time, Lois and Leroy lost nearly everything they owned. Unable to pay the mortgage, they were forced to sell their beautiful home in the Washington suburbs and move into a two-bedroom apartment. Lois recalls losing her home as one of the lowest points in her adult life. "I learned how quickly the fortunes of life can change," she recounts.

Work had become extremely stressful for both Lois and Leroy.

She decided to take action and took the $30 grocery money that Leroy had given her and had some business cards printed for Aathome Pediatrics Nursing Team. At church she heard that someone was looking for nurses to care for a sick child who was being discharged from Johns Hopkins Hospital. Lois agreed to provide care for the child and was informed that Hopkins required a contract for any agency that would care for their children. Lois eagerly signed the contract with Johns Hopkins HMO.

It wasn't long before Lois was doing marketing calls on all of the hospitals in the area. Once she shared that she was already under contract with Hopkins, one of the top hospitals in the world, doors flew open to her new business. Within the first year, Peters did more than $1 million in business. Within four years, her corporate sales skyrocketed to more than $8 million per year.

The phenomenal growth was not without growing pains. Once, Lois even decided that she had had enough. She packed her belongings and phoned her mother-in-law to inform her that she was taking the children and starting a new life without her husband.

The wise mother-in-law reminded Lois of how she and Leroy had met and that their marriage was no mistake. Those words were exactly what Lois needed to hear. God does not make mistakes; she had learned that lesson years ago.

Lois found herself supervising more than 700 nurses, therapists, and other assorted health care professionals. Peters rapidly developed a reputation for being the best home health care provider for pediatrics in the Mid-Atlantic region. What was even more amazing about Lois' meteoric rise was the fact that she had funded the company's growth solely through the firm's retained earnings. Up to that point, she had refrained from seeking any form of financing.

By 1994 the payroll had ballooned to more than $100,000 per week. Dealing with insurance companies and the state government payments were slow. By the spring of 1994, she had more than $3MM in account receivables with much of it aging rapidly. Cash flow became progressively strained and by the last week of May 1994, it seemed that the unthinkable was about to happen. Lois found herself with no funds to meet payroll for the following week. Not knowing what else to do, Lois went home and prayed. Later that day she sadly concluded that she would be forced to close the doors of the business at the end of the week.

The next day she received a totally unexpected phone call from someone identifying herself as representing Premier Health Care. "We want to buy your company," the voice on the other end of the phone proclaimed. "I'd like to fly out and meet with you to discuss the terms." Intrigued by the idea, Lois agreed to the meeting. "Buy my company." Lois laughed to herself. "Boy, are they going to be surprised when they see my small office and unpaid invoices. I don't have anything to sell." Once again she prayed for guidance.

The following day the woman flew into Baltimore-Washington International Airport for her scheduled meeting with Lois.

> When the woman first showed up at the office, Lois was taken aback. The short, heavyset white woman was so tanned that Lois thought that she was black. She had an abundant mane of thick, graying hair that hung down her back like combed sisal. She spoke with a deep, New York style, raspy voice. Most unseemly to Lois was seeing the female negotiator with a long, long cigarette that dangled between her fingers as they went out to lunch. Taking a deep breath to compose herself, the health-conscious nurse thought to herself, "Lord, are you really telling me to sell our business to this woman with such a long cigarette?"
>
> Over lunch the negotiator told Lois that she had contacted all the hospitals in the area to ask who provided their pediatric home health care. Aathome Pediatrics Nursing Team was the resounding response. "We are willing to pay your asking price," she assured Lois. "How much do you want?" Still unbelieving, Lois responded that she had to talk to someone about it and would get back to her the next day. Lois went home and prayed.

The next day Lois was led to sell the business for $3 million. Within 30 days, the transaction was completed and Lois Peters was instantly transformed into a multimillionaire.

Premier Health Care retained Lois' services as Executive Administrator for the next two years. During that time, Lois continued to grow the business and easily doubled their income. In 1996 the company was sold to Pediatric Services of America. In 1997 Lois retired from PSA to pursue her lifelong dream of traveling around the world as a consultant.

She and Leroy had just returned from South Africa when she received a call that her mother had suffered a stroke while visiting family in Jamaica. Lois chartered a Lear jet to retrieve her mother and to bring her back to Washington, D.C., for medical attention. As her mother was recuperating from the stroke Lois and Leroy reassessed their retirement plans. Needing to oversee Lois' mother's medical care, they postponed their plans to travel and started a new company, International Health Care Consultants. They purchased five assisted-living group homes in Howard County, Maryland.

Providing care for geriatric patients in a homelike setting, Lois and Leroy are once again making a name for themselves in the health care market. Looking ahead, they continue to bring healing and provide hope to those who often show up last in America's pecking order of power, the aged and the children. Lois and Leroy's entrepreneurial experiences give credence to the fact that you can do well by doing good.

5

Refining Your Vision and Setting Your Goals

The internal checkpoints for business success, which we discuss in the preceding chapter, are all tasks that you can accomplish with little or no assistance from anyone else. These are the tasks that you need to complete in order to prepare yourself individually. In contrast, this chapter summarizes the external checkpoints—those tasks necessary to take you from your dream to the reality of business ownership.

External checkpoints for business success are just as critical as the internal checkpoints for success. However, I have observed that people have more difficulty achieving the external checkpoints than they do the internal ones because they tend to have less control over the external world. The issues surrounding achieving the external checkpoints are often more complex and unpredictable. Nevertheless, any successful entrepreneur needs to work through the external checkpoints in order to establish a direct connection between the individual dream and the actual structure to support the dream. These checkpoints, as identified in the Dartmouth study, are as follows:

Step 1: Refine vision
Step 2: Hold your head high and count your blessings
Step 3: Live lite
Step 4: Revisit your values

Exhibit 5.1 External Checkpoints for Business Success

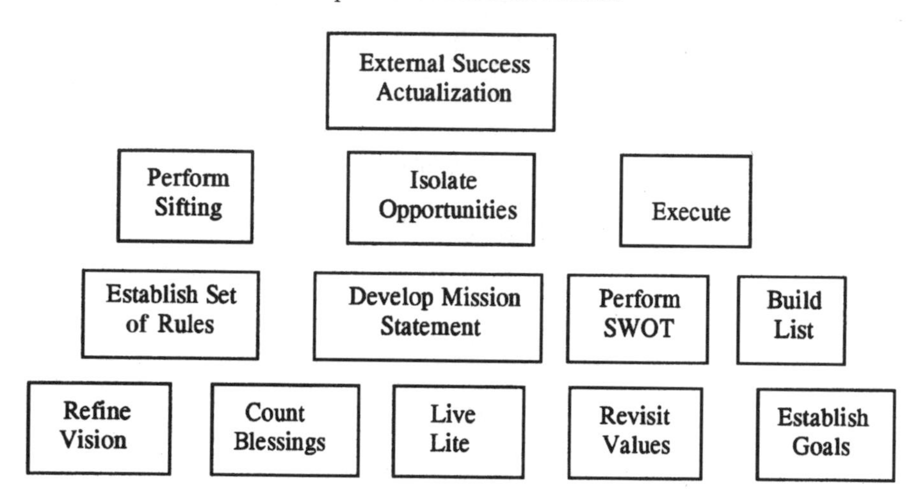

Step 5: Establish proper goals
Step 6: Establish a proper set of rules
Step 7: Develop a personal mission statement
Step 8: Perform SWOT (Strengths, Weaknesses, Opportunities, Threats) analysis of self and team
Step 9: Identify the right opportunity
Step 10: Start the sifting process
Step 11: Compile the opportunity list and compare it to your values and your SWOT list
Step 12: Execute, execute, execute

Like the internal building blocks of success, the building blocks for achieving the external requirements of success, as shown in Exhibit 5.1, are mutually dependent.

REFINE YOUR VISION

Where there is no vision, the people perish . . .

Proverbs 29:18

One of the giants of gospel music was James Cleveland. Brother Cleveland is often credited with popularizing large gospel choirs and identifying promising singing groups, mentoring them and exposing them to the public. Most people, like my mother who adored the man, probably failed to realize how much of a visionary James Cleveland was. In 1968, among other accomplishments, he founded the Gospel Music Workshop of America. The mission of this workshop was to bring together gospel talent from all over the United States and to elevate gospel music to the same level of acceptance and respect as that given to jazz, classical, and modern music. The workshop now has more than 21,000 members and boasts having more than 200 chapters nationwide. One of James Cleveland's most formidable dreams was to build an accredited college for gospel music. Imagine that, an accredited college for gospel music majors. What vision!

One of the reasons Mr. Cleveland rapidly transcended his roots in the south side of Chicago to become an internationally recognized gospel musician was that he filled a very important need that many African Americans and others shared. That is, the need to believe that in spite of the hatred, racism, poverty, and ignorance that still pervades our society, there is an omnipotent power in the universe that will change wrongs to rights and lies to truths. It's the belief that the inequalities of life are not permanent or final. If you listen to the lyrics of his songs, you will realize they all share the common mission of giving hope to the hopeless and strength to the weak. We all thrive on hope so it should be no surprise that Mr. Cleveland's music has been a phenomenal success over the years.

In spite of his obvious success, many people considered him to be an average man with average looks and talent. How could an average man with average talent be able to realize such above average accomplishments? First, because he had such clear vision, he was able to accurately gauge his market and determine which goods or services he could offer to meet the demands of the public. Second, he surrounded himself with exceptionally talented people who helped him make things happen. In other words, Mr. Cleveland became quite successful at finding whatever resources he deemed necessary for accomplishing his objectives.

We can learn a lot from Mr. Cleveland by understanding these two principles. Mr. Cleveland's vision reminds me of something Michelangelo once said about dreams that are real in one sense but not in another. On one occasion when Michelangelo began to carve a huge block of marble, he declared that his specific aim was not to construct a masterpiece but to release the angel who was imprisoned in the stone. In other words, the beauty was already there. He didn't have to create it. There also exists an angel in the visions that each of us produces that we must work to release.

James Cleveland and Michelangelo took what appeared to be plain blocks of marble and released the angels inside. Their visions became the focus of what eventually evolved into something great. Vision is simply the manifestation to the senses of something that is yet to come. Vision is an interesting phenomenon. It never lets you go, and you can't let go of it. A clear vision provides motivation, stimulation, and exuberance.

All of the entrepreneurs involved in this study actually had started their businesses years before the businesses actually materialized. Their businesses started the first day they visualized their enterprises in their hearts and minds. Although the physical environment may have told them differently, their visions or dreams convinced them daily that what they hoped and dreamed for was attainable.

Most successful people will attest to the fact that there is a tremendous amount of power in vision. The vision created in one's mind has the power to control the physical senses. Those senses then proceed to work in unison to achieve the object of your vision. I'm sure that many of you yearn to start your own business but maybe you lack a clear vision of what that business should be. Well, don't despair. I hope this section of the book will propel you on your way to allowing that dream to become real.

The first step is to try a vision-generating exercise. The beauty of conducting this vision-generating exercise is that it doesn't require any capital or supreme intelligence to make it work for you. It is appalling how few people have visions or dreams. Unfortunately, those who do dare to dream are often long on dreams but short on money and strategies. Interesting enough, most of us unconsciously visualize daily the things that we desire and the qualities that we long to possess. These images are then transferred to our subconscious for further manipulation.

For those of you who are short on vision, let's play a little game. Stop what you're doing right now. Just stop. Put the book down (I know it's difficult to put the book down and continue with this exercise but do your best), lay your head back, close your eyes, and relax. Now, let your mind wander and fantasize about the future. What do you see? Do you see a red Ferrari or Porsche 911 sitting in the driveway of your multimillion dollar estate? Maybe you see yourself relaxing on your farm in Virginia, surrounded by acres of lush forest on one side and a crystal clear lake stocked with fresh trout on the other side.

As you relax on your large rear porch, you catch a glimpse of your specially bred stallions roaming freely in front of the quaint country home that you and your spouse have built. As you look over your acreage, maybe the tall rows of corn slightly block your view of your distant apple orchard. Behind the house, you may have another garden that the kids labor in but that you enjoy watching grow as you sharpen your tennis game on the adjacent court.

Maybe your vision doesn't focus so much on material things. Your thoughts may be much more altruistic. You see yourself earning a great deal of money and then using that money to help uplift the downtrodden, feed the hungry, and provide shelter for the homeless. Can you feel the excitement and energy that focusing on your vision generates within you? Can you feel your heart start to beat a little more quickly?

Since you're reading this book, you undoubtedly desire or dream about being the president of your own business, feeling excited every day about going to work and facing the challenges of running a small business. If you're like most of the participants in this study, you'd also like to build an empire within or outside the minority community, using the resources of this empire to provide jobs and self-esteem to those members of our society who have been ignored and forgotten. Fantasizing a little further, you probably see your children inheriting a business that will give them a head start in life rather than inheriting poverty, ignorance, and a perpetual dependence on unproductive welfare programs.

Sound crazy? Not really. Everything that you can see or touch first started out as someone's vision. Your business must also start out by your active visualization of your soon-to-be enterprise. By seeing this vision of yourself on a daily basis, you force the elements of your being to fall in line with this vision and make it real.

Whenever one is forced to confront the reality of his or her situation today and the uncertainty of the situation tomorrow, he or she will find that there are only two possible outcomes: Either the reality of the present will destroy the dreams for the future or the dreams of the future will overshadow the reality of today. The present contains the reality of everyday life: your job, the household bills, college tuitions, and family issues. The future contains that vision of yourself that you'd like to make a reality. The ideal situation occurs when the vision is so strong and overbearing that it begins to take on a life of its own and quickly overshadows the problems and issues of the present. This second scenario is the one that I hope is taking place in your life because you'll never start the business if the vision isn't a powerful and convincing one.

Another perspective on the power of vision is the view that at any point in time prior to start-up, your business is both present and not present. Let me explain. The business may not exist in terms of equipment, land, buildings, and people. It does, however, exist in the sense that it resides in your heart and mind as an inner spark that creates in you large doses of inner motivation and energy.

This motivation is what forces you out of bed to work on your business idea when everyone else is still sound asleep. It's the motivation that forces you out of the house on Sunday afternoons to pursue a promising business project instead of snuggling up in your favorite chair watching your favorite football team. This vision-induced energy drives you hourly and daily to turn the focus of your vision into a reality. This spark allows you to overcome all adversity, regardless of what's put in front of you. Establish that vision, expand it, tailor it, let it take on a life of its own, and revisit it frequently.

HOLD YOUR HEAD HIGH AND COUNT YOUR BLESSINGS

Everyone has at one time or another experienced periods of depression, disappointment, and frustration. If you're like most other people, you've probably had times in your life when everything seemed to go wrong no matter what you did. Your "dry season" just seemed to stretch on and on and on. You've probably experienced failures that have shaken your confidence and made you question your value and self-worth. If you haven't had these experiences, you're either extremely blessed or not a very honest person!

Often, we spend so much time focusing on our shortcomings, our failures, our lack of material possessions, or our lack of cash that we become blind to the obvious blessings that we do enjoy, blessings such as good health, a happy and healthy family, the ability to work and dream, food to eat, and a roof over our heads. I know how you feel because I'm guilty of this type of self-pity also. I, too, have wasted time focusing on the negatives instead of the positives. If we learn to count our blessings and maintain a positive attitude, then we begin to generate positive energy instead of the negative energy that is destructive and useless. The Father often reminds us through meditation, prayer, conversation, and experiences that He does love us and that we're more blessed than we realize. One of the entrepreneurs who started a local area network consulting firm talked about a personal experience he had that shocked him back to reality.

One day, while working on an office automation project for a large East Coast client, this young man decided that he had had enough of his computer for the moment and decided to give himself a much-needed break. It was a rainy, gray day with dark, low-lying clouds. He mentioned that business was not going well and that he hadn't seen the sun in a few days. The dampness outside made the already dirty streets look even dirtier.

As he secured his overcoat to protect himself from the cold rain, he caught a glimpse of a small vehicle coming down the street where he was standing. Initially, he couldn't discern what the strange-looking vehicle was because it was raining and the vehicle was still some distance away. Out of curiosity, he slowed his normally brisk pace to a casual walk, just to get a better view of this unusual contraption. As the vehicle came closer, he began to make out the details of the vehicle and its occupant.

What he saw completely shocked him. First, the weird-looking vehicle turned out to be a motorized wheelchair and sitting in it was what appeared to be a middle-aged black woman. Yet this was no ordinary woman. To begin with she had no legs. Not only that, although she had full use of her arms, she also suffered from some visual handicaps as well. With one arm holding an umbrella providing her some protection from the rain and the other arm working the controls of her motorized chair, this brave woman maneuvered her way through the rush hour traffic of downtown in the cold damp rain.

This young entrepreneur stood there looking stupid and dumbfounded. Luckily, the amazing woman had not seen him staring at her and proceeded on her way. After regaining his composure, he once again began his trek back to his client's office to resume his work. As he hurried his stride, he began to cry uncontrollably. He later admitted that he hadn't meant to cry and he hadn't wanted to cry. But for some reason he couldn't stop the tears from rolling down his cheeks. Embarrassed, the man quickly ducked into one of the alleys to get himself together before anyone he knew saw him. He was thankful it was raining because the rain helped to camouflage his tears and the confusion he felt.

As he leaned against the alley wall, he tried to figure out why he was crying. Suddenly, it dawned on him that he wasn't crying because he felt sorry for the woman—even though he did. He was crying because at that moment he felt so ashamed. Ashamed because in spite of all the blessings God had bestowed on him, he had failed to recognize them.

Another entrepreneur shared a similar story with me. After having lost a major contract to the competition, this young man was very depressed and down on himself. As he was leaving his office late one night, he happened to walk past a homeless woman who was sitting on a city bench fishing through her many shopping bags. She was a middle-aged woman with dark hair, brown eyes, and a slender build. Like most of us, this young man tried to avoid making contact with her because she looked ragged and filthy.

As he tried to escape her sharp glances, she beckoned to him. "Excuse me, sir. I've been sitting here most of the day and many people have walked by my bench but no one has bothered to stop and help me. I'm having a hard time right now and was hoping that you could lend me a few dollars so that I could get a bite to eat."

Feeling guilty, the young man dug into his pocket for a few dollars, walked over to the woman, and handed them to her. Looking somewhat surprised, the homeless woman smiled at him and said, "Thank you, sir."

As the young entrepreneur started to walk away, the woman said to him in a soft, pleasant voice, "Sir, I have one more request to ask of you. I live on the streets and people who see me treat me like I'm a walking disease. If you don't mind, would you please give me a hug. It has been such a long time since someone hugged me, I've forgotten how it feels."

Realizing what was happening, the man walked over and with no apprehension hugged the homeless woman. As their eyes met, they both flashed a smile at one another as if to say, I understand. With no further delay, the woman gathered her shopping bags, the young man picked up his briefcase, and they both went their separate ways. As the man walked away, he suddenly had a much better understanding that in spite of all the daily problems he faced, there was still much to be thankful for. Let's move on.

LIVE LITE

One more time. Keep your living expenses low so that you have enough free cash to engage in deals. Remember, you can move a lot more quickly and travel further if you travel lite. Enough said on this matter.

REVISIT YOUR VALUES

Ralph Waldo Emerson once said, "Nothing gives so much direction to a person's life as a sound set of principles." It is almost impossible to achieve greatness without a set of principles or values. Values are what make us what we are. With the exception of our souls, it is the only thing that separates humans from the animal kingdom. Verbalizing one's values is significantly easier than writing them down. However, for your values to become integrated into your inner self and for them to control your destiny, they have to be written down. Once they're written down, they need to be reviewed on a daily basis.

Your values are your rudder in the voyage that is your life. Without values, your life is rudderless, and you will be tossed to and fro on the rough seas of life. You will have no direction and no purpose. Imagine, waking up when you're 65 years old and coming to the realization that you have accomplished nothing and your life was a waste. I shudder at the thought. However, you have time now to establish these values and let them guide you.

Values mean different things to different people. Values used in this analysis are those principles that guide our thoughts and actions. Each person's value set is different from another. However, there are usually common sets of values that everyone can relate to. These categories may include:

- Spiritual
- Physical
- Financial
- Emotional
- Intellectual

To give you an example of a set of values, the following outlines the value set used to guide me and my family:

- I love God and try to emulate the lifestyle of His son Jesus Christ.
- I love my family and provide for them financially, emotionally, and physically.
- I am financially independent and am not dependent on anyone for my financial well-being.
- I seek excellence in all that I do or am associated with.
- I am physically healthy and strong.

Believe it or not, your values will dictate what type of business you will ultimately get into. For example, let's look at the drug business (I'm not talking about prescription drugs). If you remove the emotional and ethical issues of this business, what you're left with is one of the most lucrative business opportunities of the twenty-first century. What other business allows you to make $100,000 a day profit with no major overhead, no research and development costs, a manageable payroll commitment, no unions, and no government taxation and restrictions? What other business can you invest in that doesn't require any education or special skills and that will allow you to live like the movie stars on television—big house, expensive car, and exotic vacations? Now be honest, if I told you about this business opportunity without telling you what the business was, how many of you would jump at the chance to become a part of this venture? Every single one of you would.

There are other businesses that may be very lucrative but conflict with your value structure. I recall one incident when one of the subjects of this book was approached by an old buddy of his who wanted the entrepreneur to become his partner and help him buy a local liquor store in New York. Business was very good at that particular store, which was located on the corner of one of the poorest and most crime-plagued neighborhoods in the city. It was an African American neighborhood, and market research revealed that the store was always crowded. Even though the business was exceptionally profitable, the entrepreneur chose not to invest because his value system wouldn't allow him in good conscience to sell poison to the people of his community.

The only reason more of us don't enter into these money-making business opportunities is because of our value systems. Our values tell us that these types of businesses are to be avoided at all costs. Our values dictate to us that life is valuable, and we resist participating in any venture that serves to shorten it or cause it to go in the wrong direction. See how our values direct our actions?

ESTABLISH PROPER GOALS

It never ceases to amaze me how few people have goals. Most people wander through life aimlessly with no idea of a destination. What a tragedy. God gives us only a few hours per day, a few days per week, a couple of weeks per year, and only a handful of years in a lifetime. Once that time has passed, there is no way you can ever get it back. It is lost forever. The best way to use this time is to establish goals and commit yourself to them.

Like your values, your goals must also be visualized, ultimately written down, and possess a time dimension. Your goals must be believable, clearly defined, and take on a life of their own. As with our values, we must learn to set goals for every aspect of our lives, particularly when you're working on starting your business. Set goals for *when* you'll identify what business you want to go into, how much money you want to make, how much growth you expect to realize, who your partners will be, and when and how you want to exit the business.

When setting your goals for business, it is suggested that you break down your goals into two major categories:

- Strategic goals
- Tactical goals

Strategic goals help you to set long-term goals and direction. Tactical goals help you to achieve intermediate and short-term or daily direction. Both sets of goals are critical to the overall accomplishment of your dreams.

COMMIT TO HAVE FUN!

Early in this study, I started to realize that many of the business owners interviewed stressed the importance of having fun with your business. My entrepreneurship professor, Dr. James Brian Quinn, after discussing the details of writing business plans and obtaining financing for start-ups, often stressed the importance of having fun while building and running your business. He made us understand that once you commit yourself to the business, it would in essence become your life. Obviously, if you're not having fun, you'll ultimately hate what you're doing and your creativity will suffer.

DEVELOP A PERSONAL MISSION STATEMENT

A mission statement simply articulates a specific task or set of tasks you are dedicated to carrying out. In other words, after you've exerted tremendous effort and consumed significant resources, what things must be in place before you say, My mission has been accomplished? The mission statement should be concise and crisp and should clearly delineate what it is that you're out to get. It should also be worded in such a way that it can be easily memorized.

You may find that your mission statement is dynamic in nature, changing constantly to reflect variations in your desires and means. Don't be alarmed by all of this. It is normal. Be willing to make the appropriate changes and keep the statement fresh in your mind. If you're working with a group of people, the mission statement should reflect the wants and needs of everyone involved.

PERFORM SWOT ANALYSIS OF YOURSELF AND YOUR TEAM

Those of you who recently completed business school will probably recall the famous SWOT analysis, that is, Strengths, Weaknesses, Opportunities, and Threats. This method is an excellent tool to evaluate the competitive position of any business. Although the majority of the business owners analyzed did not learn the formal technique for performing the SWOT analysis, most went through a similar exercise that provided the same results. Let's discuss this a little further.

Although mainly used to evaluate the competitive stance of businesses, SWOT is also a valuable exercise for the would-be entrepreneur when determining what kind of business to start.

To begin this analysis, look at yourself or your group very closely and assess honestly the strengths of that group. Do you have a strong technical background? Do you have the patent rights to a new technologically advanced product that no one else has? Are you well respected in your chosen profession and consequently have many contacts that may prove beneficial in helping support your business? Maybe you're young, talented, aggressive, hungry, eager, and persistent. These are all strengths that can be capitalized on during the early stages of business formation. Identify these strengths, whatever they are, and write them down.

For most people, articulating their strengths is much easier than identifying their weaknesses. Yet no matter how difficult, understanding one's weaknesses is critical. Just as you did with strengths, look within yourself and/or your group of business partners and pick out the weaknesses that exist.

The first entry on most of your lists will probably be lack of funds. Right? Maybe you're young, inexperienced, and lack direction. Are your business partners in close proximity to you or are they scattered around the country? Are you in a business environment that is already saturated with small businesses and consequently competition is fierce? What about skill set? Does your group possess all of the business skills (e.g., accounting, business law, marketing) necessary to acquire and manage a growing business successfully?

These are just a few examples of what might be considered weaknesses in a typical SWOT analysis of yourself. Keep in mind that strengths and weaknesses are all relative. What may be considered strengths by one group or person may be perceived to be weaknesses by another.

Having gone through the exercise of identifying your strengths and weaknesses, now study them for a while. You now want to look at what opportunities exist that are consistent with those strengths and weaknesses. For example, if you have a great mechanical aptitude and love to tinker with automobiles, maybe an opportunity might be to open a neighborhood gas station that provides auto maintenance. If you're the best cook in the neighborhood and you enjoy cooking, turn that love into an enterprise and open up a neighborhood restaurant.

Let's assume that you're an engineer, have worked in corporate

America for a few years, and have had numerous engineering assignments. You enjoy being an engineer, especially working in a manufacturing environment. You might want to look into the opportunity of owning a small manufacturing firm. But wait a minute. Under weaknesses you listed the fact that you're short on funds. Manufacturing businesses are highly capital-intensive enterprises, requiring in some cases a minimum of a couple of hundred thousand dollars to get started and probably more. Consequently, strengths, weaknesses, and opportunity don't quite match.

Don't despair. This analysis doesn't mean that you can't start that manufacturing business. What the SWOT analysis reveals is that for you to realize this opportunity, you will have to put a plan in place to overcome that weakness, in this case, the weakness of having no significant funds. One good thing about this exercise is that it keeps you honest!

Identifying opportunities may be the most difficult component of getting into business. Consequently, Step 9 in the following section will explore this topic in a little more detail.

The last step in the analysis is to identify the threats that would prevent you from realizing any of the opportunities that evenly match your documented strengths and weaknesses. Some examples of typical threats include rising interest rates, changing national economy, dynamic market conditions, uncommitted group members, and government restrictions. Look at potential threats very carefully and document them. Study carefully how these situations could affect your game plan for getting into business and surviving the early years.

When you've completed this analysis, you may end up with a chart that is organized like Exhibit 5.2.

IDENTIFY THE RIGHT BUSINESS OPPORTUNITY

As mentioned earlier, identifying the right opportunity is undoubtedly one of the most difficult aspects of getting into business. For this reason, more effort will be devoted to better understanding this requirement.

In a basic sense, opportunity is any good or service that satisfies a

Exhibit 5.2 SWOT Chart

Strengths	Weaknesses	Opportunities	Threats

need so vital that people are willing to pay for that good or service. Identifying where those needs are is not extremely difficult. As with most other academic exercises, identifying needs is done more easily in an aggregate sense. For example, study the national and international environments and pinpoint which industries are booming and which are dying. A day doesn't go by when you don't hear about the booming service industries and the dying manufacturing industries in our society. Be careful. Although these statistics may reveal the market dynamics of the overall society, there may still exist some gold nuggets there for minority businesspeople. This would be particularly true for industries in which minorities have been traditionally underrepresented.

Speaking of identifying a niche in a seemingly dying industry, David Bing quickly comes to mind. You probably remember Dave when he played in the National Basketball Association. He electrified audiences with his outstanding basketball skills, relentless defense, and admirable team concept of the game. However, I'm sure that few people realize that after Dave's NBA career, he started a small business in the steel industry. Based on industry statistics, this market was quickly being taken over by foreign steel manufacturers. It appeared that American steel companies were unable to compete. Yet Dave has successfully carved out a niche in this very industry and is doing well. Bing Steel was ranked as one of the 10 largest black businesses in *Black Enterprise* magazine's annual ranking.

EVALUATE VARIOUS BUSINESS OPPORTUNITIES AND START SIFTING

Not only should you be interested in which industries are booming but also where the boom is taking place. Pay especially close attention to which areas are providing opportunities to minority businesspeople. It is probably a good bet that those cities with black mayors will at least provide minorities a fair chance at winning lucrative city contracts. Also areas that have a high concentration of black and other minority people may provide a strong foundation on which to build a business. If nothing else, it may provide you a sense of comfort during the early days of your venture. For your information, Exhibits 5.3 and 5.4 list some of the states that have sizeable African American populations.

Beyond the state level, most cities, along with the federal agencies, have begun aggressive set-aside programs to assist minorities and women in starting businesses. Most cities have a list of goods and services that they contract out to small businesses. Obtain a copy of your

Exhibit 5.3 States with Largest African American Populations

1997 African American Population Ranking	State	1997 African American Population
1	New York	3,208,000
2	California	2,397,000
3	Texas	2,374,000
4	Florida	2,253,000
5	Georgia	2,126,000
6	Illinois	1,815,000
7	North Carolina	1,643,000
8	Maryland	1,471,000
9	Louisiana	1,396,000
10	Michigan	1,392,000

city's list, go through it, and pick out goods and services that you might provide. Also, get a copy of your city's minority set-aside law, study it, and make sure that you understand how it works.

One word of caution. In choosing locations, don't get caught up in what I call "chocolate city magnetism." As was mentioned, it's a good assumption that in a city where minorities are in the majority, there exists a ripe environment for minority businesspeople. However, there are many places where there are relatively few minorities, yet there exist ripe opportunities for the taking. Many of these cities are desirous of having minority businesses and can help make your investment there worthwhile. Therefore, don't write off these places too quickly.

Exhibit 5.4 Top 10 States with Largest Percentage of African Americans

Ranking of African Americans as a Percentage of Total Population	State	Percent of State Population (1996)
1	District of Columbia	65.0
2	Mississippi	35.9
3	Louisiana	31.5
4	South Carolina	30.1
5	Georgia	27.2
6	Maryland	25.5
7	Alabama	25.4
8	North Carolina	22.3
9	Virginia	19.2
10	Delaware	17.7

Studying Your Daily Routine

Not a day goes by that you don't wish for a product or service that is not being provided. Or maybe the product or service that is available doesn't meet your quality expectations. I recall one day during my bill-paying depressions when I wished there was some company somewhere that would assume the task of paying my monthly bills (I thought of starting a business around this concept but I deplore paying bills too much). A few months later, I was flipping through *PC Magazine* and came across an ad of a new company whose concept was to electronically pay bills for people. Someone had stolen my idea!

How many of you have had a great idea only to find later that someone else had the same idea? That person, however, had the vision and guts to turn that idea into a lucrative business. Look around the minority community and see what goods or services people need. In most situations the majority businesses ignore the minority community completely when searching for a business location. When you go to a minority-supported shopping center, what types of stores would you like to see that are not presently there? The answers to these questions can provide some very good business opportunities.

It's amazing to me how many business opportunities the African American community has actually created, but failed to capitalize on. Like most of you, house parties were very big when I was growing up. It seemed like every Friday or Saturday someone would host a party and everyone would "get nice" first and then enjoy the party. This was a time when we would show each other the latest dances and occasionally try to sneak a kiss from your favorite girl (or boy). Usually, the host would replace the normal light with a red or psychedelic light to provide the proper ambiance.

While we were jamming the night away, some white guys 3,000 miles away were creating a movie about an Italian kid who was to become the king of urban dancing. They even had the audacity to go to Australia to hire a white band to produce the sound track for this musical movie. You've probably guessed by now who those people were. The Italian kid was John Travolta, the group from Australia was the Bee Gees, the movie was *Saturday Night Fever,* and the missed business opportunity was the creation and economic exploitation of the disco craze.

To make matters worse, the music used was typically created by African Americans and their dances were just an imitation of what they saw on "Soul Train." As a matter of fact, it was a black man from the "Soul Train" family who spent weeks showing John Travolta how to dance like a brother! Although discos are no longer as popular as they were during the 1970s, mainstream America made fortunes from this business concept. How many blacks do you know who owned discos or made any significant money off of this short-lived craze? Very few.

What about Where You Work?

Interestingly enough, the majority of the entrepreneurs ventured into businesses in which they had some prior experience. Wherever you work, keep your eyes open for what goods and services these organizations are spending money on. Observe the small businesses that are currently filling these needs and find out what aspects of these businesses your company is unhappy with. Understand these weaknesses. If you ran that business, could you do a better job?

Even if you find that there is a large number of small businesses providing similar products, how many of them are minority owned and run? There may still be opportunities in that environment for minority businesspeople.

Start the Sifting

Once you've compiled a healthy list of opportunities, start sifting through them using the model shown in Exhibit 5.5. This model will allow you to screen opportunities quickly and visually. Evaluate each option based on the criteria shown on each of the axes. Place the opportunities in one of the four quadrants, collect the ones from the most favorable quadrant, and then run them through the next matrix. By the time you've finished the fourth matrix, you should have narrowed down your choices.

COMPILE A BUSINESS OPPORTUNITY LIST AND COMPARE IT TO YOUR VALUES AND YOUR SWOT LIST

You've just been provided with a couple of ideas about how you can begin to generate your opportunity list. Our society is rich with ways in which you can identify good business opportunities: your daily routine, dynamic market conditions, your job, the Sunday newspaper, and your friends and neighbors. By now, your list should be quite extensive, but the more difficult part becomes prioritizing these opportunities, then comparing them to your personal SWOT analysis and determining if these opportunities allow you to accomplish your mission.

Exhibit 5.5 The Sifting Process

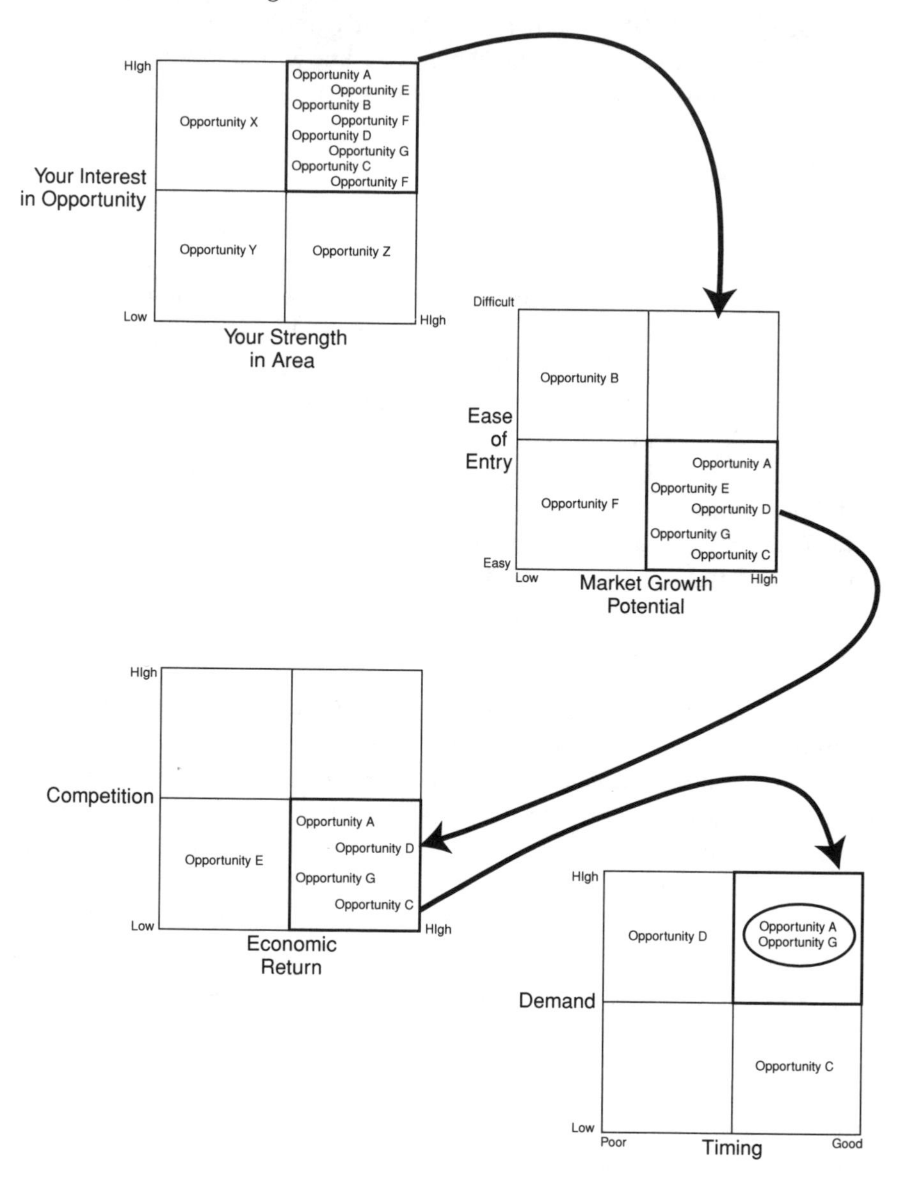

On a single sheet of paper or in your log book, begin to write down the business opportunities you've uncovered. The business ideas should now be prioritized based upon the following:

- Probability of success
- Growth potential
- Ease of start-up
- Amount of personal satisfaction
- Degree of consistency with values, mission, and SWOT analysis

Any idea that conflicts with the results of your SWOT analysis or mission statement should either be disregarded or moved to the bottom of the list. If you find that most of the ideas generated by your analysis do conflict with your values, mission, or SWOT analysis, you need to reevaluate your purpose for wanting to go into business and make sure that all the important pieces are present.

Once the ideas have been prioritized, take the first three ideas on the list and begin a more thorough analysis of those ideas. This can be done by continuing with market research in the library and talking to business owners who are already in similar businesses. Learn as much as you can about start-up costs, marketing strategies, tricks of the trade, and other important elements of that business.

After more detailed review if you find that the three options chosen hold no promise, then it is appropriate to move down the list to the next set of ideas (three to a set) and explore these in more detail. If you've been honest and diligent in developing your mission statement and in performing the SWOT analysis of yourself and if you've carefully surveyed your environment for business opportunities, you will at some point find a match.

With your freshly generated idea now burning inside your heart and mind, run with it until you're out of breath. You'll need to begin writing your business plan and seeking the appropriate counseling. Although this analysis does not discuss the specifics of writing business plans and identifying financial resources, there are a number of well-written publications that discuss these topics in great detail.

EXECUTE, EXECUTE, EXECUTE

This step needs no explanation!

CASE STUDY

This case study represents a retail business in the downtown district of a Southern city that catered to large corporate constituents. Ms. Foreman is an African American.

JOYCE FOREMAN

Founder, Foreman Office Products
Dallas, Texas

"Don't Sell Minority, Sell Business"

During a recent trip to Dallas, I visited a company called Foreman Office Products. As I waited outside the front office, I noticed a sleek, beige Mercedes-Benz roll to a stop in front of me. Out jumped Joyce Foreman, a young, slender black woman who looked like she was far too young to be the owner of such a business. Foreman Office Products is one of the few black-owned office products businesses in the city of Dallas. As she unlocked the door and entered the store, I was proud of what this young woman had accomplished, even though I hardly knew her.

BEGINNINGS

Joyce Foreman was born in Telma, Texas, but considers Dallas her home. A graduate of the Dallas Independent School District and Junior College, Joyce didn't finish her studies at the University of Texas at Dallas, citing frustrations at being a minority when there weren't many other minorities. She felt that she stuck out like a sore thumb because she was one of the few African Americans. At the time she attended college, Joyce was also working full time, which added to her difficulties.

FAMILY

Growing up as an only child in a single-parent home, Joyce enjoyed a very close bond with her mother, a relationship that she feels gave her self-assurance. Her home provided a strong work ethic. Her mother told her never to give up and consequently Joyce remained an honor roll student throughout her tenure at school. Families of black domestics are often perceived as poor, Joyce says, something that wasn't true in her family. Her mother worked two jobs to give her daughter all the comforts she desired.

A naturally enterprising woman, Joyce's mother began her own business later in life, starting an organization to upgrade domestic workers, and they worked together to get the business going. Unfortunately, just at the time when the business received the necessary funding, Joyce's mother died and the dream was deferred.

PURCHASING CAREER

Joyce accepted her first job, as a file clerk at Zale Corporation, a Dallas-based corporation. After six weeks, she was promoted to the accounting department, doing bookkeeping. She was promoted again six months later to the position of assistant to the buyer in the jewelry division. As her reputation began to precede her, she was promoted to the construction division as a purchasing agent. She left the construction division and had several other jobs in the purchasing profession. Joyce stayed in the purchasing area, working for eight years for three different companies before deciding to venture out on her own.

CAREER TURNING POINT

As the company started expanding, Joyce began to feel more insecure, particularly when a less qualified peer was promoted ahead of her. A power struggle ensued, she got frustrated, and decided to go into business for herself. After much consideration, and talking to friends and business colleagues, she decided to start a business in office products, of which she had some prior knowledge. While she put together a plan for her new business, she continued to work for large but local corporations.

Joyce was familiar with office products (having purchased them), and she was also familiar with suppliers. Initially, she spent a long time talking with office product suppliers, doing research on what it would take to set up a company and how to buy. She found that many of the companies were very receptive to her, some offering advice freely. It took about a year and a half for her to pull all the things together. Even though Joyce had no experience writing a business plan, she pooled all of her resources, finished her business plan, and prepared to step out on her own.

LOAN REJECTION

Joyce initially took her idea to the bank that she had done business with for years and requested a $50,000 loan. Joyce was familiar with the loan officer at the bank, but he had been promoted and her loan application was assigned to a new college graduate. Needless to say, they were not willing to take a chance on a young black woman with big dreams. She also felt that the loan officer was prejudiced. Joyce left the bank feeling that if a banker likes you personally, the loan will go through. The bank listed that the reason for rejection was her lack of a track record. Joyce doubted that was the real reason because when she applied for a small auto loan it was also rejected, even though she had enough collateral in the bank to cover the debt.

Later, in 1984, when the business became more successful, Joyce was angry to find certain banks courting her, asking her to move her funds to their banks. She feels that banks want to ride on a business's coattails only when it is successful and are often unwilling to take a chance on a young business that shows some promise.

START-UP COSTS

Frustrated and needing the loan money, Joyce called her real estate agent and told her she wanted to sell her home. The agent advised her not to do this, but Joyce went ahead anyway and sold her home, shocking everyone who knew her. The proceeds from the house were used as start-up capital for Foreman Office Products. She admits that this idea concerned her at first, but when she began to think of herself as a first generation black business owner she felt this was the least that she could do. She knew she had to be creative. If lending institutions aren't going to help you, she thought, then help yourself. You must have plans B, C, D, and E available and ready. She was disappointed that she could not get funding from a lending institution, but she also believed that even if they made a loan, it probably would not have been in the amount she actually needed anyway. She explains:

> The system is not set up for blacks to go into business and be successful. The system is set up for blacks to fail. Even if you do get a loan, most of the time you're undercapitalized anyway. That's why it takes minority businesses so long to grow, because they don't have the proper amount of working capital.

Later that year when Joyce went into business, she too was undercapitalized. She admits that she was scared to death. She had learned from her mother that if she did the best she could, somehow things would work out for her. As Joyce began trying to build her customer base, she realized a shortcoming that she had—she was not very sociable. Although she had excelled professionally in her jobs, she had not taken the opportunity to hone her social skills.

UNDERCAPITALIZATION

Foreman Office Products started out as a sole proprietorship with only $25,000 cash. These same funds also had to be used to pay her living expenses. Financially, it was very difficult. First, Joyce rented a home and paid a high monthly rent, then she moved in with an aunt for a year and a half. Both options took a heavy toll on her emotionally and physically.

Unfortunately, the $25,000 she had invested didn't take her very far. Her start-up costs for bringing in the first order of supplies exceeded the available capital. Consequently, she was forced to use trade credit as a means of financing her products. After a while, Joyce leveraged the trade credit strategy into a science. Her suppliers would deliver twice a day. They'd ship it in, she'd fill the order, and the merchandise was out the door the same day. She turned the merchandise over very fast. It was a creative way to get started.

EARLY MARKETING STRATEGY

Joyce stays active within the purchasing community. She is an ex-member of the Purchasing Management Association of Dallas and had worked with other purchasing managers and took the opportunity to contact them to learn tips on effective marketing strategies to use. She learned that to be effective in attracting business she had to create a professional and inviting office environment. So before she left her job to start the business, she secured office space in the same upscale building in which she was currently working.

With an idea of what she wanted to do and an office to work from, her original marketing plan was to go after minority businesses. It didn't work. She feels that it was one of the things she did wrong in the first year. Joyce says you can sell minority businesses only to companies who have programs and know what minority business means and understand it. If you just call XYZ Company and say you're a minority business, they don't want to hear it.

After the first year, she realized that being a minority business was limiting and started selling to all businesses while targeting minority business where it made the most sense. She did telemarketing on her own, setting up appointments, saying who she was and her interest in doing business. She never mentioned that she was a minority business. Later, after she started attracting new accounts, she started hiring salespeople to assist with the marketing side of the business. Her theory is that her company sells business, and sells minority where it has to sell minority:

> Minority business has a negative connotation, which is hard for minorities to understand. You can't sell minority because some companies may have used a minority business before and been disappointed because the firm may have made a mistake. In their warped thinking, if one minority firm makes a mistake then all minority firms cannot be trusted to do quality work.

Joyce is a businessperson first and a minority businessperson second. She asks only for a fair shake because she's aware that white firms make mistakes but they almost always get another chance. She asks only that potential customers give her the chance to fail, but she knows she'll succeed. People have to know that all businesses make mistakes. Yet they refuse to let minorities make mistakes.

Joyce encourages all minority businesses to take the rifle approach to targeting business opportunities. Find out where you are most competitive and go for those opportunities. Second, Joyce explains, you have to find your niche in the market. She recently asked a client, "If we can go direct on orders of under $500, why aren't we directing some of those opportunities to minority businesses?" Joyce continues:

> The amount of $500 means a lot to some minority businesses. State law says that on any bid under $10,000, you must call up three people on the phone. Are you assured that one of those three people is a minority business? The manufacturer is probably not going to fool with that $10,000 order. So the level of competition becomes greater for that minority business enterprise (MBE). For too long, we've gone out there and said, "Give me some business." We haven't been able to identify what we want. We need to ask for specifics and not let them identify what our specifics should be, leaving it totally up to them to define.

Joyce's niche is noncontract items. She explains why:

> What customers say to me is we sent you a bid; but what they don't say is that they also sent a copy to my suppliers as well. They don't know that I realize that every time they send me a bid my suppliers get a copy also. Obviously the manufacturers are not going to let me beat them out unless they have a commitment not to sell direct, and few manufacturers honor that commitment. They get any business that they can. They'll sell to my customers, too!

She admits she can't compete with those from whom she buys. So her selling technique is saying, "You sent me a bid. What other way do you purchase?" Joyce explains her point of view:

> Any order under x amount of dollars, I'll pick up a telephone and call and say, "Give me some of that business," because I can't compete on that level and what they have historically done is knock us out because we can't compete against the people we buy from. Why send me a bid that I can't competitively bid on?

KNOW YOUR BUSINESS

Historically, Joyce says, a person will see Joe Blow in a business making money and think that's great. Under the illusion that there is easy money to be made, he or she attempts to go into his business without finding out how Joe is really making money. Joyce says it's key to know something about what you're going to sell and what you're going to do. Learning how to be in business, how to control your employees, how to deal with banks, and so forth is very difficult, she explains. You can't learn how to be in business and understand the nature of what you're doing at the same time. That's why she used the experiences from her prior jobs to prepare herself for getting her business off the ground, and it worked well for her.

A CENTRAL LOCATION

Her start-up materials were expensive, and she felt that being a minority, she was watched very closely by suppliers initially because she feels they were concerned about her paying her bills on time. Many were put at ease once they saw her store and saw that she was right in the middle of the business district. She had initially rented a place on the eleventh floor of a building. Her suppliers were a bit miffed; getting all her supplies to the eleventh floor caused problems, but the downtown address was important. Her particular commodity was to sell to major corporations and they can identify with a downtown address.

She fought for a street level walk-in location for a long time. People thought she wasn't ready for that kind of exposure. She talked to a building office manager about getting a street level walk-in location in the building. Joyce later was pleasantly surprised that the office manager was a white female who liked her and agreed to give her a fair chance. The two women negotiated a satisfactory deal. The overhead was extensive, but the identity of a street level downtown address means more than the overhead, says Joyce.

THE DOOR IS ALWAYS OPEN

Joyce's office door is always open. Some well-meaning business associates advised her not to leave her door open so that the public would not know that the owner of this business is a black female. Joyce rationalizes that if people see her only as a black and female, then she isn't interested in their business anyway. She believes that people come in to see her because she is available.

Joyce thinks of herself as an affirmative action baby. She went through the process of working for large corporations and learned how to do it their way. She's a firm believer in doing it their way. You can't make up the rules yourself, she says.

CONFIDENT IN THE FUTURE OF MINORITY BUSINESS

Foreman is optimistic about the future of minority business in America. In the past five years, she has seen a dramatic increase in minority entrepreneurs' awareness and preparation, but believes that the structure of minority businesses has to change. "If we start putting minorities to work, look at what happens to the development of the city as a whole," she says. Joyce believes we have to move quality minority vendors from level one to the next level where they can begin generating millions of dollars in business. We need to create businesses that will put more people to work. The more people we have working, the broader our tax base becomes. Full employment provides members of the community with a heightened sense of security and well-being. People who feel secure are better positioned to address the other issues facing their community. If people are not working, they aren't going to get involved. Joyce thinks you have to be in a position to give back to the community, not necessarily working out of the minority community. This is her mission.

Joyce sees minority businesses that have been around for seven years and thinks they need to be pushed to another level. For the minority business owner just starting out, she sees a need for education. "From the minority business standpoint, we've got to convince the business owners that they need education." She pushes education. She is convinced that her purchasing background helped her into another level, providing her with an education. She feels her background helped her to be successful.

LACK OF BUSINESS EXPERIENCE IS NO SWEAT

The most important trait to success, according to Joyce, is attitude. She simply believes in being the best. Once she made the commitment to seeing her dream through, she stuck to it. She sees herself on one side as nonthreatening, but on the other side as forceful, sometimes pushy.

"If people know that you will work hard," says Joyce, "they will tend to get on your bandwagon. You've got to maintain high morals and strong work ethics," she preaches to minority businesses. Joyce says she'll work seven days a week or all night. She doesn't care. She feels that Foreman Office Products is committed to excellence and will push until it gets its fair share. She demands quality from her workers and nothing less. "Just because you're black doesn't mean you expect things that are substandard. That's a bunch of crap," she says. She wants people to see that she's doing good, quality work, and that her standards are high by anyone's standards.

DON'T SELL MINORITY, SELL BUSINESS

"Don't sell minority, sell business," Joyce says. She just happens to be black and female. She refuses to go into a corporation and say that she wants her 10 percent. She knows that it has to be earned. Joyce suggests that if you're going into an account for the first time, try to identify the problem and understand the customer's business first. She says you are not going to solve problems overnight that have been going on for years. "The minority business problem, or solution," says Joyce, "is the collective input from both sides." That's basically what works for Joyce Foreman. Joyce emphasizes that she is not pushing minorities for minorities' sakes; she's pushing quality minorities.

FINDING AND MANAGING YOUR STAFF

Joyce has 10 people working for her. Women, she thinks, manage differently from men. She concludes that men like to carry the big stick. "Maybe it's a macho thing." Joyce does not use this approach. She prefers using the family approach, and the workers tend to support one another. However, the family approach doesn't always work, especially when men want to test her. When she speaks, she feels that everybody listens; what she says goes. Before hiring, she asks potential workers how they feel about working for a female. Most people say that it's no problem. She insists that all her people either fit in the fold or look for employment elsewhere. The bottom line is that Joyce demands excellent performance and respect.

Joyce is firm, but fair. When workers have failed to perform she lets them know that she expects excellence and that they've worked too hard to get put under. She also feels she's a very loving, caring person. Joyce has taken the added responsibility of nurturing her employees. She insists that they do their best. She knows that if the business folded tomorrow she could get a job and wants to ensure that they could also. She talks to her employees about being a minority business, telling them they are an example and that they aren't allowed to make mistakes. She believes the family management system has worked well for her. Joyce also recognizes that it doesn't work well for everybody.

BEING A WOMAN IN BUSINESS

Many associate the family style of management with female managers. Unlike some other female entrepreneurs, Joyce doesn't think you have to lose your femininity to be in business. While she is petite, she believes that her size can be an advantage. Although most view her as nonthreatening, when challenged, people look up to find themselves bleeding. She is single with no children and doesn't think she would have gotten where she is if she had been married. Joyce believes that typically women take the role of supporting their husbands rather than taking that step forward. If married, she wouldn't have been able to sell her home or spend adequate time developing Foreman Office Products. Joyce feels that understanding your constraints is key. She gets calls all the time from women interested in going into business and gives them the Foreman Story. She has no commitments to tie her down.

Foreman also expects commitment from female employees. She believes female employees are more difficult to manage. "Women tend to be more nitpicky," she explains. "Men don't have time."

BUILDING THE PROPER SUPPORT SYSTEM

Most minority businesses are first generation, and a strong support system is critical for success. Although she had extended family support, they were unfamiliar with what she was trying to accomplish; therefore, their ability to support was limited. However, the support Joyce's family couldn't provide was adequately provided by other local minority business owners. Joyce's support group of local business owners meets regularly to discuss critical issues and problems. "It seems like our problems are the same," says Foreman.

Fortunately, the support that Joyce's group provides her will ultimately be provided by Joyce to the next generation of minority businesses. She explains:

> The process is going to be a lot easier for them because when my generation came through there was no one to talk to. At least the next crop of entrepreneurs will have a lot more potential role models to choose from.

START-UP ORGANIZATION

When Joyce first started her business, she did everything herself. She had to because there was no one else. Her resources were so scarce that she had to deliver merchandise in her car. Owning a minority business, you have to be willing to do grunt work because you are usually undercapitalized. Just for those occasions, she keeps a pair of jeans in her office should she have to assist in the warehouse. In the beginning, she was the marketing person, the salesperson, the telephone operator, and the delivery person. Jim Washington and Ken Carter were her confidantes and they offered support, telling her what to do, and where to go. She attended lots of seminars and workshops and believes that one never stops learning.

"All successful businesses," explains Joyce, "need to have clear and well-defined goals. This is especially true from a marketing viewpoint. The owner needs to understand where he's going to go to get his business, who you market to, and why you've chosen that particular market." She has two salespeople, far fewer than what she should have. She won't put people on the payroll whom she can't afford. It goes back to being undercapitalized. She tries to keep things in perspective. She's trying not to grow too fast. If she hires five salespeople and they go out and get $5 million worth of business, it would be difficult. "There's nothing worse," says Joyce, "than having too much business. If for some reason you can't perform, you will probably never get a second chance."

GROWTH PROJECTION

Joyce sees Foreman Office Products growing by leaps and bounds. She has good reason to be confident. First of all, Joyce feels she's already proven herself and shown the value that her firm can bring to her customers. However, Joyce is uncertain how long she'll remain in the office products business. She has always believed that getting into the office products business was just a stepping-stone to bigger and better opportunities. Now that she knows how to start and manage a business, it would be very easy for her to start branching into other businesses. Joyce is quick to admit that the office products business has been very good to her. But if something better came along, she'd sell Foreman Office Products in a heartbeat.

She believes that once you're in the network, people bring the deals to you. If you're perceived as the "in" minority business, then they all will be talking to you. Even the banks will beat a path to your door to loan you money if you're a part of the deal stream. Joyce insists that she could easily obtain a loan now, but when you owe the banks, they own a part of you and Joyce is reluctant to get into this situation.

TEN-YEAR PLAN

During the last couple of years that Joyce has been in business, she has purposely grown the business slowly. Joyce has a long-term greedy mentality. She had no intention of getting rich in the first 10 years because when you start out undercapitalized, the chances of your making big money in the short-term are slim. Usually it will take approximately 10 years before things start to really cook. To remain within that 10-year plan, Joyce pays herself a small salary to cover living expenses:

> In the first 10 years, you take care of the business. During the next 10 years, the business will take care of you. After 10 years, if I'm still getting up at 5:30 A.M., then I've failed. Right now I'm taking care of the business. If it was easy, everybody would be doing it. It's a hard job, worse than anything. You don't have one boss, you have many bosses, your customers.

She'd like her people to emulate her, leave their jobs at Foreman, and start their own businesses. Joyce hopes that her employees have learned some valuable skills while in her employ. She'd like to have an incubator for minority businesses. This would entail creating an environment with a building and a handpicked group of minority businesses that she thinks would be successful:

> What sometimes happens with minority businesses is that you'll get guys leaving corporate America with very strong skills in certain areas but not always in critical areas like accounting, billing, invoicing, and things of that nature. Somehow these people need to learn these lessons quickly, and the incubator concept might prove helpful in situations like these.

GETTING IN AND STAYING IN

Joyce cautions all would-be entrepreneurs to first know why they want to go into business and to know something about the business they're getting into. She warns that it is extremely difficult to run your business effectively and learn it at the same time. There are business development centers around the country specializing in helping small businesses, and people should take the opportunity to use them instead of trying to learn everything on their own.

Those who choose to run their own businesses need to have strong organizational, social, and leadership skills. These skills must be applied at all times:

> Most deals are cut in places where you'd least expect them to be cut, so you always have to be on the alert for opportunity. I recall a situation where I attended a meeting in Dallas on economic development within the city. The president of one of the local corporations was in attendance and was impressed by me for some reason. Even though I had been calling on this man's company for years with no success, he and I struck a deal that afternoon—on the spot.

Joyce Foreman's commitment to minority business development and survival is unwavering. In her opinion it goes far beyond just the businesses themselves, but to the African American community in general. African American businesspeople provide role models for young people and gainful employment for some struggling adults. Joyce logically concludes that if there are more businesses created in the community, then there will be more people employed.

When people are transferred from the welfare rolls to the job rolls, an amazing thing happens. First, their self-esteem is restored and their self-hate and negative attitudes are diminished. Second, they begin to focus on other critical issues within their community.

As Joyce works her way to the front door of her store to receive her first customer of the day, she looks back at me and in an almost trance-like state utters, "Clearly, there is a direct correlation between black economic empowerment and the level of social problems facing that community." This is a relationship she understands well.

CASE STUDY

This case study epitomizes the business opportunities that exist working with the Internet. Wayne's company specializes in Internet security. Mr. Armour is an African American.

WAYNE ARMOUR

President and CEO, OFO Technologies, Inc.

"Just Find a Void, Fill That Void and Do Not Be Afraid to Take a Chance"

Wayne Armour, president and CEO of OFO Technologies, an Internet security firm, has spent a lifetime in a quest to fulfill this destiny. As a successful and innovative entrepreneur, Wayne embodies the American dream elusive to so many others. Just before taking a plane to some business venture, I caught up with Wayne in an effort to gain his perspective on the importance of the entrepreneurial spirit.

Success has left him unspoiled and willing to share his story though, like many of his counterparts, he finds himself more focused on the present. "I guess I am trying to grow up a little more, businesswise," he opens. "So I'm trying to get from a point where you just have a very small company incrementally increasing its value. If you want to make a real step, you have to have a serious plan. My plans in the past have been more personal. I want to be at a certain level, but now I'm looking at how I can really come up with a coherent plan so that I can describe very concisely what my company does." He trails off into a business tangent unfolding the importance of analysis. When I ask about the origin of his company, OFO, he refocuses. "First of all OFO [has] accents under the Os and means *vision* in Igbo, a Nigerian language. A friend of mine was trying to help me find a name. I wanted it to be tied to Africa, but I also wanted it to be concise. This friend, who is Nigerian, revealed that in a Nigerian village a successful man who has a son might name him Ejiofo meaning *one with vision.*" Wayne shortened it to OFO to complement his vision of entrepreneurship.

THE INTERNET: LAND OF OPPORTUNITY

"In the Internet arena there are so many things that can be done and you have to make sure you don't delude yourself. Especially with a smaller company, you must find a noncommodity niche to maximize the earning potential of the company. Several years ago, we decided to focus on Internet security infrastructure. Our term for this is Secure Web Immersion Methodology (SWIM). The first stage of SWIM is assessment. This is accomplished via penetration testing and host-based vulnerability analyses. Then we can go to a client, talk to them about what their current web infrastructure is, and then come up with a plan to build them to where they want to be." Wayne promises no easy road in his service-oriented market. He stresses the importance of incremental steps for the business. "It may not happen immediately for time or cost reasons . . . but every quarter we want to get closer. So we start to pull in countermeasures and then do follow up assessments every quarter to make sure that [the company] is on track."

BORN TO BE AN ENTREPRENEUR

Perhaps Wayne has a genetic link to his success. Entrepreneurship permeates his family history, like many other African American families who proudly entered the marketplace as early as the turn of the twentieth century. Wayne preferred to embrace the maverick spirit of the entrepreneur rather than the family business. "My first actual job out of college was working with my father. He's an entrepreneur and I really enjoyed working with him, but I wanted to move ahead a little faster than even he had in mind."

In no time, Wayne found an opportunity. "That was the first time my mother said, 'Why are you leaving? You're working with your Dad. Why are you going to take a risk with a company you don't know?'

"I said, 'Look, I don't mind taking the risk. If I fail, then I have to do something else. I'm not afraid of doing any job.' "

Never truer words were spoken as Wayne left that opportunity for another with a prestigious oil company. Despite the high profile and turnover of the job (and the threat of termination), once again Wayne took the risk. Yet courageous risk taking is far from the key to success. Wayne also implemented his vision to "build a business over a small number of years . . . and by the time the company was successful, I would get out." Keeping his vision clear means maintaining control and Wayne understands that "once a company gets to a certain level, you really do lose control. I'd be back in the situation that I really didn't want to be in, in the first place. So I'd probably take my money and then start some other small concern."

Like many other prosperous businesspeople, Wayne has a solid physical, intellectual, and spiritual preparation. Even legacy is a preparation for him. He attributes exercise, particularly jogging, to keeping his energy level up and alert. Many other entrepreneurs such as Oprah Winfrey have enjoyed jogging at the start of a competitive business day. He credits his voracious appetite for business as the fuel for his intellect. Ingesting every form of information from newsletters to online publications, Wayne keeps his head fed. He cites one of his goals as to become a domain expert, which he is certain creates more indispensability with clients.

A SPIRITUAL FOUNDATION

Most important to Wayne is his spiritual foundation. "I've talked to God. I've always felt that I was more spiritual than religious. I believe that whatever religion someone practices is fine. If they love God then I love them and I have no problem with that." While his spiritual foundation is Christian, it is bolstered, in his own words, by the coming birth of his daughter. The notion of his legacy sustains him. "I think that having a child is a gift from God. I feel that with that gift comes a certain responsibility. There is a responsibility to do the best that you can [with all] the gifts that God has given you. Just have the faith and know the opportunity God has given you, with the capabilities and the blessings He's given you individually."

Wayne's definition of success is simple: "being on track, being fulfilled, and being able to pay the bills." He deepens when he discusses what he believes are principles of success. The most prominent is ethics.

> Let's say you're in business in a small market. People know you. I worked for a large company providing support to IBM. They were paying us a certain amount of money because we were to have a certain number of people working on the project. I got to be a manager and instead of having eight people, I had three. We fell behind on a number of problems, so we got called down to a meeting.
>
> I was there with my new boss, the head of this new company. The IBM guy asked me point blank, "Wayne, do you really have eight people working on this project?" I was in a dilemma, because my current boss was like "Listen, if they ask say yes we do but they aren't all full time blah, blah, blah."
>
> At that point, I said I couldn't answer that question. "Why don't you ask my boss?" I think the point got across to this guy that I wasn't going to lie to him. I just wasn't going to do that.

Wayne explains that the two companies ceased a relationship not long after. "I think that the lesson for that company is that they really shouldn't sell themselves in an area [for which] they aren't prepared. I found out that in other situations like that, where hard decisions have to be made, the best advice is: don't lie to people."

STRIVING FOR EXCELLENCE

Wayne testifies to his personal mantra, "go into a job every day ready to leave" and that it has kept him from overestimating the importance of working for any company. This mantra granted Wayne freedom from compromising his ethics and/or morals to keep a job because: "I can tell people what I think and I don't have to accept any b.s."

Wayne cites striving for excellence as the second most important principle of success. He muses that sometimes his clients do not know exactly what they want and so are rarely happy with the job done unless you educate them first.

> [A major investment firm] once brought me in. "Take the application as it is. Don't make any changes. Maybe there's a program that can just automatically translate [client/server] so it's on the web."
>
> My response: "There is no magic wand." We were under time constraints, but instead of just trying to do [the job] exactly like it was I said, "Why don't we break the mold a little bit . . . ," which has this company ready to take it further.
>
> [Now they are saying] "Let's redesign the whole thing. Let's try to do it right."
>
> I think by saying it over and over again if you really want a quality product, you can't squeeze the time. You can't throw people on and then cut it by any amount of people. I think what they really learned is they can depend on me to deliver a quality product.
>
> They said, "Wow, you came in here and now you're telling us how our systems work." I think that [striving for excellence], not by just doing what someone tells you but what is rational, is what really works here.

Though he was hard pressed to come up with a label for a third principle, Wayne waxes about being unafraid, "not from the point of being fearful but from the point that says you are going to do the best job you can. If by doing that people don't like what you're doing or don't want to hear what you're telling them, what you believe is true, move on." Wayne recounts a situation in which a former senior executive with militaristic style attempted to exert command over his project. Wayne returned the suggestions with one of his own: to communicate with his direct supervisor about any changes. "It ended up that they said, 'You have one week.' I went from there to an even more substantial company so it was a good move for me." Each of the principles Wayne listed has directly benefited his career, but he isn't totally dependent on them to assure his success.

TRAITS OF THE SUCCESSFUL

He outlines a few traits of highly successful people that he has observed and cultivated. The first trait is big egos. Business is a minefield of competition, but Wayne believes that self-esteem is key. "They really think that they can do it better than others. That's why they really do it themselves. Because whether they are right or not, they all say, I can do this better than IBM, AT&T or whatever company." Wayne exclaimed that he understands the rigors and precariousness of being "responsible for your own being, not just by going to work every day, doing what someone else wants you to do, but by determining what you are going to do. I think you need a pretty big ego and a lot of confidence." Second, "I see people who really love what they do. My mother-in-law sells stockings, pantyhose, socks, and things like that at a flea market. She is an entrepreneur and she loves what she's doing. It doesn't matter where she is, she's always commenting on someone's pantyhose, or in the mall she'll say, 'Let me look in this store.' She's always talking about this.

"My wife used to tell me I was always talking about 'Internet, Internet, Internet.' Now she's been bitten by the Internet bug almost as much as I have. If you're in your own business, you're an entrepreneur. You're living it. You're not 9 to 5 any more. You're always working or thinking about what you should be doing." The final trait is highly significant to all would-be business moguls: understanding your shortcomings. It comes with a few words that are all too telling. Wayne illumines that his shortcomings are constantly under construction as he seeks direction through spiritual means.

My time ran short with Wayne, who offered insight into his vision of the future. Wayne thinks the disintermediation of Internet commerce is the wave of the future:

> The middle man is basically going to disappear. You won't have to worry about [whether] a store is open, insurance, assembly line. Maybe you can sell a small amount of goods you make yourself. I am planning [an e-commerce site] with my mother-in-law, who also makes items for cribs, right now. [I believe] she is talented. Let her make these things.
>
> Disintermediation is key where you don't have a big company, you just have a product that you own yourself, that you're not trying to resell [for a manufacturer]. My hope is that this site, eUjamaa.com, will become a portal for many African American-based products and services. The

> other term I hear from venture capitalists is *e-commerce or elimination.* [Companies] are going to have to be on the Internet. They are going to have to sell some of their products there . . . [or] lose.

Wayne cites an example of a Fortune 500 investment banker whose reputation for repudiating the notions of online trading and discount brokering has drastically changed due to e-commerce or elimination. Currently, the same company offers online trading with the perk of financial advisement from brokers at the firm.

Before he is off to another lofty venture, Wayne offers a final term on an advisement to potential entrepreneurs. "You have to make those strategic partnerships with people who are in the service end. [They] can enhance it. They can even feed things back into your central development strategy. Strategic partnerships are important. Those are the people who are going to be winning." Wayne's vehement independence, his grounding and willingness to take a risk, his lofty goals, and his solid foundation have all combined in his strategy for success.

CASE STUDY

SSI has perfected the essence of government contracting and teaming with diverse business partners. Mr. Curry was a Hispanic American.

EUGENE CURRY

Founder, Seven Systems, Inc.
Gaithersburg, Maryland

"You Have to Have a Long-Term, Well-Thought-Out Business Strategy"

The Alpha Phi Alpha fraternity has produced some of the most notable African American leaders in this country. Great Alpha men like Dr. Martin Luther King Jr., Thurgood Marshall, and Jesse Owens, just to name a few, have left such an indelible mark on our nation and the world that no amount of bigotry or ignorance can ever erase their memories. Eugene Curry has certainly followed in the tradition of excellence that most other Alpha men espouse. Eugene seems to enjoy the high level of activity that most successful government contractors experience daily. Like many of the other Beltway Bandits, as some government contractors are sometimes affectionately known as, Eugene's (b.k.a. Gene) firm is comfortable being in the midst of the business fray.

BEGINNINGS

Seven Systems, Inc. (SSI) started out as a software/data processing systems company in statistical analysis, the brainchild of three partners who had begun as computer programmers. Primarily their work involves utilizing data that are already stored in computing systems to prepare statistics, analyze trends, or perform inventory analyses. Ninety percent of their contracts are in government. The business focuses on many areas, most notably health care—drug abuse, mental health, and infectious diseases. Recently, the National Institutes of Health (NIH) in Bethesda, Maryland, has become a major client.

SSI'S STRUCTURE

SSI became incorporated in 1978. At that time the three partners were working together as officers for a major data processing firm. When the company broke up, the three partners united and started their own company. The new partners quickly carved out niches that allowed each to work in his or her area of expertise and to contribute most effectively in making the business successful.

Their excellent relationships as partners have been assimilated into SSI's culture as a very informal, tight-knit team trying to achieve common objectives. One of the partners proudly shares:

> The company is informal, with the majority of SSI's 75 employees knowing each other on a first-name basis. Everyone knows what's going on and no one is working in fog. We hold board meetings and keep everybody abreast of major company decisions.

One of the partners works primarily in hardware and software. He's also treasurer of the board, Accounting Department, and serves as corporate coordinator. A second partner is expert in Java programming and contract coordinator in health and imaging. The third partner, who is Eugene Curry, serves as CEO while still maintaining a respectable amount of billable hours.

By wisely dividing the company's duties among themselves, SSI's leaders developed a very good reputation. Every contract is assigned to one of the vice presidents or principals who has day-to-day responsibilities, making sure the project's on budget, on time, and helping resolve any issues that arise. Due to their excellent reputation, they get most business by word of mouth. They pride themselves on providing services that are on time, on budget, and thorough.

SSI'S FINANCIAL PLANNING

SSI's basic financial strategy is always to stay one step ahead of its financial requirements. They try to maintain large lines of credit with numerous banking sources. The company has done business with the local banks for so long that the firm has never been denied credit whenever it needed it. The company prides itself on its ability to estimate its cash requirements as a function of what contracts they're awarded and the anticipated duration of those contracts.

RURAL ROOTS

Eugene Curry grew up on a farm outside Lawrenceville, Virginia, which was purchased by his grandfather during the early 1900s. Eugene and his eight brothers helped to work the farm, where they grew mostly cotton and corn, although corn was the more profitable of the two. Although farm work was very hard, it provided the family with a certain level of security and prestige. Eugene's grandfather worked very hard to provide the family with that security. He not only had a farm, but also owned a country store and one of the few cotton gins in the community. Although farmers by trade, Eugene's parents understood the importance of education, so when Eugene turned 17 they ushered him off to Hampton College in Virginia, where he studied mathematics.

After graduation from college, he didn't know what he wanted to do. He knew what he didn't want to do—work in the post office or become a teacher. These were two of the few areas that minorities were allowed to work in but neither paid especially well. Disappointed but not willing to give up, he ended up waiting tables in Richmond, Virginia.

In 1959 he was drafted and later that year he married his lovely fiancée, Juliet. Since he had a college education and was technically skilled, Curry was assigned to the Pentagon to work on building economic models to predict the performance of the Eastern bloc countries and monitor their economic indicators. During his stint at the Pentagon, Eugene decided to take advantage of living in Washington and later enrolled in Howard University to earn his master's degree, after which he accepted a new position as a FORTRAN programmer. At this point in his life, he maintains, he wasn't thinking about going into his own business, but he was satisfied he had found a good government job. Besides he had finally found a profession that he enjoyed—computer programming.

> Computer programmers in the late 1960s and early 1970s were like little angels; everybody wanted them. You could leave a job confident that you could get another job. Computer people were in demand just as Internet and web technicians are in great demand today.

CONSULTING

It was the high demand for consulting services that eventually wooed Eugene away from his job with the government. In 1962 he got a job offer from a private company for $13,000. At that time, he was a GS9 with the government at only $9,000 per year and felt that he could use the increased pay. Eugene accepted the offer and worked there for five years before leaving to join another firm called Delta Corporation. In 1967 he agreed to venture out and form a new company with three other people. The venture was short lived for Eugene, as the group had great difficulty working together. Eventually Eugene left the start-up firm and returned to Delta.

After getting his job back at Delta, it wasn't long before he heard about consulting opportunities from the guy sitting next to him. Shortly thereafter, that guy quit and later called Eugene to ask him if he wanted to do some consulting. Again Eugene left Delta, this time to do a $25,000 contract. Gene felt that this situation was no risk, because even if business didn't do well, he could always get more work. After a few months, he and his partner, Danny Gwynn, decided to form SSI.

SSI'S CAPITALIZATION

Before setting out on his own, apart from Gwynn, Curry had already secured a deal for approximately $1 million worth of business. Unlike many other fledgling businesses, Curry started from a position that was well capitalized. Based on the nature of his business and on Eugene's philosophy to have twice as much as he needed at the outset, he found himself able to promote his business from a position of strength. Eugene's belief about strong capitalization cannot be overemphasized. He asserts:

> You have to have capital—your projection of what you need is only as good as how well you know your business. Get more than what you need—almost twice as much. When you've exhausted the bare minimal money, no one is going to give you more. Our business lost $90,000 the first year but I had borrowed twice the amount I needed, so we survived. You have to have a long-term, well-thought-out business strategy.

The other key factors that Eugene believes contributed to SSI's success were knowledge of the business and their competition.

> You have to have some feel for what people make doing comparable jobs and what their overhead rates are. What do people load their spreadsheets with if they are selling people's time? Ask friends that are hiring contractors. Look at the contracts you have lost and ask why. As a bidder, you have the right to find out why. Remember, you can't rely on other people to protect your interest.

Besides a good capital basis, SSI had other strengths from the outset. Most importantly, Curry was working in his area of expertise.

> You can't rely on other people to protect your interest—you have to protect it yourself. You have to work your butt off to make sure it's the way you want it to be. One thing that the banking people look for is the ability to run the business. I had nine years of running an active business, during three of which I was the president. You have to know when you're making

> money and when you're not. The key to starting a small business is to know what you're doing.

Eugene has learned that sometimes you don't have to sell the best mousetrap, especially in hard times. Often in contract bidding situations, they don't want the best mousetrap but maybe the most polished mousetrap. As an executive, you must learn what works and use it.

ONE SUCCESS WON'T MAKE YOU

When asked what it takes to be successful in the long run, Eugene replies:

> Learn to work hard and stay with it. Do not let early successes get you off track. One success won't make you. You need to develop a pattern of success. Save your cash. No one wants to bother with a five-year-old business that needs money. Try harder to accumulate cash. If you're in a personal service firm, get qualified personnel.

Besides remaining persistent, attracting good people, and remaining focused Eugene further recommends that the entrepreneur not spread himself or herself too thin. He warns:

> Don't be in a hurry to serve on too many boards and committees at the beginning of your venture. Back off and let someone else serve on them for you. It is critical to focus on the needs of the business until it's strong enough to stand on its own and not on your shoulders.

6

Success Factors for African American Entrepreneurs

As was mentioned earlier, my trips around the country interviewing entrepreneurs required me to keep records of my conversations. I tirelessly sifted through the experiences of each business owner to identify the secrets of success. Like Ponce de Leon searching for the fountain of youth, I searched for turnkey solutions to complex challenges, which, if adopted, would quickly lead one to wealth and fame. Well, I'm sorry to report that there are no secrets of success. There is nothing known to humans that guarantees success. As a matter of fact, the same strategies that may bring one person success may take another down the path of failure and destruction.

However, it has been my experience that serious emerging, embryonic, and established entrepreneurs are not looking for easy formulas to follow or for someone to hold their hands and protect them from the cold realities of owning and managing businesses. These entrepreneurs are willing to take the risks on their own and want only to learn from the experiences of those who went before them so that they don't make the same mistakes. They have learned that to be successful, they must do what successful people do. The United Negro College Fund says and summarizes the desires of this special breed, "We're not looking for a handout, just a hand."

For those entrepreneurs who are looking for a hand, I'm happy to report that although there may be no magical secrets of success, there are some common traits among African American in particular and minority American entrepreneurs in general that I observed from interviews, frank conversations at quiet moments, and just general observations that will definitely help you. Don't look at these traits as an all-or-nothing deal you assume that if you possess only a few of them or none at all, you're unfit to become an entrepreneur. Absorb all the information initially, review your situation carefully, extract the parts of this analysis that you find beneficial, and pass the rest on to someone else. For others, the information on traits of African American entrepreneurs may help to fill some void in your understanding of how successful businesspeople create and manage thriving enterprises.

It is difficult to discern which characteristics of black entrepreneurs are unique only to this group and not to mainstream entrepreneurs as well. Obviously, there is a common set of traits associated with all successful entrepreneurs regardless of their race, creed, color, or religion. However, due to the unique circumstances that define the African Americans' experiences, they have been forced to develop additional traits just to survive. I've tried diligently to focus only on these unique qualities. I'm afraid though that no matter how hard I tried, there is still some degree of overlap. Regardless, blacks often must call upon unique strengths within themselves to fight for what is rightfully theirs in an environment that is increasingly hostile. It is these special qualities that I've attempted to capture in this book.

This chapter describes three phenomena that contribute to successful entrepreneurship in the black community: the *first hit* phenomenon, the *water bucket* theory, and the invisible *sixth-person* phenomenon. The chapter then compares three tiers of entrepreneurial businesses and describes which are more successful for entrepreneurs regardless of race, versus which are more successful for blacks in particular. Finally, the chapter introduces three archetypes of black entrepreneurs. Chapter 7 continues this discussion by describing 20 traits of successful African American entrepreneurs.

THE FIRST HIT PHENOMENON (SIGNIFICANT EVENT)

Early in my analysis, I began to uncover an interesting phenomenon. Almost without exception, all the businesspeople in this study struggled during the early phases of their venture. Usually during this phase of the journey, the entrepreneurs were forced to make major sacrifices and faced major disappointments. In many situations, the minority entrepreneur worked diligently for years without ever reaping any significant benefits or rewards.

For those strong enough to persevere through those dark and uncertain periods, an interesting phenomenon usually occurred. These people would score their first hit ultimately. What do I mean by the *first hit*? I have characterized this as any event that is preceded by a difficult and tenuous period and culminates in a success of significant magnitude. The first hit could be the awarding of the first contract from a client who's been marketed to for years. Or it could be the successful purchase of and the ultimate turnaround of a small struggling manufacturing company. In some instances it could be resolving an operations problem that's been negatively affecting customer satisfaction and operating efficiencies at your company. With the problem solved, you go on to produce high-quality products at a brisk production rate.

As shown in Exhibit 6.1, after the first hit, the entrepreneur usually finds that the second, third, and subsequent hits come along more frequently and often with much greater impact and potential for reward. Experiencing the first hit is like making a difficult shot at a critical point in a championship basketball game. Prior to taking the shot you may have been burdened with self-doubt and low confidence. However, after the shot, you become buoyed with confidence and anticipation of making even more difficult, but exciting shots.

The tragedy in this situation is that many aspiring entrepreneurs never hang around long enough to experience their first hits. They usually

Exhibit 6.1 Investment/Return Curve

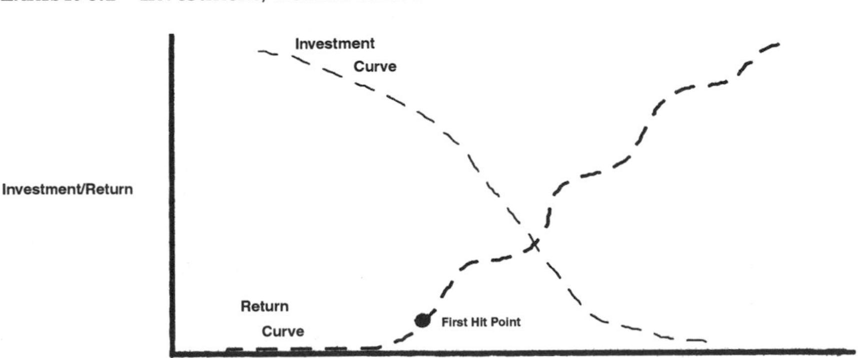

get so disgusted and disillusioned with the seeming lack of progress, they give up on their dreams and settle for a life of mediocrity. They fail to understand that the process of achieving your goal requires that you pay some dues first and that you maintain your course (assuming it is the correct one) until you experience your first hit. Beyond the first hit, your return for paying your dues begins to multiply.

THE WATER BUCKET THEORY

Understanding the first hit phenomenon is critical because it provides aspiring entrepreneurs with linear guidelines for maintaining perseverance and commitment to their business goal. The water bucket theory takes the first hit theory one step further and attempts to explain the process of business formation from a two- or three-dimensional standpoint.

As shown in Exhibit 6.2, obtaining business success is analogous to pouring water into a bucket and eventually using that water to nourish the flowers you've planted. If we assume that the bucket remains stationary, the simple act of pouring water into the bucket will not suffice to pro-

Exhibit 6.2 The Water Bucket Theory

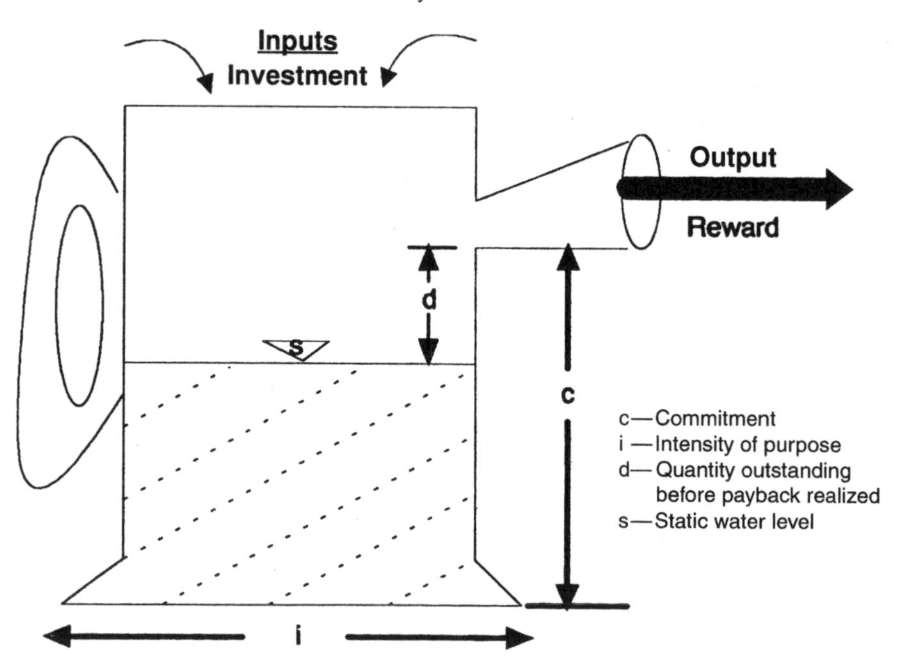

vide water to the flowers. There is a certain amount of water that must be poured into the bucket before the static water level is high enough to overflow through the spout.

Every man and woman who wants to start and own a business has a unique bucket to fill to some level before seeing benefits and rewards from his or her inputs, investments, or costs associated with making the business dream a reality. The costs or investments considered in this analysis include things such as time, capital, frustration, recreation time, disappointments, stress, opportunity cost, and others. The sum quantity of these costs helps fill each individual's bucket.

For the sake of this discussion, if we assume that intensity of purpose (i) and commitment (c) are the basic ingredients, then i times c equals the quantity of investment made. D represents the quantity that is still outstanding before the individual will begin seeing some payback or reward. It is my assumption that the quantity of each person's investment is cumulative. This idea implies that if an entrepreneur starts filling his or her bucket and for one reason or another stops filling the bucket, the quantity in the bucket remains stagnant until the entrepreneur picks up where he or she left off and resumes work on making up the quantity d. There may be some losses in the content of the bucket depending on the goal being sought, but in general the contents of the bucket should remain stagnant for some time, as shown by Exhibit 6.3.

Although I submit that the opportunity buckets for each individual are different, I also suggest that the size of the opportunity bucket of African American businesspeople and other businesspeople of color are much larger than their white counterparts.

There are numerous reasons the bucket for businesspeople of color is much larger than that of whites but the two most apparent reasons are

Exhibit 6.3 Water Buckets Commensurate with Goals of Entrepreneurs

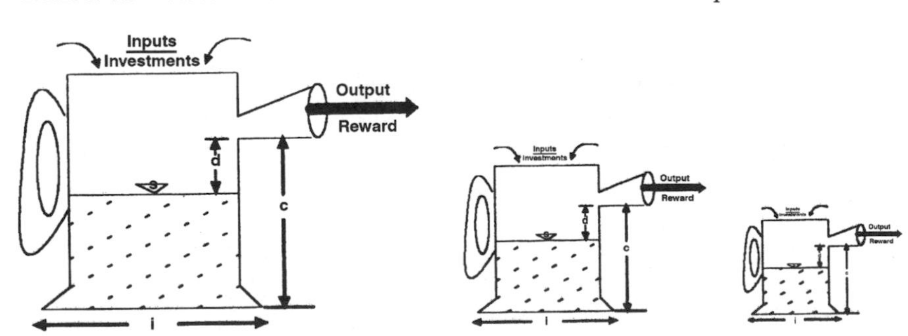

overt and institutional racism and oppression of the mind. Before aspiring African American entrepreneurs even get a chance to present their ideas or business plans, they must first burn valuable resources justifying why they should even be listened to!

Beyond this first step things become even more difficult: (1) Black entrepreneurs' access to capital is much more limited than whites; (2) They have to work longer and harder to build a strong customer/client base; (3) Blacks normally don't travel in the social circles of their prospective customers and therefore must develop strategies for working their way into those circles; (4) Blacks have more people telling them that they can never be as successful as their white counterparts; (5) Family members of black businesspeople probably don't have any experience in the specific business area so black entrepreneurs are usually out there all alone; and (6) African Americans are constantly bombarded with negative images of themselves and their community, and after being told enough times that blacks can't be successful in this country, the subconscious mind will actually begin to believe it.

In spite of the inequalities in bucket sizes outlined earlier, there is a silver lining to this seemingly dark cloud. Because blacks in business are required to fill bigger buckets before they reap any rewards, the quantities invested are greater; therefore, over the long term, the outputs or rewards also will be greater than those of many of their white counterparts. This assumes that black entrepreneurs will have the strength and fortitude to see the process to the very end. At times it may appear that justice doesn't prevail, but it really does. Sometimes, it just gets delayed. The biblical teaching that "you reap what you sow," is valid even in business.

THE INVISIBLE, SIXTH-PERSON PHENOMENON

The third phenomenon identified in this study is the sixth-person concept. I happen to adore the sport of basketball. Although I once played the sport seven days a week, I'm lucky now if I get to play once or twice per week. Anyway, one of the observations I've made over the years in watching thousands of basketball games on the streets and on television is the number of times that a mediocre team of players ends up kicking the butt of a team of so-called superstars.

For a long time, I couldn't understand how this could happen. I became enlightened one day when my friends (all over 35 years old) and I were challenged to a game by some yo boys (i.e., young, urban teenagers). As the game commenced, I observed that on our team, even though we were slower, weaker, and clearly not as physically gifted as our younger counterparts, we communicated well with one another, supported one another, and developed a strategy and stuck to it as a team. We encouraged one another when one of us made a mistake and praised one another when one of us made a good shot or showed a little more hustle than was expected.

The yo boy team, on the other hand, while loaded with unbelievable talent, was fraught with chaos and mayhem. First, it was clear that the boys didn't respect one another. They called each other names, refused to pass the ball to the open man, had no game strategy, took stupid shots, and refused to support one another. Well, you probably guessed it. We embarrassed them so terribly that they never came back to that court.

The reason a team of old, slow, balding, overweight basketball players could defeat a team of young, quick, and talented players was due to the help of the invisible sixth person. The invisible sixth person is an energy source that is created whenever a group of people who work well together and care about one another come together as a unified group to achieve a common goal. Do not underestimate the power of the sixth person. It will often determine the success or failure of a particular engagement.

When attempting to build a strong team to go after a business, many people tend to focus only on where the person went to school, degrees earned, and work experiences, to determine their fit in the group. Although these qualities are important it is probably more critical to ascertain the individual's ability to work within the group, his or her style of conducting business, and whether you like the person.

MANAGE THE LOWS AND THE REST WILL TAKE CARE OF ITSELF

Vince Lombardi once said, "Success is not in never falling, but in rising every time you fall." How true this statement is. History has shown that the process of achieving any worthy goal is a cyclical one—there will be temporary periods of successes and temporary periods of failure. Ordinary people can generally figure out how to manage the success intervals that occasionally come their way. However, it takes special individuals to be able to manage through the uncertainties of the failure intervals. This fact is especially true when there is a great amount at risk—home, job, family, independence, and perhaps sanity.

Successful African American businesspeople have learned to anticipate the low periods and prepare themselves for managing through them. They understand that if they can make it through the tough times, the good times will be a piece of cake.

THE THREE TIERS OF ENTREPRENEURIAL BUSINESS FORMATION

When analyzing any event or object, it is usually helpful to evaluate it within the framework of a model. In studying black entrepreneurs, I've created a set of models that I've used to describe in some logical way the differences within the group. Like all other businesses, enterprises owned and operated by blacks come packaged in many different ways. In positioning the businesses within the African American community, I've identified three categories in which each business could be accurately placed: Tier 1 Businesses, Tier 2 Businesses, and Tier 3 Businesses (see Exhibit 6.4).

Tier 1 Businesses

Companies that generally fall into this category are very small businesses. Tier 1 usually includes most start-ups, small franchises, and the mom and pop operations. As a group, these firms tend to generate less than $500,000 per year in revenues and often cater to the basic needs of the community in which they're located. The owners of these businesses have a tendency to be very active and visible within their local communities but not as visible in the mainstream community.

If minority communities are to recapture control of local economies, most likely this effort will be spearheaded by the players at the Tier 1 level. Although it is possible for a Tier 1 business to migrate to a Tier 2 or even a Tier 3 business eventually, it appears that most Tier 1 businesses remain at Tier 1 for the duration of their existence unless they are sold to someone who has Tier 2 intentions.

Tier 2 Businesses

Tier 2 businesses tend to generate significantly more revenue than Tier 1 businesses, producing somewhere between $500,000 and $15,000,000 per year. This level of business activity does not necessarily make its base physically within the minority community and typically operates somewhere on the periphery of the community. The products or services it

Exhibit 6.4 Types of Business Enterprises

Characteristics	Tier 1 Businesses	Tier 2 Businesses	Tier 3 Businesses
a) Revenue	•Sales less than $500,000/year	•Sales between $500,000 and $15,000,000/year	•Sales over $15,000,000 per year
b) Typical businesses in this tier	•Corner grocery •Gas stations •Small restaurants •Liquor stores •Janitorial services •Accounting/Legal services •Consulting	•Transportation •Fast foods •Steel fabrication •Plastics fabrication •Low tech manufacturing	•Medium/high tech manufacturing •Trucking •Biotechnology •Computer services •Railroad car manufacturing •High tech applications
c) Customer set	•Minority community	•Minority and majority communities	•Predominantly majority community and Fortune 500 companies
d) Recognition within the minority community	•Strong	•Strong	•Weak
e) Recognition within the majority community	•Weak	•Medium	•Strong
f) Requirements for success	•Good service •Respect for customers •Grass roots involvement within community •Recession-proof product (e.g., gas, food, clothes)	•Strong contacts within majority community •Politically active •Competitive product or service	•Strong contacts within the majority community •Strong political ties •Strong ties to financial community •Competitive product or service

produces are consumed both by the black community and the mainstream community. Although these types of businesses are active in both environments, they are still recognizable within the black community. Well-managed Tier 2 businesses that survive the early years have a good chance of migrating to a Tier 3 business at some point.

Tier 3 Businesses

The interesting fact about Tier 3 businesses is that there are sublevels within this group of enterprises. Although this tier of businesses generates upwards of $15,000,000 per year, it also includes big deal makers like the deceased Reginald Lewis, former CEO of Beatrice Foods. Last year

Beatrice Foods had sales approaching the $2 billion mark. Typically, customers of the goods or services produced by this group of businesses are mainstream consumers, usually large corporations or the federal government. Unfortunately, the majority of these companies are not recognizable within the African American community.

Consequently, the accomplishments of these firms (with the exception of companies like Johnson Publishing Company and other household names) go unrecognized by a large percentage of the community. Because of the types of businesses usually operating at this level, it is essential that these companies maintain strong ties with the mainstream community, particularly the financial community.

It is rare for a new entrepreneur to immediately migrate to a Tier 3 type business. An entrepreneur starting out would usually come in at the Tier 1 or maybe a Tier 2 level and then build that business into a Tier 3 enterprise over time. However, I believe that early in the new millennium, we will see many young, black entrepreneurs taking over mainstream businesses and positioning them as Tier 2 or Tier 3 businesses.

These would-be entrepreneurs are the best of the breed and are recipients of some of the best on-the-job training programs in the world. Some have strategically embedded themselves in the Fortune 100 companies, in boutique consulting firms, and even at mid to senior levels within the federal government. Like sponges, soaking up every bit of knowledge and technical expertise that they come into contact with, they patiently await the opportunity to make their move. This special group of people is also like water behind a dam. As time goes on they rapidly scale the walls of the dam. As Wall Street continues to open up for minorities and females and society once again seeks to satisfy its insatiable appetite for new goods and services, these young professionals will spill over, like the water behind the dam and assume their positions as prominent business leaders. The 2000s will be the decade of Tier 3 businesses. Exhibit 6.4 summarizes the differences among these enterprises.

TYPES OF MINORITY ENTREPRENEURS

Similar to evaluating the types of businesses within the community, it is equally difficult to define the types of entrepreneurs present in today's environment. However, it is important to segment the various types of entrepreneurs within the community and attempt to define them in some way. Specific strategies then can be formulated to assist these groups in not just surviving, but excelling in their respective areas. Grouping of entrepreneurs also helps would-be entrepreneurs to evaluate themselves and maybe align themselves with one of the groups in order to formulate their entry strategy effectively.

Again, the use of a model to define the different characteristics of the various types of entrepreneurs is helpful. Exhibit 6.5 segments the types of African American entrepreneurs into three distinct groups. Depending on the level of detail desired, the number of groups defined

Exhibit 6.5 Traits of Successful African American Entrepreneurs

Characteristics	Brown Bomber	Blood and Guts	Daring Dashing Dan
a) Age	•All ages	•All ages	•Young
b) Sex	•Majority male	•Male and female	•Majority male
c) Educational level	•Up to 12 years	•More than 12 years	•More than 16 years with Ivy League exposure
d) Business vision	•Make ends meet	•Make ends meet •Build empire on his/her own	•Build empire using his/her brain, but other people's money and sweat
e) Strengths	•Honesty •Respect for individuals •Humble •Worldly •Excellent people skills	•Diligent •Worldly •Attention to details •Tactical strategist •Multitalented •Capable of multitasking	•Leadership skills •"Slicster" •Team coalition builder •Brave vision •Skilled at delegating •Wall Street connected •Embraces new and young talent •Strategic thinker •Superb decision maker
f) Weaknesses	•Naive •Short-sighted •Refuses to think strategically •Runs business day by day •Suspicious of young, well-educated talent •Puts out fires	•Weak delegator •Suspicious of young, well-educated talent •Afraid of failure •Weak strategic thinker •Impulsive decision maker •Distrustful of those around him/her	•Operates close to being ruthless •Impatient •Fails to pay close attention to details •Blinded by ambition •"River boat gambler"
g) Reason for going into business	•Necessity	•Dream •Right opportunity	•Lifetime dream •Dissatisfaction with corporate old boy system
h) Work background	•Frequently moved from job to job	•Fortune 500 training •Multi-functional experiences	•Experience working with Fortune 500 companies •Recipient of executive/management training program

could have been much greater than three. However, within the scope of my analysis, the three groups within my model adequately define the subjects. The basis of this model assumes that the majority of the African American entrepreneurs can be defined by one or a combination of the following types of entrepreneurs: Brown Bomber Entrepreneurs (BBE), Blood and Guts Entrepreneurs (BGE), and the Daring, Dashing Dan Entrepreneurs (DDDE).

It would be an erroneous assumption to assume that the three groups are separated by their degree of success, with the BBEs being the least successful and the DDDEs being the most successful. Although the term Brown Bomber Entrepreneurs may not sound as glamourous as the Dashing Dan types, there are many BBEs around who make more money and live far more fulfilling lives than most of us. Likewise, there are some DDDEs who tried to play ball in the big league and ended up worse than when they started. Keep in mind that each type of entrepreneur can be as successful or unsuccessful as he or she wants to be.

Brown Bomber Entrepreneurs

Joe Louis (a.k.a. The Brown Bomber) was arguably the greatest heavyweight fighter in history. He came at a time when blacks had to fight to retain even the smallest amount of dignity and respect. In spite of these formidable challenges, Mr. Louis won the 1934 Golden Gloves championship in the light heavyweight division and three years later took the heavyweight title from James Braddock, becoming the second African American to hold the world championship. He later successfully defended his title 25 times in 12 years, knocking out 6 world champions.

My father knew Joe Louis and often told me of how honest and kind, but somewhat naive, Mr. Louis was. Of all the millions he earned as a fighter, much of it was stolen by crooked managers and fast women. Yet Mr. Louis continued to love and have faith in people and was always humble in his personal and business dealings.

Like Joe Louis, the Brown Bomber Entrepreneurs are honest, worldly people who maintain strong respect for individuals. In their minds, their greatest assets are their trust and their word. Typically, the members of this group tend to be male with little or no formal college training. Although they usually are able to generate and maintain loyalty in their customer base, they often are short sighted and refuse to view their businesses strategically. They prefer to make short-term decisions and often are suspicious of the young, well-educated talent available to them within and outside the community.

Blood and Guts Entrepreneurs

Blood and Guts Entrepreneurs come in all ages and both genders. This group is characterized by its members' strong desire to make it on their own. They like to show the world how tough they are. These folks take pride in the fact that no matter what the world throws at them, they can take it. Women entrepreneurs are prominent within this group primarily because of their belief that they must be twice as good as men in order to get the same breaks and recognition that men of lesser skills receive (which is probably true).

Their vision of the business is that its primary purpose is to satisfy the needs of today. Members of this group could be considered potential empire builders. They're often open to building an empire, but only if it's done with their blood, sweat, and tears. Successful Blood and Guts Entrepreneurs pay great attention to details, usually at great cost, and excel at being strong tactical thinkers. However, like the Brown Bomber group, this group tends to be suspicious of young, well-educated talent and tends to be distrustful of those around them. "No one can do a job better than I can," is their motto. Therefore, they end up doing most of the jobs instead of delegating to others.

Daring Dashing Dan Entrepreneurs

The new millennium will reveal a cadre of young, swashbuckling, Daring Dashing Dan Entrepreneurs (DDDEs) or "new jack" entrepreneurs. This group of young, well-educated, aggressive, risk-prone entrepreneurs will consummate deals that will surpass even the Beatrice deal in terms of size and complexity. Certainly people like Christopher Williams and C. Michael Gooden are headed in this direction. Individuals who fall into this group are basically empire builders. But they're not normal empire builders. These are people who want to build an empire with their brains, but with other people's sweat and capital.

As shown in Exhibit 6.5, people in this group will perform well in the new world order of competition because they tend to be strong leaders with brave, bold visions and the heart to go with it. They are strong, strategic thinkers and consequently will embrace new young talent if they see how such people will help them achieve their goals. In this fast-paced environment, DDDEs find themselves not having the time to learn the details of the operation, which requires heavy reliance on the management team. This group of entrepreneurs goes through wide swings in their performance. When they hit, they hit big. However, when they fall, they typically have a long and painful fall. Occasionally, the fall ends up being fatal.

CASE STUDY

This company has been operating for over one-half century. It speaks to the secrets of business longevity. Mr. Grimes and Mr. Parham are African Americans.

PETER PARHAM AND CALVIN GRIMES JR.

Founders, Grimes Oil
Washington, D.C. and Boston, Massachusetts

"We Have to Learn to Utilize Our Own Resources"

Although Calvin Grimes Sr. had been selling oil since the mid to late 1930s, Grimes Oil officially began operating as a corporation in 1940. Through providing quality service, competitive pricing, and maintaining excellent visibility within the minority communities, Grimes was very successful in building and retaining a large and diverse residential customer base. He was particularly successful at developing the black residential market because prior to his movement into this business, the black consumer base was, for the most part, ignored by the major oil distributors.

For a long time, Calvin Grimes Sr. refused to pursue the commercial markets for development of a commercial client base. Business in the residential sectors was going strong and showed little signs of slowing down. However, when the Small Business Administration's 8(a) program was initiated in the mid 1970s, Grimes saw an opportunity to develop a commercial customer client base that held the potential to surpass the residential client base that he had spent so many years nurturing. As Calvin (Kern) Grimes Jr. began to assume more of the day-to-day management of the operation, Grimes Oil aggressively sought to develop its commercial clients and did so with much success.

Part of the reason Grimes Oil was successful at developing these new markets was because of the advice and entrepreneurial instincts of a marketing consultant, Peter Parham. Calvin was no stranger to Peter. Parham had known Kern all of his life and was very close to the Grimes family. One day while in Boston, Kern met with Peter to discuss ways in which Grimes Oil could begin to expand its market into other geographic locations across the country.

Kern believed that based on the size of Grimes Oil and the company's relative success to date, he would be well positioned to meet the fuel oil needs of major corporations and municipalities that sought to do more business with minority oil companies. Peter concurred with Kern's assessment and agreed to work for Grimes Oil on a retainer basis to help the company expand its market share beyond the Boston and other New England areas.

Peter was so successful at accomplishing this task that Kern later asked him to join Grimes Oil on a permanent basis as vice president of marketing. The markets that Peter engaged in included Washington, Boston, Philadelphia, New York, and New Jersey.

Parham has his eye on an even bigger pie. He explains:

> We have many cities where blacks hold positions of power and can make decisions that could favorably impact on black businesses. Unfortunately, there are not many black owned oil companies comparable to Grimes Oil to respond to these opportunities. What good is it to have legislators who might know that there's going to be an economic or business opportunity that could help the black community if you don't have the companies in place to take advantage of it? We've developed a strategy where we go into a place like Hartford, Connecticut, identify the local minority oil company there, which may have only one or two trucks, and work with him to deliver on a $4 million job. We could bid on the job ourselves and subcontract a piece to him. The end result is that we get to go, he gets to go. That's part of what I'm doing.

Although Kern Grimes runs the company in a low-key fashion, it is by no means a simple mom and pop operation. Kern has been in business a long time and has built a strong organization that has weathered some severe storms over the years. The company faced one of the most difficult times after its graduation from the 8(a) program in the early 1980s when a decision was made to focus solely on its commercial client base at the expense of its residential base. Unfortunately for Grimes, shortly after the firm began focusing on its commercial clientele, conditions affecting the oil industry began to impact negatively on Grimes' business. As oil prices went into a spiraling decline and winters were consistently mild for a number of years, the demand for oil at a profitable price fell sharply. During that period, Grimes saw a significant drop in sales while his expenses remained the same or showed even slight increases. Within a short span of time, Calvin saw his margins being squeezed to a point where it was becoming increasingly difficult to service his debt.

Grimes Oil was able to weather these storms, in large part because of the company's reputation, the relationships it had built over the years, and the honesty and perseverance of Calvin Grimes Jr. Another factor that made the company's survival possible was the corporate structure that Calvin had put in place prior to the troubled times. He had strategically dissected the business, attracted talented people, and placed them in strategic positions within the corporate structure. As Peter explains it:

> The sign of an educated man is not that he has it all up here, but that he knows where to go get it. A good administrator is one who can have good people around who know how to do a multitude of things. Both Kern and I have been successful at attracting good black people and helping them grow.

Despite Grimes' successes, there are those who still have complaints about the company. The oil business is a tough business with its high volumes and low margins. Consequently, business owners sometimes have to make tough decisions, which may not always be very popular. Clearly, Kern has had to make some difficult decisions of his own, which may explain why Kern Grimes' contribution to the community is not unanimously recognized by its residents. Few understand the struggles he's forced to go through on a daily basis and most don't make the extra effort to even communicate their concerns. However, Kern seems to be unaffected by the miscommunication or even the jealousy that exists. He understands that he can't be all things to all people and he doesn't try to be.

FINANCING

The fact that Grimes Oil has been in business for more than 50 years has helped the company attract the financing it needs. The company has developed an outstanding reputation in the Boston area and Grimes has been successful in developing a long-term, mutually beneficial business relationship with his major supplier. As it turns out, the oil company that supplied Grimes his oil also became his biggest financier. In the oil business a distributor who has earned the trust of his supplier and who has established a good reputation can often use supplier credit to fund his transactions on a short-term basis.

In the case of Grimes Oil, the supplier also benefited from this flexible financing arrangement. Although Grimes Oil may be a small company, it provided a conduit through which the supplier could channel its product to the minority community. This client base is one of Kern's priorities, which results in suppliers knowing that he can deliver.

Kern has built such a good relationship with the oil companies because he is basically a very honest and hard-working man. He has built the business to a point that he's responsible for moving more than 35 million gallons of oil per year.

CONTROLLING WEALTH

Peter Parham agrees with a comment Rev. Jesse Jackson made when they were once traveling together: "I don't think that African Americans understand how much wealth they have at hand." Too often blacks assume that mainstream America owns more than it really does. If blacks only learned to reciprocate in their business transactions, there would be a noticeable improvement in the number and quality of minority businesses in America. Peter recalls a particular situation:

> Grimes Oil gets letters from development offices of black colleges around the country asking us to fund scholarships for their kids. Well, I went to the annual meeting for the Black College Association to give a presentation. I concluded by asking, "If you can write to Grimes Oil about scholarship money without even knowing him that well, then why can't you let us have the opportunity to bid on your oil contracts?" Rev. Jackson once challenged the administration of North Carolina A&T, who were in the midst of a major building project, asking them if they were giving contracts to any black firms. We have to learn to utilize our own resources.

Kern Grimes also has urged local black groups to channel their wealth to the benefit of the black community. Peter once organized a meeting with black administrators of New England colleges including MIT, Harvard, BU, and Northeastern to discuss how each of them could work together to benefit their institutions' students and the community. Peter doesn't mind that the school's minority programs expect some financial support from Grimes Oil, but he asks in return that they support his efforts to compete on heating oil contracts from these same institutions. Grimes Oil now has established contracts with many of these schools. He continues to build long-term business relationships with the black administrators of each school.

Kern has consistently acted on the belief that the black community should control its own wealth. When Senator Edward Brooke and Ron Homer opened up Boston Bank of Commerce, Kern took all of his money out of First National and put it into their bank. Grimes Oil is one of the main reasons that the Boston Bank of Commerce remains open. Although Grimes Oil was not financially involved when William Cosby and Julius Erving bought a major Coca-Cola franchise through the Economic Justice Campaign, the company was a steadfast supporter of the concept and the campaign.

LEVERAGING FINANCIAL INSTITUTIONS

Peter contends that one of the most important things that the African American community can do to build up black-owned enterprises in their community is to create black owned and operated financial institutions. These institutions are much more sensitive to the needs and problems that face minority people. Peter adds, however, that the only way to make the government do what it should do to help create black financial institutions is by using our ballots and our political strength. Blacks should demand that their tax dollars be leveraged effectively to benefit their community. Peter hastens to add:

> As long as we allow banking institutions to shut us out from the level where decisions are made, they will not be responsive to our needs. We might have a black person in a good job downtown, but if he does not pave the way for somebody else, then we are missing the point. When a bank refuses to consider our loan application, rather than change banks, we often continue to maintain our savings and checking accounts with them. We have to fight this thing on many fronts.

Peter concludes that those people who have benefited from the community have an obligation to give something back. Returning value to the community is a responsibility that blacks must recognize. If resources are pooled, greater deals can be consummated. Unfortunately, Peter feels that some black businesspeople are afraid of being open with one another and end up wasting a great deal of time. Black businesspeople need to look at themselves, be honest, and fix the things that need fixing.

THE IMPORTANCE OF AFRICAN AMERICAN BUSINESSES

Like many young men in today's African American community, Peter never saw black businessmen when he was growing up, except for the funeral director. Because he didn't see anyone else, his subconscious eventually began to tell him that this was the only business option available to him. Peter learned differently as he grew older and became exposed to more situations. However, he still contends that African Americans need to do a better job of teaching their children about business and how to start enterprises. More people need to do what Kern Grimes does for school-age children. Grimes Oil produced a film that tells the Grimes Oil story. Depicting him as a minority businessperson and showing how he runs his company, the film is shown in schools nationwide and has become so popular that Kern gets numerous requests for the film from colleges throughout the country.

PLANNING

Peter often finds himself speaking before groups of young people and his message is always the same—prepare, prepare, prepare. Prepare to meet all of one's goals and dreams. Peter encourages young, aspiring entrepreneurs to engage in every avenue open to them. Academics is critical, but people need to remember that success with academics is only one element of success. Equally as important is a person's sense of responsibility, integrity, and willingness to get a start somewhere, anywhere. Peter quickly gets to the point:

> So many young entrepreneurs want to start at the top but usually it doesn't work that way. People need to spend more time volunteering and picking up as much free information as they can. There are certain things that don't change. I often see white kids starting out in the mail room in Washington, even those whose parents have money. Next thing you know they've moved up and are now administrative assistants or something even higher. Listen and learn; you might need the information to get a job. And most importantly, have a plan.

Peter also strongly urges those people who are already in business not to judge others in the community by the way they dress, where they were raised, or where they went to school. There is a wealth of talent in the community that needs only to be given a chance. Grimes Oil has had its chance and has done quite well with it.

CASE STUDY

This case study depicts the nuances of managing a manufacturing business in a competitive corporate environment. Mr. Artis is African American.

WILLIE ARTIS

Founder, Genessee Packaging
Flint, Michigan

"I Never Sell Minority. The First Thing I Do Is Sell Myself"

Political and business deals are cut every day in the nation's capital. Men and women in designer suits frantically make their way throughout the many hotels initiating and closing business deals. It was no surprise that Willie seemed to fit right in with all the hustle and bustle that surrounded him in the lobby of one of Washington, D.C.'s most elegant hotels. As we sat down to discuss Willie's ascent from his humble beginnings in Memphis to his successful manufacturing business in Flint, Michigan, his calm demeanor and soft voice quickly put me at ease. His relentless smile was only a precursor to an important meeting he was hosting that evening. Due to his proven track record, he had been invited to Washington by some local businesspeople to discuss a joint venture. How convenient. Having deals find you versus your chasing them is just one of the fringe benefits of owning and managing a successful business enterprise.

Although Willie looked comfortable in the successful CEO role, his advent into the business world had been anything but comfortable. Early in his career, Willie accepted a job with a large manufacturing company. Because of his experience, he was given a significant role in managing the operations. It didn't take long before the owner of the parent company decided to expand his operation by spinning off a new subsidiary. The uniqueness of this new subsidiary is that he wanted it to be a minority company so that he could take advantage of all state and federal minority set-asides. There was only one problem. He didn't have any minority participation and needed to find a few minority players. Because Willie was already working for the parent company, he was a perfect candidate to become a silent partner of the new enterprise.

Although Willie did not perform any day-to-day functions for the new firm and continued to carry out his duties at the parent company, his participation in the venture legitimized the firm's claim of minority status. Consequently, by taking advantage of minority programs, the subsidiary was able to increase its annual revenues quickly from $250,000 to $4,000,000.

It didn't take long before Willie realized what had taken place. After confronting the owner about the improper company, Willie promptly resigned. He began looking for a way that he could seek revenge on the greedy businesspeople who took advantage of programs that were specifically geared toward building the commerce base within the minority communities. After careful and deliberate thought, Willie concluded that the best way to punish this company was to go out and compete against it. Why not? He knew the business inside and out.

He knew that particular company's strengths and weaknesses and where the exposure points resided. But wait a minute! He had never started a business from the ground up. Yes, he knew the corrugated cardboard manufacturing business, but what about capitalization, marketing, financial analysis, and all the other functional skills necessary to be successful in business.

To his surprise, Willie received his most ardent encouragement from an unlikely source. A General Motors buyer with whom Willie and his associates had done business was the first person to suggest that Willie leave the company and venture out on his own. Not only did this man make the initial suggestion that Willie start his company, he even went as far as to help them obtain financing, set up the proper business controls, and accompany them to strategic business meetings. Later, he proved to be instrumental in helping the new company obtain its first three contracts from General Motors. It became evident that this man believed in Willie and his partner and sincerely wanted to see them succeed. As is usually the case with new entrepreneurs, Willie was marching into unfamiliar territory and his friend in General Motors helped him to bridge the experience gap during the early days.

What Willie supplied was constantly changing. When he first started the company, he and his partner initially started in the contract packaging business. Nine months into the first project, they decided to try their hand in the corrugated paper business. Moving into the paper industry was a natural progression for these men because of their previous experiences with their past employers. At the time neither thought they would ever get back into that business again. However, fate stepped in and revealed an opportunity they could not refuse. As Willie recalls it:

> In the city of Flint, there was a corrugated business that was supposedly owned by an American Indian. However, in reality it was a front minor-

ity business that was really owned by five nonminority businessmen. Again, these people thought that they could take advantage of minority set-aside dollars, but the company was clearly doomed for failure. My partner knew one of the owners, happened to meet him in the lobby of one of the local hotels, and suggested to him that if he and his partner ever decide to sell, we would be interested. My partner was only joking but the man took him very seriously. My partner and I joked about this little episode and didn't think much more about it. However, we learned shortly thereafter that the owners of this company were serious about selling their business. They kept coming back at us with different proposals, and it became difficult not to accept their offer. At this point in time, they were doing about $250,000 of business per year and employed 10 people. We were able to purchase the business for $65,000 and agreed to pick up the $80,000 debt. This business now generates more than $4,500,000 in sales per year and is more profitable than the packaging company! I know that this is an unusual story, but it is certainly true.

If Willie were to be judged on his finesse at finding and consummating deals, one would think that he was a seasoned entrepreneur with strong and deep entrepreneurial roots. This assumption couldn't be further from the truth. Willie was born in Memphis, Tennessee, the youngest of five children. Although his parents were loving and patient, they didn't have much money and everyone in the family was forced to work and help make ends meet. Most work that his family could garner was working for someone else and consequently no one in his family ever seriously considered creating a business of his own. Even Willie never had any particular desire to go into business.

After high school he went to work and attended college at night. He never was one to change jobs frequently and consequently ended up having only four different employers (including his present business) in his life.

In 1956, to obtain his first work experience in the corrugated business, Willie had to tell some untruths. On his initial job interview, when the employer asked him if he had any experience in the corrugated business, he replied yes, although he had none. Somehow Willie convinced the employer that he knew what he was talking about and was ultimately hired.

That was his first experience in this industry. For most of his working life, he has been in the corrugated business and really learned his trade while working for a corrugated manufacturing company in Chicago. Between all of this job experience, he did manage to attend college for a few years but didn't seriously consider becoming an employer until 1975.

THE SEEDS OF DISCONTENT

By the start of 1975, Willie had gained enough experience that he felt confident of his ability to start and run his own business. After finding himself a partner who was outside the parent company that he had been working for, he decided to start a wood pallet business. This was to be his first attempt at starting his own business. Unfortunately for Willie, it became apparent that he and his new partner had great difficulty working together. While Willie's partner thought solely in terms of minority set-asides, Willie had a much more grandiose view of the company and made it very clear that he wanted to be able to successfully compete on all fronts—minority and nonminority. Willie had a more practical view on the proper use of minority programs:

> I do believe in minority set-asides as a start. Then after you've participated in these set-asides for a while, if that's what you want to do, you should then move out and participate in the other 90 percent of the business. You then become a normal businessperson with no minority stigmas attached to you whatsoever. Genessee competes with everyone and not just other minority companies. We have our own affirmative action program, which is unusual for a minority company.

After two years of trying desperately to make the partnership work, Willie and his partner went their separate ways. It didn't take long before Willie was able to identify another business partner with whom to go into business. Fortunately for Willie, this time, the two men were quite compatible and thus, this man became Willie's partner for his current business, Genessee Packaging, Inc.

GENESSEE TODAY

Genessee's present organization is broken into two distinct business units. One is the Corrugated Division, which produces corrugated paper containers for many different products for different industries. The other is the Packaging and Light Assembly Division. This division obtains numerous subcomponents of a product (some of which are sent to them by GM, but the majority of them are purchased by Genessee) and assembles those components in-house to produce the final component. The end product is then sent to the customer and in most cases is used in the assembly of automobiles and other pieces of equipment. This second unit also repackages automotive parts along with assembling final automotive parts.

They are currently tied into the GM Just-In-Time (JIT) inventory system which helps to minimize inventory expenses for GM and keeps Genessee well connected with GM's business flow opportunities. The accelerators used in some of GM's newer vehicles were assembled by Genessee. This accelerator has about 11 different component parts. Willie ships out about 8,000 of these parts per day. Another product that Willie assembles is the MacPherson Strut Suspension System that's used on the Buick LeSabre, which is produced in Flint, Michigan. Genessee also assembles many of the oil filters that are produced by AC Spark Plug, which are used in automobiles and heavy equipment. With sales surpassing the $18 million per year mark, the bulk of the business is coming from the packaging side of the business.

STAFFING AND FINANCING

When discussing the staffing of his company, Willie is quick to point out that in the early days of his company, the key positions were staffed by nonminorities. At that time, there was not a sizeable minority population to choose from nor was it easy to find the skills that he needed in the minority community. Consequently, several nonminorities held key positions.

In 1979 Willie and his partner went to one of the local banks in Flint for additional financing. This bank agreed to loan them $250,000, which was just enough money to drive them out of business. The GM buyer who was assisting them at the time tried in vain to convince the bank that this was not enough money to capitalize a business like theirs and that it was important that they be able to finance their inventories, payroll, and receivables. Even the SBA tried to reason with the bank to increase their level of financing, but it was all for naught. The bank refused to approve additional funds, and so Genessee reluctantly accepted the deal and the loan was guaranteed by the SBA.

Undaunted, at the suggestion of their CPA, Genessee decided to go across the street to another bank and apply for a business loan. The new loan officer understood the issues that faced this new business and tried to defend their case before the loan committee but his decision was overturned. This episode was terribly upsetting to the team that Willie had put together. As expected, the $250,000 did not provide the company with enough capitalization to support the business throughout the year and consequently forced Willie to revisit the last bank with which he had tried to do business. This time, however, the loan officer submitted a written proposal instead of the verbal one used the first time. As fate would have it, the loan was approved! According to Willie:

> The loan was approved the second time around because of someone's name. My last name is Artis, and it just so happened that there was a very prominent family in Flint whose last name was Artis. I am not a part of that family, but one of the bank directors thought I was. The director looked at the application, saw the name Artis, and stated that he knew this family, it's a good family, and that he thought that the committee should approve the loan. Just like that, the bank approved the loan for $750,000, without any guarantee from the SBA. They paid off the first loan and provided us a $500,000 line of credit. Since that time Genessee has had a fantastic relationship with that bank.

This experience epitomizes the hardships that minorities face when dealing with most financial institutions. Unless you know someone inside who will support you and that person is a part of the decision-making process, your chances of getting loans approved are significantly diminished.

THE EQUITY COMPONENT

The equity participation in the initial funding was quite low by recent comparisons. The first bank wanted both Willie and his partner to put up $5,000. Willie strongly believes that if a business has a known business leader running the company with an established track record, 100 percent financing from a reputable bank can be obtained. With his present business status, right now, every acquisition that requires outside financing is financed 100 percent. For example, there is a $400,000 machine that they just obtained that will be shipped and installed into his plant at no significant cost to his company. He recently opened up a new plant in Milwaukee, Wisconsin, which again will require very little up-front capital from Genessee. Clearly, the right businesspeople know of his accomplishments and view doing business with him to be a low-risk venture.

SUCCEEDING AS STATED BY ARTIS

Profit Motivation

> Whatever business you get into, pursue it with one thought in mind—make money! Everything you do must be profitable. You must think in terms of profits. If you have any philanthropic motives, put them on the back burner until you're able to enhance the corporation's profitability. If you pursue all of your business dealings with the idea of generating profits, all the other things—goodwill, job creation, support for the community and other niceties—will fall into place.

Genessee presently has 300 people working within the organization. The only other company, other than hospitals and banks, that employs more people than Genessee in Flint is General Motors.

Business and Marriage

Business can sometimes play havoc with an owner's marriage. Willie warns young entrepreneurs:

> Your thinking will change as you work to make your venture successful. You're often away from home, and you can't expect to spend normal working hours with your business and still succeed. Unforeseen problems occur all of the time, sometimes causing havoc with the business. The process of going from an employee to an employer is a difficult one that is just as difficult for a spouse.

The growth that takes place changes one's social habits. Willie found himself mingling with nonminorities on a more frequent basis and making more social commitments. Unfortunately, his spouse had not shared in this growth and consequently stress soon developed within the marriage, resulting in divorce.

Business Conduct

Never, never, never, flaunt your wealth, once you've obtained it. Often minorities will hurry out to buy fine cars, diamonds, and furs as soon as the first profits come rolling in. This is the worst thing that a minority businessperson can do—particularly if he or she does a lot of business with buyers from the large corporations. When at work, Willie is rarely seen wearing jewelry or any other eye-catching accessories. He adds:

> People need to remember that in most cases when you're trying to establish a customer base with corporations, you'll be dealing with the little guy (buyer) in the little cubicle. This person will most likely be a white male who may have three or four kids and a home in the suburbs that he's struggling to maintain. The worst thing that a minority person could do is to flaunt their wealth in the face of the buyer. You can bet the buyer knows that you're either a millionaire now or that you'll be one some day in the future. You never talk about that. If you need to flaunt your wealth, do it somewhere else, but never where you do business. Many minority businesses fail because they failed to follow this simple principle.

Dealing with Competition

"I kill competition regardless of whether it's a minority or non-minority company."

Willie Artis

Willie is very clear on how he handles competition. It doesn't matter what race, creed, or color his competition is. He treats them the same. He goes for blood and often gets it. Competition is also beaten by playing the niche game. Creating a niche is very important and once it's created you take steps to keep other people out. Many companies will try to come in and steal your customers. Willie becomes very political when he needs to be and always tries to become the sole supplier for most of his customers, sometimes quite successfully. His determination to remain competitive is revealed by the fact that at one point he was leasing the same facility that his former employer also leased. Additionally, it was the same building that was used for the fronted minority company.

Genessee is also protected from downturns in the automotive industry. Willie has wisely diversified his customer base and has included many nonautomotive industries in his client portfolio. This diversification has also served to help keep his competition on the defensive and less able to absorb any of his market share. Willie is a firm believer that you kill competition before it takes hold. This should be done regardless of the competition's ethnic origin.

ESTABLISHING A SOLID CUSTOMER BASE

In the long run, a business, whether it's minority or nonminority owned, establishes a lasting customer base by leveraging its own reputation. Willie has followed this strategy by taking his profits aggressively and plowing them back into his business to buy new equipment, hiring young, bright engineers to implement the latest in technology, recruiting good people to help make the business strong, and providing some form of competitive edge. Basically, Genessee implements the same intelligent business strategies that all well-run businesses do. When potential customers hear of Willie's success and his format for conducting business, they often seek to establish business relationships with him! It is not suggested, however, that a new business sit back and wait for business to come its way. But it does illustrate again some of the perks of being a successful and established businessperson.

As wonderful as this all sounds, it was pretty tough for Willie to develop a strong customer base in the early days of the company. Although he was fortunate to get off to a good start, having won three major GM contracts, to begin really generating business, he had to go from door to door, selling himself and his company. He states emphatically that this is not always an easy thing to do. Establishing business relationships with nonminorities is sometimes difficult because of the cultural differences between the two groups. These differences sometimes cause suspicion, uneasiness, and distrust. However, no matter how difficult, the minority businessperson must stay in the buyers' and nonminorities' faces. He must pursue continual social contact with potential customers so that the comfort level is enhanced.

As for which levels of the purchasing hierarchy new entrepreneurs should focus on, well, it depends. Although Willie spends significant time wooing the upper purchasing executives, he does not neglect the many front-line buyers in the little cubicles. The cubicle with the little guy is where the action really is. Recently, executives of some of the larger companies have mandated that their companies increase the percentage of goods and services that are purchased from minority businesses. While Willie sees nothing wrong with taking advantage of these opportunities, he adamantly refuses to use his minority status as a marketing tool. He says:

> I don't want anyone to be forced into doing business with me. I never sell minority. I never talk about it, and I never mention it. I don't wave the flag. The first thing that I do is sell myself. Then I move ahead and sell Genessee.

Willie reasons that except for corporate minority purchasing goals, why should this buyer want to buy from a business solely because it is minority owned? Why would he or she buy from someone whom, on a normal basis, he has no business or social contact with? Concurrently, if he has racist tendencies, how is that handled? Willie, in his usual style, attacks these issues head on. He continues:

> After making an appointment to see this buyer, I walk in and the first thing he says to me was that he didn't need any minority dollars and that his quota for minority purchases was already met. He kept using the word *minority* in everything that he said. He never stopped using the word. This was enough to drive me through the roof. However you can't let this type of reaction affect you. Although I never did business with this particular buyer, he did refer me to another buyer who held more promise for me. This guy would talk about golf, his grandmother, everything else except the business that I came to discuss.

In spite of this disappointing first encounter, I never stopped coming to see him. I went to see other buyers at this company, but I never stopped visiting this particular buyer. Every Friday, I would see this man for lunch. It became a standing appointment. In many cases I would take him and his girlfriend out to dinner and we'd talk some more. Well, it took me nine months to get a contract from this man. The contract was worth only $1,100, but it was my first contract from this company and I was very appreciative of it. I was just as happy to receive this purchase order as I would have been had it been for one million dollars. I later framed that purchase order and placed it on my office wall. I look at it every day. It tends to keep me humble. That $1,100 has now grown to more than several million dollars of business.

Perseverance and staying power are of the utmost importance. Buyers will turn you off, say things to try to turn you away, and try to beat you down. Most feel that if you want the business bad enough that you'll stay around. This is exactly what Willie Artis plans to do.

7

Twenty Traits of Successful African American Entrepreneurs

As mentioned earlier, with such a diverse group of businesspeople, it is difficult to paint a picture of the characteristics of the super-successful, minority entrepreneur. However, there are some traits that appear to be present to varying degrees. Those identified traits include:

Trait 1: Spiritual fortitude
Trait 2: When in doubt, do something!
Trait 3: The amoeba effect
Trait 4: Leveraging the buffalo soldier legacy
Trait 5: Managing the ride
Trait 6: Intensity of purpose
Trait 7: Ghetto cunning
Trait 8: Feeling at home on the Nile
Trait 9: The X factor is a big factor
Trait 10: Learning from the conversion of Saul to Paul
Trait 11: Resisting the herd instinct
Trait 12: Living by the pain don't hurt point of view
Trait 13: Long-term greedy versus short-term greedy
Trait 14: Experiencing a gut-wrenching event
Trait 15: The natural high from making money
Trait 16: Being comfortable with being uncomfortable

Trait 17: Correlating exactitude with chaos and bringing vision into focus
Trait 18: Believing that competitiveness usually defeats sexism, racism, and classism
Trait 19: Perpetual dream chasers
Trait 20: Ascending the incremental energy levels of success

TRAIT 1: SPIRITUAL FORTITUDE

Most African American entrepreneurs readily admit that they've seen and experienced the power of God in their lives. It has probably been the most successful means of helping them withstand the forces of injustice and oppression, and they appreciate how this same power will guide them to even higher levels of achievement.

It is my observation that African American businesspeople, due to their volatile and uncertain position in American society, possess a greater appreciation of the frailties of human existence and have been more successful than their white counterparts in putting the relationship of God and humans into its proper perspective. African American entrepreneurs appreciate that the reason black people have been able to survive more than 200 years of terror, torture, oppression, violence, poverty, and hatred was because of the love and power of our Father in heaven. It is no accident that the civil rights struggle in this country was for all intents and purposes orchestrated from the pulpits and boardrooms of our churches. His presence and power, whose manifestation has allowed us to endure, struggle, fight, and hope, also has helped blacks survive.

The survival of the African American community cannot become limited only to our pursuit of dignity and justice. Although the fight for justice has not been concluded, it has now moved to different and sometimes unfamiliar battlegrounds. On the battleground of economic empowerment, we're fighting a formidable opponent, but God is there and guess what? He's still in charge. He is guiding our brave and fearless entrepreneurs just as He did our brothers and sisters during our quest for basic respect and human dignity.

Successful African American entrepreneurs seem to welcome this spiritual ally with open arms and great anticipation. They know that this power, if used effectively, can help them chart their courses clear through the new millennium. As any other intelligent businessperson will do, these businesspeople use all the resources at their disposal, including spiritual resources, to help them achieve their business objectives and to keep their successes (or failures) in the proper perspective.

TRAIT 2: WHEN IN DOUBT, DO SOMETHING!

Whatever city you come from, daily life for people living in the projects is a tough and brutal one. Between the violence, drugs, police brutality, and self-hate, it is amazing that anyone is able to survive the environment yet alone become a productive member of society. I remember my days in a project community in South Baltimore called Cherry Hill. Contrary to popular belief, I never was much of a yo boy. I took school seriously and concentrated much of my time on preparing for college and playing sports.

During the fall semester, when I played football, my home boys always helped me celebrate after a victory. This one Friday in particular, we were especially happy because I had just won a big game and really wanted to celebrate. We wanted to locate a party to meet some girls and have some fun. It just so happened there was a party in an adjacent low-income community called Westport.

Westport was like Cherry Hill in many ways. It was an area that was predominantly populated by African Americans. There were some whites living in the area, but their numbers seemed to dwindle daily. Like Cherry Hill, Westport had a number of federal project developments in which low-income people lived. The community faced the same social problems that most other urban centers faced, and had difficulty solving most of them. One thing was certain. There existed an old rivalry between the young men of both communities, which often bordered on lunacy. The two groups despised one another. So it was for many years.

It was my misfortune that the only party happening that night was in Westport. Determined to have a good time, all four of my buddies and I jumped into my friend Donnie's car and sped away to find the party. After we arrived within the boundaries of Westport, it soon became apparent to us that we were very drunk and very lost. Due to the poor design of the Westport area, there is only one way in and only one way out. The streets are arranged in a haphazard fashion with many of them being dead ends without warning or logic. As we weaved our way through the maze of streets and alleys, we finally arrived at a street that appeared to be the correct one. As we made a right turn onto the street, we all began to breathe a sigh of relief as we thought we had finally arrived at the party.

A few seconds later, to our dismay, we not only learned that this was not the correct street, but that the street abruptly came to a dead end. Donnie cursed as he yanked the transmission into reverse to back out of the street. Unbeknown to us, while we were weaving our way through the neighborhood, one of the local gangs had recognized us as Cherry Hill kids and had organized a mob to teach us a lesson about trespassing on their turf. This mob was waiting for us at the entrance to the street. Donnie, still unaware of what was unfolding, backed his car to the entrance of the street before coming to a halt due to a truck's blocking the exit.

As the mob began to surround the car with bats waving and shanks (knives) glistening under the dim light of the lamp post, the four of us sat there terrified, contemplating our fate. I don't know what my buddies were thinking, but thoughts were racing through my mind as I searched to find a quick solution to our deadly dilemma. I don't know why, but I immediately thought about some advice that my father had given me after a football game in which I had showed a great deal of indecision. My father said, "Son, when in doubt, do something!" What he meant was that there are often times in our lives when we're temporarily confused and uncertain about which choices to make. Most people in this situation usually choose not to make a decision because they're concerned they'll make the wrong one. My father's view was that in those times you need to make a quick decision—even if it is not the best one.

With my father's words ringing in my mind, I began to cry, pray, kick, curse, yell, and punch, all at the same time. My buddies must have had the same thought because they started doing the same thing. To make a long story short, by the grace of God we made it out of Westport alive that night with just a few cuts and bruises. It was a long time before I ever set foot back there again.

If you are serious about becoming a successful entrepreneur, as sure as you're born, you will be faced with situations in which you are confused and uncertain about what your next step should be. You will sometimes travel down uncharted avenues that may dead-end at any time. The difference between those who are successful and those who meet their demise is that when in doubt, successful businesspeople do something. They refuse to allow the changes and vicissitudes of the situation to paralyze them into a state of indecision. They quickly analyze the facts, review their options, and make decisions. They have enough confidence in themselves to believe that most of the time they will make wise decisions.

TRAIT 3: THE AMOEBA EFFECT

While a student at the University of Pennsylvania, my wife, Carolyn, a pre-med major, was extremely fascinated with biology. She was especially fond of the lab sessions in which she studied the world of microorganisms under the amplifying eye of the microscope and then presented her findings to her classmates.

Of all the millions of organisms known to humans, none aroused her curiosity more than the amoeba. The amoeba is a tiny, one-cell organism that can be seen only under a microscope. Amoebas vary in size from about .001 inches to .01 inches across. Some amoebas live in water and moist soil. Others live in the bodies of animals and human beings.

Only one cell makes up the amoeba's whole body. The cell is a shapeless mass of protoplasm, the living, jellylike material found in the cells of all other living things. A thin, elastic membrane surrounds the protoplasm and holds it together. Water and gases pass in and out of the amoeba through the membrane.

In order for the amoeba to move from one point to another, it must change its body shape. The protoplasm pushes out the elastic membrane to form a fingerlike pseudopod (false foot) and seemingly without much effort, the protoplasm flows into the pseudopod. For every step that it takes in any direction, it must first form a pseudopod, and the protoplasm then must flow into that new member.

The successful entrepreneurs reviewed in this study reminded me of those amoebas. Often very fluid, these businesspeople do not allow themselves to be categorized in a specific area that will ultimately minimize their ability to compete and move into new areas. In a way, these people are shapeless, continually molding themselves into various shapes and forms to accommodate very dynamic and often volatile business environments.

When successful businesspeople recognize opportunities, they marshal all of their resources and direct them in that direction, much like the amoeba squeezes its protoplasm into its newly-created pseudopod. They then move as unified entities in the direction of the new opportunities. Generally, the entrepreneur makes this transformation without much thought, and the transfiguration is usually transparent to those around him or her.

TRAIT 4: LEVERAGING THE BUFFALO SOLDIER LEGACY

One of my favorite comedians is Richard Pryor. During the 1960s and 1970s, he was one of the hottest entertainers around. I believe I must have all of his albums, including the one in which he talks about the differences between black folks and white folks. I recall in one dialogue he was joking about the way black folks can buffalo situations in order to get what they want. Although Richard may have been only poking fun at our community, I think that he stumbled onto a characteristic that is rampant throughout the community—especially among African American entrepreneurs.

This characteristic, which I've termed the Buffalo Soldier Legacy, was epitomized by the group from which this characteristic derived its name—the buffalo soldiers of the American nineteenth-century army. Our businesspeople who are stubborn, strong, brave, and relentless epitomize these characteristics and follow in the legacy of their ancestors. Because an analogy can be drawn between the African American businessperson of today and the rough riders of the past, it seems appropriate to draw the comparison.

Let's briefly step back through history. At the end of the Civil War, the United States government created several black volunteer army units. The two black cavalry regiments were the Ninth and the Tenth Cavalry. By 1871 the majority of these soldiers were stationed at various posts in Texas and the Indian Territory. The Indians gave these soldiers the name Buffalo Soldiers partly because of their dark skin and curly hair and partly because of their great strength and the superior fierceness of their fighting. Although these soldiers fought with great valor, they were often treated worse than the horses and other livestock owned by the United States Army. Punishment for the least infraction was severe; food was often rotten; respect was nonexistent; and death was forever near. In spite of these conditions, the desertion rate of the buffalo soldier was often the lowest in the army.

With few exceptions, the entrepreneurs profiled in this book display the traits characteristic of our military forefathers: bravery, tenacity, the unwillingness to accept defeat, and the beliefs that their equitable sharing of this country's resources is just and right, and that capitalism is good and that it works.

The experiences of today's black entrepreneurs are quite similar to our buffalo soldiers of yesterday and their reaction to overwhelming adversities is also comparable. Although the weapons and battlegrounds are drastically different, the battle is a familiar one. Like their ancestors, the entrepreneurs depicted in this study remain proud, confident, and mentally tough despite persistently demoralizing conditions. Their challenge, which they readily accept, is to make the system work for the African American community as well as it works for everyone else.

TRAIT 5: MANAGING THE RIDE

Business is like life—one big roller coaster ride. Sometimes you're up and sometimes you're down. Those who are wise quickly realize that these changes are a part of the process and are not unique to them individually. Some people have the mistaken belief that to be successful you need only to be able to manage the tough times, and the good times will take care of everything else. This is just not the case. Successful black businesspeople understand that you must also manage the good times as effectively. You must know when to spend or when to save. It is understood that additional resources generated during good times need to be leveraged for the upcoming roller coaster ride.

TRAIT 6: INTENSITY OF PURPOSE

When discussing this trait, one of the entrepreneurs was reminded of a young man with whom he worked at IBM who had an impact on most people who got to know him. He was a personable young man, highly educated and warm, yet very intense. He always seemed to have a serious look on his face and had a brisk walk that made it difficult for normal people to keep up with him. When he went through IBM's marketing school, unlike many of his other classmates, he refused to cheat on the exams and laboratory exercises and often had to work by himself late at night to ensure his understanding of the principles and guidelines being taught.

When in the District Branch this young man seemed to have little time for chitchat and always took his work seriously. Indeed, this fellow was intense. People often commented that he was on a mission. As it turns out, while all this was going on, this young account marketing representative was actually making plans to leave IBM to start his own business! Each day he was driven by his vision of starting his business and nothing else mattered.

Successful black businesspeople possess an intensity of purpose just like this young IBM account marketing representative. Once they commit to a dream or vision, they have the ability to focus all of their energies on realizing that vision. They let nothing stand in their way. Even when they're uncertain about how to go about achieving whatever it is they're after, they're intense enough to become unconcerned about making the wrong decision.

Just making a decision becomes a good decision because it often opens up other opportunities at the same time. Intense people understand that time is short and that you must squeeze all you can into that time. Their intensity of purpose serves as a generator for added enthusiasm and as a compass for plotting the next steps.

TRAIT 7: GHETTO CUNNING

Some of us who were born and raised in the ghetto often expend great amounts of energy trying to forget it. In our attempt to forget, we sometimes try to change the way we dress, the way we talk, the crowd of people with whom we associate, and most importantly, the way we think. In our haste to change ourselves to become more acceptable to our mainstream counterparts, we often give up certain elements of our ghetto experience that would serve us well in our professions, our businesses, and our lives.

Some successful blacks who were raised in the ghetto or on the streets have learned to leverage the lessons they learned growing up in the slums and apply them within the business world. These people possess what has been romantically called street smarts.

For example, in the ghetto, you learn early on (or you don't survive) that if someone doesn't like you, that person will eventually come after you. To protect yourself, you never turn your back on that person or let him catch you in a position where you're vulnerable. You keep the person at bay until you can figure a way to get him. Even when a truce is called, you remain alert for that person whenever he's in striking distance.

Black entrepreneurs realize that these same principles of survival apply in the business world. There is a toughness that being raised in the ghetto provided some of the entrepreneurs and they're not ashamed of it. On the contrary, they leverage it to their advantage.

TRAIT 8: FEELING AT HOME ON THE NILE

The Nile River is the longest river in the world. It flows for 4,145 miles (6,671 kilometers) through northeast Africa. The Nile rises near the equator and flows into the Mediterranean Sea. It irrigates about 6 million acres of land in what is now known as Egypt and about 2.4 million acres in Sudan. Majestically embedded in the Nile valley, the river runs from what used to be the ancient nation of Kemet northward to the Mediterranean Sea, in what was once called Upper Egypt. Unlike the sometimes erratic Euphrates River, the level of the Nile River rose and declined with such predictable regularity that the Nubians of the area developed calendars, agricultural strategies, and construction projects based on the river's movements.

Each year the Nile flooded, nurturing the crops that lined its banks. The monsoon rains dumped enormous amounts of water causing the river to swell and feed the major tributary, the Blue Nile. The now aggrandized river rumbled northward before eventually merging with the White Nile. The predictable flooding of the Nile River led to the development of irrigation technologies thousands of years before being used by Europeans. The process of irrigation along the Nile promoted a significant agricultural surplus and a spirit of collective discipline. The need to develop additional irrigation projects up and down the Nile promoted communal links along the river and helped unite the region known as the Nile valley.

Successful African American entrepreneurs are familiar with this irrigation effect. They understand that the flow of resources runs in both directions. There is some degree of irrigation from the majority community. This irrigation may have come in the form of a partner, business advisor, friendly banker, elected government official, concerned corporate purchaser, or just a friend with ties to the local business community. Conversely, these entrepreneurs understand that they must supply nourishment to their communities so that they remain vibrant and the seeds of entrepreneurship and business formation are fertilized in the minds of coming generations. This nourishment may take the form of adopting local schools, conducting workshops or seminars on entrepreneurship, providing scholarship funding to needy students, or just using their influence to effect relevant local policies to their communities.

Clearly, any attempt to start and grow a minority-owned business using only the resources found within the boundaries of the minority community is doomed to failure. Yes, it sounds good to say that all the resources necessary to grow a business reside within the African American community, but reality tells us different. The fact of the matter is that all subeconomies are usually mutually dependent on one another and on the aggregate economy as a whole. Therefore, one subeconomy cannot prosper without developing irrigation channels to the others. This is especially true given the fact that the world has moved from a local economy to a global one. Dr. Sybil Mobley, Dean of Florida A&M's Graduate School of Business Administration, while speaking at Dartmouth College's Tuck School of Business Administration, once shared that the fact that Americans don't hesitate to buy Japanese, Taiwanese, and other products produced by foreign countries indicates the existence of a world economy that has no allegiance to any country or any group or any race.

The business leaders who contributed to this book understand the impact of a global economy and make extensive uses of resources within and outside the minority community. For the most part, they view themselves as astute businesspeople first and as minority businesspeople second. A few didn't view themselves as minority businesspeople at all! Just businesspeople. Typically, when it was determined that additional resources were required, these people made every attempt to identify sources within the community. However, if the particular resource was scarce, they had no difficulty seeking the appropriate resources elsewhere.

Whether the irrigation is taking place from within the minority community or external to it, the flow of resources will dwindle unless the proper channels are developed and kept open. Just like our ancestors of ancient Egypt (Kemet) built channels to tap into the rich and fertile Nile River, the participants in the Dartmouth study consistently work at building the proper channels to tie into the information and financial resources found in the mainstream and within the community. They tend to belong to strategic civic and professional organizations. They understand the importance of supporting the appropriate politicians of both parties. By serving on the boards of specific corporations and nonprofit organizations, they tap into resources that would normally not be available to them.

This irrigation effect that I speak of takes place not only in business settings, but also can take place in social settings. Basically, people do business with people they know, trust, and like. As odd as it may seem, it is difficult to develop a long-term business relationship with a client with little social contact. Therefore, most businesspeople use social functions to learn more about prospective business associates. These functions could include golf outings, baseball games, dinner parties, political functions, and fund-raisers.

The challenge that minority businesspeople face concerning irrigation through social channels is that whites tend to socialize with whites and blacks tend to socialize with blacks. Consequently, minority contact with potential white business associates through social channels tends to be limited. However, as awkward as it may have been, successful minority businesspeople develop social irrigation channels effectively and feverishly work to keep existing channels open while working on opening new channels to yet untapped resources.

TRAIT 9: THE X FACTOR

One of the most interesting observations made during this study was an issue that's been around a long time and one that most of us are familiar with. After careful thought, I decided to call this observation the X factor because it specifically reminded me of some of the painful issues that Malcolm X dealt with during the early years of the civil rights movement. In keeping with my belief that the destiny of all African Americans is indelibly linked to all people of color in the struggle, past and present, I've chosen to define this observation relative to Malcolm X.

To appreciate this analogy, one must first understand Malcolm and what he stood for. By some accounts, Malcolm had to be the most misunderstood African American leader during the turbulent civil rights movement. Malcolm spent the majority of his public career in dedicated service to Elijah Muhammad, the then-fiery, controversial leader of the Nation of Islam. With the support of the Nation of Islam behind him, Malcolm almost single-handedly moved the message of Elijah Muhammad from the temples where the Muslims worshipped across the nation's airwaves and onto the university lecture circuit.

Malcolm's message and its delivery prior to his break with the Nation of Islam alienated him from a large segment of the black community and from most of the white community. Black leaders of the nonviolent movement, led by Dr. King, viewed Malcolm as a serious threat to the civil rights movement. Concurrently, white Americans were fearful because early in his career Malcolm had preached that white people were a race of devils whose sole purpose was to torment African Americans. As would be expected, the majority of white Americans saw Malcolm as an apostle of violence and hate.

Malcolm's message changed drastically after his break with Elijah Muhammad and his subsequent visits to Africa and Mecca. Inspired by his experiences in Africa, Malcolm would later say with great dignity and humility:

> Because of the spiritual rebirth which I was blessed to undergo as a result of my pilgrimage to the Holy City of Mecca, I no longer subscribe to sweeping indictments of one race. In the future, I intend to be careful not to sentence anyone who has not been proved guilty. You may be shocked by these words coming from me, but I have always been a man who tries to face facts, and to accept the reality of life as new experiences and knowledge unfold it.

The core of Malcolm's message changed from espousing a separate black nation to his advocating that blacks gain control of the institutions, politics, and economics of their community. Unfortunately, at the time of his death, he was still to some degree confusing to some members of the black community and remained a wild man and a segregationist in the eyes of many white Americans.

Data from my Dartmouth study reveal that African American businesspeople often find themselves wedged between the confusion of the black community and the fear and hostility of the white community. The black community is confused because although they'd like to support the minority businesses in their communities, they feel that shoddy service and disrespect for its minority customers is the trademark of most black-owned businesses. The belief that anything produced by black people is inferior has become so prevalent that even some blacks themselves are convinced that it is true.

Concurrently, the white community, which in general has very little contact with the minority community, espouses similar beliefs, in most cases unjustifiably. Many whites have only limited exposure to African Americans, usually within the formal structure of a work environment. For others, their only contact is through television and films. All too often though, the white-dominated media choose to sensationalize the failures of black businesses instead of magnifying the many successes. The unsophisticated among them often write off minority businesses as fronts for majority businesses. They're quick to attack the special programs designed to bolster minority enterprises (the same way the government designed special programs to bolster the aerospace companies during the Eisenhower years) as merely giveaways that will ultimately amount to nothing.

The unfair assessment of black businesses by both the black and white communities places the African American entrepreneur in an awkward position. Like Malcolm, many possess a sincere desire to build and strengthen the black community through various enterprise initiatives. This desire is partially responsible for their opting to go into business instead of pursuing the leisurely corporate existence. Yet they face a community that seems baffled at times and often divided about how it should deal with its own businesspeople. Although the white community doesn't fear minority entrepreneurs as it did Malcolm, it nevertheless doesn't understand them. This lack of understanding forces the minority businessperson to expend additional resources to address these misconceptions instead of using these same resources to produce jobs and wealth.

African American entrepreneurs recognize the predicament they're in and are beginning to put strategies in place to neutralize these concerns. Forums to bring together the minority consumer with the minority businessperson have become common in most cities. Most large corporations have specific units in place to help bridge the gap between the white corporate structure and minority businesses.

TRAIT 10: UNDERSTANDING THE CONVERSION OF SAUL TO PAUL

One of the most powerful sets of passages in the holy Bible is the Epistle to the Romans. Written by Paul, this book covers justification by faith, spiritual counsel, God's plan for Jew and Gentile, and what Christians and Jews must do to gain the road to salvation. It's hard to believe that this inspirational book was written by Paul since he was one of the most vicious persecutors of Christians in his community.

Although Paul (then called Saul) was a Roman citizen, he was a Jew of the tribe of Benjamin. As a typical Jewish boy, brought up in Tarsus, the capital of Cilicia, he learned the trade of tent making. In his youth, his devout parents sent him to Jerusalem, where he studied under the renowned Jewish scholar Gamaliel. Thus, Paul became a Pharisee, devoted to the strict observance of the law as a means of salvation. Unfortunately, as a Pharisee, Paul became an arch-persecutor of the Christian community. Paul was part of the group who stoned Stephen. He often breathed murderous threats against the disciples of the Lord, later obtaining special permission authorizing him to arrest anyone he found who followed the new way that was Christianity.

However, God was not finished with Paul. One day, while he was on the road and nearing Damascus, a light suddenly flashed from the sky all around him. He fell to the ground and heard a voice saying, "Saul, Saul, why do you persecute Me?"

"Tell me, Lord, who are You?" asked Saul.

The voice answered, "I am Jesus, who you are persecuting. But get up and go into the city, and you will be told what you are to do."

Meanwhile, the men who were traveling with him stood speechless. They heard the voice, but could see no one. The Lord made Saul blind for three days, at the end of which a man named Ananias healed his blindness and Saul, who became Paul, soon began proclaiming Jesus publicly in the synagogues.

Successful black businesspeople have an uncanny ability to change what on the surface appears to be bad and unchangeable into something that is worthwhile and rewarding. These businesspeople usually found themselves in dire situations at some point during their business careers. In some cases, they couldn't find the financing to maintain and expand their businesses, or as in the case of Earl Chavis, put trust in a business partner who turned out to be dishonest.

No matter what the ordeal, talented minority businesspeople tend to have the foresight to take what appears to be a hopeless situation and convert it into a promising and exciting opportunity.

TRAIT 11: RESIST THE HERD INSTINCT

I interviewed a businessperson from New England who talked about how so many people possess the herd instinct. These people, he said, are constantly on the move, but end up nowhere. His perspective reminded me of the sheep farm just down the road from where I live.

Each morning as I drive by, I fondly watch the sheep marching out to the corners of the meadow to feed. Usually, there is one sheep out front leading the herd while the others, apparently oblivious to their surroundings, blindly follow the herd out to pasture. I suspect there is a group of leaders within the herd who take turns leading the sheep to eat in the mornings and then leading them back to shelter at dusk. Without exception, each morning that I drive by, the sheep herd seems to carry itself as if it is one big monolithic unit versus hundreds of individual animals. This phenomenon has been termed the herd instinct.

Successful African American businesspeople have made it a habit to resist the herd instinct. True leaders chart their own courses. Charting their own course has become the trademark of Ron and Cynthia Thompson. The Thompsons own what I believe to be the only railroad car manufacturing company owned and managed by African Americans. Although it would have been safer for the Thompsons to pursue more traditional small businesses, they chose instead to study the market, understand their strengths and weaknesses, and chart their own course.

TRAIT 12: LIVING BY THE "PAIN DON'T HURT" POINT OF VIEW

Sparky Anderson, former manager of the Detroit Tigers, had a knack for making some of the most profound statements in baseball. I recall reading a comment he made to one of his players, who was nursing an injury he had received during the previous season. The player, while going through spring training, was obviously in a great deal of pain. Sparky, in his infinite wisdom, tried to encourage the young player to continue playing despite his injury by saying to the player, "C'mon, you can do better than that. You know the pain don't hurt."

In a way, this is very true in the lives of successful black entrepreneurs. When they commit themselves to their business goals without holding back, even with the many disappointments, failures, and uncertainties, they refuse to let the pain stop them. They continue to work their plan and plan their work as if the pain don't hurt.

TRAIT 13: LONG-TERM GREEDY VERSUS SHORT-TERM GREEDY

Eliot Powell, a friend and former president of SDGG Holding Company, often stated that minority businesspeople need to become long-term greedy instead of short-term greedy. Although the word greed usually conjures up negative images in the minds of most people, it is one of the most essential elements for survival in the business world. Greed, properly applied, serves to keep the struggling entrepreneur motivated and somewhat frightened. A healthy dose of fear acts to keep the adrenaline flowing and also sharpens the senses. Those entrepreneurs who get in trouble because of greed do so because they allow it to cloud their judgment and coerce them into making short-term decisions that produce short-term gains and end up causing them to fall short of their long-term goals.

It has often been said that the race is won, not by the swiftest, but by the runner who is steady and who perseveres to the end. Those African American entrepreneurs who survive have learned to pace themselves in terms of reaping the rewards from their labors. They possess a quiet confidence about them that echoes out every so often that if they continue to do the right things at the right time and if they never give up, they will eventually win. Not only will they win but the rewards that are commensurate with the degree of effort, patience, and commitment invested will be theirs ultimately. These people have learned that being short-term greedy may feel good but the euphoria generated by these temporary gains normally dissipates soon thereafter. Successful African American entrepreneurs have adopted a long-term greedy strategy and it's paying handsome dividends for them.

TRAIT 14: EXPERIENCE A GUT-WRENCHING EVENT

As is true with most other projects in life, getting started is usually the most challenging hurdle to overcome. For most, the reason it's so hard to get started is because doing it requires us to expand our comfort zone. All of us like to operate in our own little comfort zones. There are certain places that we're use to, certain groups of people we're comfortable with, and specific tasks that we're confident and comfortable in doing. We fail to realize that the tasks we become accustomed to doing on a routine basis begin to dictate for us the dimensions of our comfort zone. Unless we force ourselves to venture outside that comfort zone or to expand it, we will never grow, expand our skill base, or try new things.

The transition from an employee to an employer requires a major leap outside our comfort zones, and the catalyst for such a leap is generally a gut-wrenching event in the life of the converted entrepreneur. A gut-wrenching event is any occurrence in your life that causes you such pain, anxiety, fear, and apprehension so that you are forced to make a decision that, under normal conditions, you are unlikely to make. Some examples of gut-wrenching experiences that I've had are:

- I was fired from my job and had no visible way of paying my bills or feeding my family.
- Someone I knew who had far less talent than I started a successful company and has since become a millionaire.

- My father died, left me the business, and made me promise to run it and not sell it.
- My company had a lucrative early retirement program and suggested that I participate in it.

Of course, what may be a gut-wrenching experience for one person may mean nothing to another person. However, you will know when you've experienced a gut-wrenching event.

The beauty of gut-wrenching events is that if they're accepted in the proper way, they can be used to your advantage as events to stimulate you to redefine your comfort zones. Those black entrepreneurs who ultimately accepted the entrepreneur challenges generally experienced one of these events before venturing out. To their credit, instead of letting it demoralize them, they used it to stimulate and to motivate them to make their dream a reality.

TRAIT 15: THE NATURAL HIGH FROM MAKING MONEY

Successful black entrepreneurs enjoy making money. Although money is not always the primary motivator for these people, making it is fun and exciting. Often it is the process of making money that provides them the most satisfaction, or high, versus the end result of putting the cash into the bank.

TRAIT 16: BEING COMFORTABLE WITH BEING UNCOMFORTABLE

The transition from being an employee to becoming an employer is full of twists, turns, and surprises. This usually results in entrepreneurs being thrust into unfamiliar situations; nevertheless, entrepreneurs must still perform. Times such as these require black entrepreneurs to appear comfortable, even though in fact they are extremely uncomfortable.

TRAIT 17: CORRELATING EXACTITUDE WITH CHAOS AND BRINGING VISION INTO FOCUS

At the University of Pennsylvania's two hundred fiftieth anniversary, the dean of the engineering school, Dr. Joseph Bordogna, a friend and mentor, was asked to describe the role that engineers play in society. His response was to say, "Engineers are people who can consistently and effectively correlate exactitude with chaos and bring vision into focus." Like their engineering counterparts, successful African American entrepreneurs possess the ability to translate their visions of an idea, product, or business, and bring them into focus. They are good at turning the dreams into reality. While attempting to translate the dreams into something real and concrete, they often find themselves in chaotic situations that require some degree of exactitude before progress can be made. These people have a keen ability to absorb the chaos and in turn structure and set direction so that the venture is able to develop and mature.

TRAIT 18: BELIEVING THAT COMPETITIVENESS USUALLY DEFEATS RACISM, SEXISM, AND CLASSISM

To accelerate the closure of World War II, the United States government released a horrible weapon on the world that created an inferno that even the mind of Dante probably could not have imagined. This terrible weapon was the atomic bomb. When released over the blue skies of Japan, the bomb rained death and destruction on the Japanese people in two of Japan's major industrial cities. Japan was bombarded into submission and with much of its industrial infrastructure destroyed, surrendered to the Allied forces, and thus the final chapter of World War II was closed.

As expected, it took the Japanese people a couple of decades to rebuild their country and their technological/industrial complex. Although Japan was able to produce and sell some products during the transition, the products that made it to the market were usually rejected and ridiculed as being inferior and not up to U.S. standards. I suspect there also existed a certain amount of American animosity, racism, and mistrust toward the Japanese people.

Undeterred, Japan never gave up its quest to rebuild its infrastructure and continued to look for help from the West through people such as W. Edwards Deming, who worked feverishly and assisted them in modeling their industrial complex after that of the United States. Persistence eventually paid off for Japan and despite an obliterated infrastructure and Americans' blatant racism against people of color, Japan rebuilt its economy and developed into one of the premier manufacturing forces on the face of the earth.

Successful African American businesspeople have learned from the Japanese experience and understand that regardless of race, gender, ethnic origin, social/economic position, or scarcity of resources, if they can produce competitive goods and provide value-add services at competitive prices, customers will buy the product or services, regardless of the seller's skin color. In most situations, competitiveness is the great race equalizer in business.

TRAIT 19: PERPETUAL DREAM CHASERS

> *Dreaming is an act of pure imagination, attesting in all men a creative power, which, if it were available in waking, would make every man a Dante or Shakespeare.*
>
> H. F. Hedge

During the late 1960s, Robert Kennedy, well on his way to becoming a successful politician and national leader at an unusually young age, explained, "Some men see things as they are and say why. I dream things that never were and say why not."

In this short but insightful comment, Bobby defined the differences between people who chase dreams and people who don't.

Black business leaders who enjoy various levels of success always focus on events that are not yet and not only ask why not, but take it one step further and implement strategies to make the dream a reality. Ron and Cynthia Thompson of General Railroad Equipment & Services, Inc., conjured up the dream of owning and operating one of the few, if not the only, black-owned railroad equipment and services company in America. They didn't have any role models in this area to guide them through the rigors and difficulties of conquering such a herculean task. Unlike the franchise route, the road for Ron and Cynthia was uncharted and uncertain. Yet, they continued undaunted because they were chasing a dream.

The dream chasers are an interesting group of people. First, they never have just one dream, but instead have a steady progression of dreams. Each successive dream appears to get much bolder and more encompassing than the prior one. It is not unusual to find a much larger, loftier dream unknowingly dissected into smaller dreams that work in harmony to achieve the bigger dreams. This often happens without the successful businessperson's even being aware that this is taking place.

This progression of dreams that seems to define successful black businesspeople usually starts at some point during their childhoods and remains a part of their lives until they die. Although most experience this phenomenon at a young age, it is unlikely that they are born with this trait or that it can be taught. In general, it appears that the trait is assimilated into black entrepreneurs through two channels: personal experiences and the proper types and amounts of exposures. Successful businesspeople take seriously the issue of exposure because they realize that the dream-chasing virus is extremely contagious. Consequently, they try to surround themselves with other dream chasers.

Whether through personal experiences or exposure, these dream chasers learn early on that it is not the object of the dream that brings them joy, but the rush they experience just knowing that the object of their dream is achievable and clearly within their grasp. Getting closer and closer to the object of their dreams is more exciting than the actual achievement of the dream itself. That is why dream chasers conjure up new dreams every time an old dream is realized.

The process of moving closer to making a dream reality is in itself magical. During the process, the dream chaser is injected with high doses of energy, excitement, creativity, and serenity that often spill over into other aspects of the dreamer's life. Thus, these dream chasers tend to be a pleasant and charismatic lot that act as magnets to other people and whom other people enjoy being around.

TRAIT 20: ASCENDING THE INCREMENTAL ENERGY LEVELS OF SUCCESS

Cecil and Donna Stevens of Early Morning Software, Inc. learned years ago how to leverage the incremental energy levels of success. For years, they struggled to build an information technology and software development firm to support clients in the mid-Atlantic region. Although it took them years to achieve the dynamic and growing enterprise they now own and manage, they quietly and confidently achieved and accepted the smaller levels of success during the process of achieving the aggregate success component. Like most other successful business leaders, Cecil and Donna get stronger and more determined as they ascend more levels.

What are the incremental energy levels of success? As shown in Exhibit 7.1, success, or the achievement of one's dreams, does not come in one big chunk. Successful businesspeople understand that to achieve ultimate success the individual must make his or her way from one success level to the next. After some specific period of time, if the entrepreneur's plan is sound and the commitment unwavering, the successful busi-

Exhibit 7.1 Success Levels to Goal Attainment

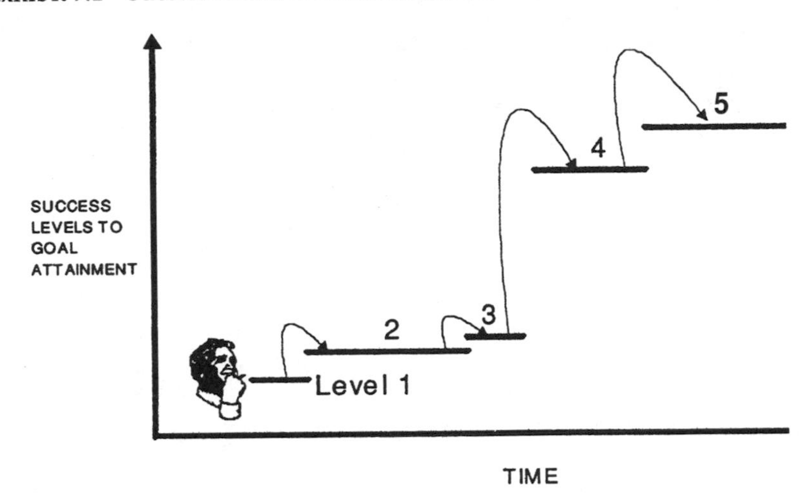

nessperson will go through a series of level jumps as he or she slowly makes the way to the objective.

Although all successful African American businesspeople set a steady course of ascending these energy levels, they also understand that the duration of each level may vary and that the incremental jump to each successive level can be either very small or very large. However, he or she is committed to making the jumps regardless of the distance and duration of each successive level.

CASE STUDY

This case study illustrates the enormous opportunities on Wall Street for blacks and other minorities. Mr. Williams is the epitome of the Daring Dashing Dan entrepreneur. Mr. Williams is Ivy League educated and is an African American.

CHRISTOPHER J. WILLIAMS

President & CEO, The Williams Capital Group, L.P.

"If You Believe in Your Heart That You Are on the Right Path, Push Even Harder"

Christopher Williams looks like a man to whom success comes easily. He owns a rapidly growing investment bank with offices on Fifth Avenue in New York City and in the West End of London, a large apartment in the upper east side of Manhattan, is married to a lovely woman who is also his business partner, and has two healthy and happy children, a son and a daughter. In June 1999 *Black Enterprise* described him as appearing more like an NBA star than an M.B.A. To look at him, you would never know that less than five years ago, his phone hadn't rung for months, his business was crumbling day by day, and he was only weeks away from turning out the lights permanently on his less-than-one-year-old company, The Williams Capital Group, L.P. How did he turn the business around? By following his own principles for success.

GROWING UP

Chris Williams was born in 1957 in Norwalk, Connecticut, and was raised in a traditional middle-class home. His mother, a native of California, stayed at home to raise Chris, his older brother Allen, and little sister Reina. His father worked in heavy labor for Connecticut Light & Power. The family was middle-class, and like many other small-town working families during that time, only on occasion ventured outside the surrounding communities. In addition to his parents, Chris found his early professional role model to be his fraternal grandfather. While his grandfather held an associate's degree and was trained as an accountant, a rare distinction for an African American in the 1940s, his less qualified peers surpassed him professionally due to the company's unwillingness to hire blacks in professional positions, and he was directed to a career as a laborer. Even in his youth, Chris could sense his grandfather's frustration with having to compromise his dreams and goals. This awareness was one of his first lessons in the differences that race can cause in one's ability to succeed.

Chris attended New Milford High School in Connecticut, where he was one of only a handful of African American students. At 6'4", and as one of the few black students, he played numerous sports, including basketball and track.

After considering several different career options, Chris decided to choose architecture in order to marry both an interest and aptitude for art and a means of making a viable living. He decided to attend Howard University for his undergraduate studies in architecture, encouraged in part by his father, who felt Chris needed to be exposed to an environment in which he could have a range of African American role models. The Washington, D.C., campus provided an urban environment that met Chris' needs, and he found his experience at Howard to be a positive one.

While many other blacks who have attended predominantly white secondary schools before attending a historically black college or university find the transition difficult, Chris thrived in this environment. In fact, even though the school is predominantly composed of minority students, many choose Howard for similar reasons to Chris'—to get more exposure to their heritage after being raised and attending school in communities where they were among a very small minority. In addition, Howard offered its own intrinsic benefits. Chris received a first-rate education in his chosen field as well as exposure to African American professionals who were also positive role models. In addition to gaining exposure to these role models, Chris developed friendships, which he expects to last a lifetime.

PROFESSIONAL CHOICES

After graduation from Howard in 1980, with a master's degree in architecture, Chris went home to New Haven and practiced architecture for three years. His former boss, also a Howard graduate, remains a friend and business associate to this day.

After three years of practicing architecture, Chris decided to leave the field for one that he believed offered greater economic upside. Without a specific career goal in mind, he decided to pursue an M.B.A. to maximize his income earning potential.

The decision of which of the top M.B.A. programs to attend was a challenging one. In addition to Dartmouth's Amos Tuck School of Business Administration, Chris considered attending the University of

Pennsylvania's renowned Wharton School of Business, as well as the also highly competitive M.B.A. program at Columbia University in New York City. Chris put as much energy into making this decision as he did on his future entrepreneurial pursuits, and in the end made his decision based on two essential factors.

> I visited all three of the schools that I was seriously considering. An essential selling point of Dartmouth was the positive interaction that I was able to have with both students and faculty during my brief visit. I was impressed with the opportunity to forge relationships with both students and professors. This was due in part to the smaller size of the program. The second reason I selected Dartmouth was my recognition that learning would need to be my priority for the next two years and that I didn't need the distractions of large cities like New York or Philadelphia.

Chris began his studies at Dartmouth in the fall of 1982. He originally planned to pursue a career in real estate development, but a summer internship with Morgan Guaranty Company offered him a glimpse of the lucrative careers available on Wall Street. After graduation in 1984, with a variety of offers in hand, he accepted a position with the Wall Street partnership of Lehman Brothers Kuhn Loeb, one of the largest and most prestigious investment banks on The Street at that time.

Investment banking was the field to be in during the Roaring '80s, but African Americans were focused in the area of public finance and Chris was no exception. Blacks were beginning to assume leadership roles in the political process in urban areas, and these municipalities were looking to work with investment firms that had blacks employed in visible roles. These hundred-year-old investment firms hadn't achieved their successes without being politically savvy, and focused many qualified African American employees in that area of the business. "Unfortunately," Chris notes, "the public finance area was experiencing declining margins, and not surprisingly, declining paychecks." However, this was a great intrapreneurship opportunity, with great training, and plenty of experience and autonomy early in a professional career.

PERSONAL NEEDS MEET PROFESSIONAL OPPORTUNITIES

During his tenure at Lehman Brothers, Chris met, and eventually married, Janice Savin. Janice was an employee of Shearson American Express, and they first met during the Shearson-Lehman merger. Janice shared Chris' values and entrepreneurial spirit, and supported him fully while maintaining her own professional career.

> Getting married and starting a family certainly had an impact on me. I had always been driven toward financial success. But having children, first my son Chris while I was still employed by Lehman, and later my daughter Jillian after I started my own business, was a constant reminder of what I wanted and needed to accomplish. I was concerned not just for myself, but also for my family's future.

At this point Chris again decided to pursue increased financial opportunities, a vastly underrated career strategy in the African American community. His next step was toward Corporate Finance. Around that time, 1987, Lehman began to increase its presence in the derivatives market, and Chris became involved in this area of the business as well. While derivatives can be complex financial instruments, in their simplest forms they are merely agreements between two parties requiring specific performance based on preset variables (i.e., expectations about future market movements). Lehman Brothers, and Chris as its agent, designed and developed new derivative products to help corporate clients use derivatives to manage market risk.

Chris thrived in the derivatives area for several years. However, following a restructuring that did not provide the desired increase in responsibility, Chris decided to evaluate alternative opportunities, concerned that professional growth opportunity might be limited at Lehman. Knowing that annual bonuses were granted in February, Chris began preparing his business plan, and ultimately presented his plan to acquaintances at Jefferies & Company.

Jefferies is a midsize national firm of about 1,200 people, based in Los Angeles. The firm was willing to expand into both derivatives and investment grade bonds, making Williams an ideal candidate for building a partnership.

> This was not just about the money, although that was certainly a driving factor. It was about the lack of upside that I felt existed at my old employer, and by then, I had my plans in place. With my business plan coming to life with the relationship with Jefferies, I believed that the potential financial rewards of entrepreneurship outweighed the benefits of remaining in the corporate structure. Of course, upon learning of my plans to leave Lehman, my bosses made the usual counteroffers and proposals—all of which were too little, too late.

With his bonus in hand (Wall Street bonuses for someone at Chris' level are typically in the six figures), Chris left Lehman Brothers to officially become an entrepreneur. Derivatives were hot, and Chris and the two other Lehman colleagues—one a market technician and the other an experienced marketer—brought major clients along with them to their newly established enterprise. Following a successful 18-month relationship with Jefferies, Chris decided to become totally independent and formed The Williams Capital Group, L.P. Unfortunately, within months after the operation began, the derivatives' market received extremely negative national attention, belying the old saying that there is no such thing as bad publicity. Procter & Gamble, Gibson Greetings, and, most spectacularly, Orange County, California, all had issues associated with the management of derivatives:

> Derivatives were not inherently bad financial instruments; however, they were best used for mitigating risk as opposed to establishing speculative positions. When used for management of risk, they were excellent financial tools and remain so today. However, the bad publicity associated with derivatives had an immediate impact on the entire industry. Because of our complete reliance on a single line of business, derivatives, the industry caught a cold, and my business, Williams Capital, got pneumonia—almost a fatal case.
>
> The worst year of not only my career, but also my entire life was nineteen ninety-four. The telephone literally would not ring for *months*—and this in offices the size of a small conference room. We'd all look at one another—I remember that the phone rang on one occasion, and it turned out to be a potential client, telling me in great detail, why he *wouldn't* be able to sign on with us. I remember thinking that I could not believe that it came to the point where the only telephone call I received was a long-winded rejection.

When asked whether he ever considered giving up, Chris gives an answer that might be considered unusual in this day and time. He replies:

> I never seriously considered folding my business. In fact, I had an opportunity to do so when a former boss offered what would have been a very attractive financial package. I checked with two original partners, and we all independently agreed to stick it out. I literally intended to stay until—as in the old cartoons—they turned the lights out on me and pulled me offstage with the big hook.

Fortunately, it did not come to that for Williams Capital. In October 1994 the firm was able to increase business and break even for the first time in its history. By the following March, the firm was back on track, and the business has been moving in a positive direction ever since. Notably, the firm even eventually signed the client who had called during their darkest days to inform them of why he would not do business with the firm.

> I learned a lot about myself during this period—particularly that I had more confidence in myself than I ever would have suspected. While certainly part of my motivation was the fact that I had others depending on me, especially my family and my employees, ultimately I was successful because I believed in myself.

However, Chris does not take all the credit for turning the business around. He adds:

> My wife and I strategized, supported one another, and prayed day *and* night, for not only direction, but also that we did not let the stress ruin our health. This type of business downturn takes a physical as well as an emotional toll, at a time when you are least able to spend time taking care of yourself.

PRINCIPLES FOR SUCCESS

Chris developed his personal success principles through his entire career, but not surprisingly, he learned the most during the most difficult times.

1. The first of these principles is:

> Be straightforward and honest—treat people with integrity. Treat them in a way that allows you to earn, and deserve, their *trust*. Not just your clients, but as importantly, your employees. When the business reached its lowest point, in the summer of 1994, I spoke to each of my employees individually and asked them to take reductions in their salaries. I asked them to take a leap of faith with me, and committed to them that we would accrue the difference and pay them back the lost income as soon as we were back on our feet. Everyone recognized that we were all working hard, we were all in this together, and we were doing our best, and *everyone* stayed—not a single person left. Their leap of faith was rewarded, and they were paid in full within the first quarter of the following year. Not surprisingly, many of those employees are still with me today.

2. His second principle is to set a clear vision and goals, such that your organization knows where you are going. Chris believes:

> Not everyone wants to be a leader. There are many people who expect to achieve success by following, and it is a good thing that there are people like that. What many people really want is to know where they are going and what it will take them to get there. As the President and CEO, it was my responsibility to provide my team with this vision, and to live it every day.

3. Not surprisingly, Chris leads by example, his third principle. Especially during the difficult times, but even today, he stays in the trenches working closely with his employees.

> You should never ask anyone to do anything you're not willing to do yourself, whether it's taking a pay cut, calling on clients, or if necessary, mopping the floors. Not only is this a way to build sound relationships with your employees, it's good business sense. As a leader, there is no question that I need to be a strategic thinker. However, it is just as important to think short term, especially in a business like finance where you may have to react quickly to changes in the markets. Being in the trenches has the added benefit of giving me that short-term perspective.

4. Chris' fourth principle for success is a very practical one. He ensures that at any point in time, he has at least five major business ideas in the works. A few are focused on maintaining his current business, while others are designed to grow his firm. Two examples of the latter are his recently opened London office, designed to build business overseas, and the planned purchase of a seat on the New York Stock Exchange. At more than a quarter of a million dollars annually, a seat is hardly an insignificant investment. However, Chris expects it to pay big dividends. He notes, "A seat on the exchange not only improves my ability to service current clients, by providing me with direct access to information, but it also builds credibility for my firm, which will help me attract new clients."

KEY CHARACTERISTICS OF SUCCESSFUL ENTREPRENEURS

Chris believes that there are essential traits that lead to an individual becoming a successful entrepreneur. The most important of these is to be both aggressive and tireless, traits that go hand in hand for successful business owners. He says, "As exhausting as it was to manage the business during the hard times, it takes just as much physical and mental energy, perhaps even more so, to maintain and build a business." The second characteristic is consistent with his principles: "Have a vision and a plan." The third and one of the most important is stubbornness.

> Almost by definition, an entrepreneur is pursuing an opportunity that the masses may not consider viable. Moreover, one of the reasons that it may not have been done is because of all the naysayers, who do not believe it can be done. So you need to be stubborn, and when people tell you no, if you believe in your heart that you are on the right path, push even harder in that direction.

FUTURE BUSINESS OPPORTUNITIES FOR MINORITY ENTREPRENEURS

Chris' first recommendation for aspiring minority business owners is first and foremost, not to think of themselves as *minority* business owners, or to limit themselves to *minority* business opportunities. Instead, they should focus on meeting needs that have not been met, regardless of whether they are the needs of the African American community or of the community at large. A second area that Chris recommends in the current environment is exploring the potential of Internet businesses, or e-commerce. If you have the background and qualifications, Chris believes this is an area where race truly should not matter. In addition, while it is certainly not true that everything that can be done already has been done, he believes that there is significant opportunity in making the way current businesses are run better and more efficient.

NEXT STEPS

Where will The Williams Capital Group and its President and CEO go from here? At 41, just beginning to gray at the temples, Chris gets thoughtful as he ponders the future.

> By the time I am 50, less than 10 years from now, I would love to be in a position where I could play a more passive role in the management of the firm. There are so few minority-owned firms that are institutionalized to where the principals can pass on their organizations to the next generation, with Johnson Publications being a notable exception. While my children will still be a little young at that point, that remains an ultimate goal.

When asked what he would do with his time if his business reached the point where he did not have to be involved in a hands-on manner, Chris does not give the typical answers of traveling or relaxing. Instead, he dreams of the opportunities available to a business that achieves that level of success. "If the business reaches that level, the opportunities for this type of growth and partnerships would be wonderful. It would be impossible to resist pursuing them."

FOLLOW THE PLAN

One of the success traits of successful entrepreneurs is to Know thy plan, and of course, to follow it. It appears that Chris' plan was to follow the dollars, a strategy often adhered to by the majority, but one that blacks are often ashamed to admit to or do not even consider. When asked about whether this was his plan, Chris pauses. After a few moments' consideration, he shares one last piece of wisdom:

> Any field you might choose has its own challenges with its own unique pressures. Why not choose the path that offers the most financial benefits?

Why not indeed?

CASE STUDY

This case study illustrates the nuances of starting a business through acquisitions and securing funding through traditional and mainstream sources. The case study also speaks to the challenges that are inherent in building a partnership. Messrs. Sanders, Powell, and Wallace are African Americans.

JEROME SANDERS
ELIOT POWELL
ROBERT (BOB) WALLACE

Founders, The SDGG Holding Company, Inc.
Summit, New Jersey

"If We Don't Kill Something, We Don't Eat!"

The noise coming from my three sons horseplaying in the back seat of the car could not stop me from thinking about the exciting business opportunity I had just uncovered while attending Dartmouth's annual Minority Business Executive Program (MBEP). For the past five years, I had been attending the MBEP, hoping that eventually I would locate a medium-size manufacturing company that the owner was ready and willing to sell. I and my buddy from my DuPont days, Jerome Sanders, had planned for such an acquisition for a long time. When I called Jerry from New Hampshire to share with him the good news, Jerry insisted that I stop by his home in New Jersey to explain the details of the deal. After a long six-hour drive, as I and my family finally rolled our old, green Volvo into Jerry's driveway, my wife, Carolyn, kept wondering aloud, "Is this the deal? Is this the deal?" I shrugged my shoulders and replied, "I hope so, honey."

It was no coincidence that this meeting took place on Labor Day 1987. Jerry was hosting a picnic at his home and had invited another friend, Kevin Brown, to attend so that the three of us could discuss business opportunities. Kevin had been a classmate of Jerry's at the Wharton Business School and was also interested in creating wealth through business formation. Jerry would later admit that he purposely invited Kevin and me to his home so that we could size each other up as potential business partners. We three planned to spend much of the afternoon discussing our entrepreneurial interests and how the three of us might work closely together to pursue acquiring a business. Another twist of fate revealed—unbeknown to all attendees—a friend and classmate of mine from the Tuck School at Dartmouth College, Eliot Powell, lived within a few blocks of Jerry's home. Feeling Eliot would be interested in discussing possible business ventures, Jerry also had invited Eliot to the picnic. Shortly after Eliot arrived, it became apparent that he had his sights on starting a business and had developed strong financial connections during his tenure at Goldman Sachs. The four of us discussed our entrepreneurial dreams far into the night under the watchful eye of the moon. This chance encounter was the beginning of SDGG Holding Company.

THE DREAM

As the four of us shared our entrepreneurial visions, all of us agreed that the key to developing wealth and achieving success was through equity ownership in a company. Although no specific business or industry was identified, we believed that we could use our educational background, creativity, energy, work experience, and minority ownership in the company as leverage to acquire, build, and manage a portfolio of businesses.

Indeed, our shared view was that the business should be based on the collective strength of the individuals. Both Jerry and I had undergraduate engineering degrees and each had worked in the Engineering Services Division at DuPont. Having received our MBAs, I went to work for IBM in its Marketing and Systems Engineering Division while Jerry chose the consulting life and took up residence at Cresap, McCormick and Paget in New York. Kevin's background was in marketing and Eliot's background was in finance. After earning his MBA from Tuck, Eliot chose the high finance route and cut his financial teeth at Goldman Sachs on Wall Street.

BUT WHAT BUSINESS?

Besides the metal fabricating business that I had so excitedly rushed to Jerry's home to discuss, another business that seemed equally promising, based on the discussion that night, was contract manufacturing and contract packaging. Given the high concentration of pharmaceutical and personal products companies in New Jersey and the contacts of the individuals on the team, it was felt that this would be a promising area to exploit. Over the course of the next two to three months, Jerry, Eliot, and I kept in contact and slowly developed an interest in pursuing contract manufacturing and packaging deals in New Jersey and elsewhere.

THE BIOTECHNOLOGY OPTION

As the team quickly wrapped itself into the deal loop, we identified an available pharmaceutical freeze-drying facility just outside Chicago. This particular plant was owned by Zenith Laboratories, a generic pharmaceutical manufacturer. SDGG realized that this was an opportunity that could not be passed up. The facility was underutilized, running far below its known capacity. While producing only approximately $3 million of generic pharmaceuticals per year, the facility was capable of handling a far greater capacity. Further research revealed that there was a limited national capacity of qualified freeze-drying facilities for pharmaceuticals; thus supply was far out of line with demand. In contacting several biotechnology firms in both the Boston and San Francisco areas, it was discovered that this type of facility was often required by biotechnology firms that could not afford the time or expense necessary to build and maintain these types of facility for experimental products. Such companies often require short-run, freeze-drying capacity under FDA-approved specifications. In fact, the team's market research indicated that there was only one other contract manufacturer in the country who provided freeze-drying services, and this vendor was operating at capacity all year round and was booked solid for the next couple of years.

The team felt confident that they had stumbled upon a lucrative business opportunity. As we quickly learned from talking with experts, attending biotechnology conferences, and conducting extensive industry research, most biotechnology products have shelf lives of less than 90 days, and the advanced planning required for this primary freeze-drying vendor was at least 90 days or more, leaving little or no alternative for many of the bio-tech companies to preserve their products. The team realized that the freeze-drying facility in Rosemont, Illinois, could easily be converted to a contract manufacturing company servicing the biotechnology industry.

Excited about their new diamond in the rough opportunity, the team set out to explore financing options for the proposed acquisition. Because I still lived in Baltimore, I focused on identifying sources in the Baltimore-Washington area. Jerry and Eliot, who had worked in New York City for many years, pushed on the contacts that they had made in the consulting and investment banking businesses. To their surprise, many of these contacts showed a strong interest in working with SDGG, and thus they were able to quickly secure soft commitments to finance the acquisition of the facility and to develop their contract manufacturing business. Little did they know the challenge that awaited them.

The next two to three months were fast paced and grueling. The team spent a large amount of time developing a business plan and negotiating with the company to purchase the freeze-drying plant and other strategic facilities. I spent thousands of dollars commuting back and forth between Baltimore and New York City on the train and conducting research. Concurrent to negotiating this deal, some of the owners of SDGG were still employed, so the team had to be careful about how it communicated information about the deal to one another. To keep their identities a secret and to inject some fun into what was rapidly becoming an intense engagement, the three of us (Kevin Brown had left to pursue other opportunities) adopted code names. Jerry's code name became N-man because of the network he had developed over the years. Eliot's code name became Storm because of the intensity he displayed when transacting business. My code name became Neutron because of my earlier disdain for unions and the missionary zeal I displayed in my attempts to neutralize unproductive workers.

REDUCING THE EXPOSURE

Although the freeze-drying deal was showing some promise, the team wanted to minimize its exposure so it decided to look at other business opportunities should the freeze-drying facility not work out. In April 1989, Jerry and Eliot had scheduled a meeting with the president and CFO of Zenith Laboratories to discuss the acquisition. Zenith was a troubled company nearly in bankruptcy. This sale would have provided a means for Zenith to raise capital for its primary business, generic pharmaceuticals. Two days prior to their meeting with the officers of the company, they learned of the CEO's dismissal by the board members and their replacement by an interim consultant. As a consequence of this series of events, the acquisition of the freeze-drying facility in Rosemont was no longer feasible.

With operating expenses increasing and no steady revenue being generated, SDGG was confronted with a major dilemma. The team had to decide how to divide its time between pursuing acquisitions, which tend to have long payoff horizons, and diversifying into other businesses that could generate a quick cash injection for the firm and that require little start-up capital. After the team again reviewed its strengths and weaknesses, it decided to diversify into the auto/equipment leasing and consulting businesses. The new organization is shown in Exhibit 7.2.

Diversifying into these two businesses was a natural fit for the

Exhibit 7.2 SDGG Holding Company, Inc.

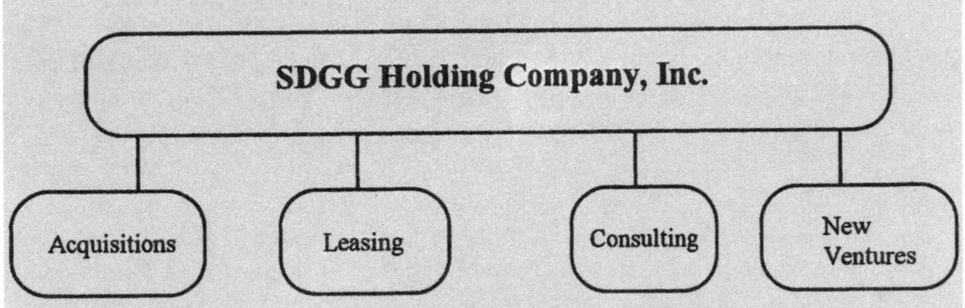

team. First of all, one of Eliot's and my classmates at the Tuck School of Business had recently purchased a tractor manufacturing company in Wisconsin. This company made tractors for specific commercial applications and special Department of Defense uses. To assist his clients in financing their purchases of these tractors, our classmate wanted to provide a leasing option to his customers. We agreed that SDGG would start a leasing company (Atlantis Leasing) and that Atlantis would provide the leasing arm for the financing of tractors. The consulting division of SDGG sprouted roots after the advent of the Atlantis Leasing Company. Consulting came easy to the team because Jerry had many years of consulting experience and generated an extensive network in which solid consulting leads could be developed. The little cash generated from these two ventures would help prolong the life of the SDGG Holding Company.

LAWYERS, ACCOUNTANTS, AND FINANCIAL SOURCES

Now that the three divisions—acquisitions, leasing, and consulting—had been set up and the Zenith business plan had been prepared, SDGG spent a substantial amount of time searching for accounting, legal, and financial assistance to complete the rounding out of the team. Because the majority of the activity up to that point revolved around the New York City area, Jerry and Eliot focused on identifying legal and accounting consultants in the city. They interviewed all six of the big six accounting firms looking for assistance in developing the business plan, financial contacts, and references. Each of the firms had a small business group dedicated to assisting start-up companies like SDGG. Although the accounting firms understand the huge risk they assume when they bet on start-up firms, they also appreciate the tremendous returns they can achieve if they bet on the right company. The only way they can realize the benefit is by finding these companies while they're still in their embryonic stages. After numerous meetings with some high-ranking officials at Ernst & Whinney (now Ernst & Young) accounting firm, SDGG chose this firm to handle all of their accounting and financial work. As the two companies became more comfortable with one another, Ernst & Young would go on to play a major role in SDGG's pursuit and evaluation of other acquisition candidates.

In addition to searching for accounting support, a search was also performed throughout greater New York City for qualified legal firms to assist SDGG in managing the legal aspects of its business. Although at first a qualified minority firm was sought out, the search was broadened to include all firms that could provide appropriate acquisition services at competitive prices. Having interviewed over a dozen firms, Cleary, Gottlieb, Steen and Hamilton was selected. To the group's chagrin, very few minority firms were qualified to handle the type of work that SDGG was interested in pursuing. In fact, the only minority firm that came close to meeting SDGG's requirements were the law offices of Lewis and Clark, headed by Reg Lewis. Unfortunately for SDGG, Lewis and Clark had their hands full working through the Beatrice acquisition which at one time was the largest black business in America until it was sold.

Although cost was a major consideration in choosing a law firm, it turned out that Gottlieb was not the cheapest legal firm available. In fact, it was the most expensive of those interviewed by SDGG. However, their abilities and insight into the merger and acquisition process were the strongest. This criterion, along with their established presence in the Wall Street deal flow, was the basis for their selection by SDGG management. The exposure that SDGG ultimately received to senior partners of the firm would help the struggling company weather the many stormy issues that would soon appear.

FINANCIAL SOURCES

Another key aspect of selecting Cleary Gottlieb was their connection into the financial community. Cleary provided inroads to Drexel, Burnham and Lambert, the Wall Street firm that was doing substantial junk bond financing in the mid to late 1980s. Drexel, at the time headed by Michael Milken, was a source of equity dollars badly needed by SDGG. For the size and quality of transactions that SDGG was interested in pursuing, smaller companies like MESBICS were incapable of providing adequate financial resources.

ADDITIONAL SEARCHES

Throughout the rest of the year, Jerry, Eliot, and I looked for other companies to buy. The spectrum was broad and the company's intensive research included evaluating a small precision glass company in Connecticut, capable of financially supporting only one of the three owners. The largest acquisition candidate was a food wholesaler and distributor based on the East Coast that did $500 million dollars in annual sales. While this acquisition looked promising initially, the deal collapsed when the family who owned the business changed their minds and decided not to sell. Undaunted, SDGG continued to evaluate deals across the country. They analyzed trucking companies, oil companies, energy management companies, and a variety of other opportunities. However, near the end of 1988, the team grew frustrated and fatigued for not having successfully located the type of company that would adequately provide the vehicle for the growth envisioned by the three. Would this be the end of the line?

PREPARING FOR THE NEW YEAR

After committing themselves to seeing the process through to the end, the team agreed to conduct a planning session during the first weekend of the new year. Jerry and Eliot joined me at my home in Baltimore for a weekend to discuss the successes and failures of the past year, revisit our mission, and try to map out a plan for SDGG to achieve its goals in 1990. The trio also chose to meet in Baltimore so that they could continue negotiations on the $500 million food distribution business. As mentioned, this deal failed to close due to seller remorse.

Contract manufacturing still held an allure for us. As a result of the intensive weekend discussion we decided to focus on building or creating a primary assembly or subassembly company that focused on high-quality manufacturing and had substantial growth capacities. We did not expect to find such a business in the near future. Instead, the strategy was to build the business from the ground up.

Coincidentally, one week later, the team heard of a small finishing and assembly company available in Newark, New Jersey. This unknown company turned out to be a perfect acquisition candidate. It was a very profitable family business owned and managed by two brothers who had operated the company for more than 30 years. This multimillion dollar company consistently paid $2 million in salary to the two brothers along with healthy net incomes to service any debt and support projected growth. In addition, the brothers were able to take out of the company at least $350,000 in lifestyle expenses. Clearly, the company had sufficient cash flow to support a leveraged acquisition.

Yet in spite of the strong financials, there were inherent problems with the transaction. First, a high percentage of the business in the company came from one customer, IBM. This firm was the primary vendor for furnishing the computer covers for many of IBM's systems. This, however, represented 75 percent of their business. Moreover, the profitability of the company made it difficult to negotiate a price in terms favorable to the buyer. Additionally, the company's financial statements were merely compiled, not audited.

The company's CPA had only one client, the two brothers, their real estate holdings, their personal finances, and the assembly company. The business had been run for many years as a family enterprise and the challenge for SDGG was to try to identify the true corporate profits and convince the lending community of the veracity of those profits. For a $12 million acquisition price, $2 million would be taken back by the brothers, in the form of purchase money financing, $5 million would be provided in the form of mezzanine financing from Drexel, and $5 million would come from senior debt bank financing. SDGG was to provide limited hard equity into the transaction, but would devote three full-time employees to the success of the company. In essence, this was a sweat equity deal for us. At this point in time, the three partners were getting very little sleep and were becoming quite fatigued from the process. However, as each day drew to a close, we felt ourselves moving closer and closer to owning this assembly company. Unfortunately, unseen events were occurring that were out of our control, but would serve to close the door on the transaction.

During 1990, several events occurred that reduced the likelihood of this deal's being completed. First of all, IBM had a poor operating year and sales were down. This company was totally dependent on IBM and suffered along with it. The positive aspect of buying a company in an off year is the downward pressure on the purchase price. The negative side was trying to demonstrate that the company had sufficient cash flow to sustain this transaction price of $12 million.

Concurrently, Drexel had substantial problems following the Dennis Levin case, the Milken insider trading probes, and the weakening of the economy. The so-called credit crunch was in its early stages, and the ability to finance a transaction, as had been routinely done only a few years earlier, was now very difficult. This was no more evident than in the due diligence process when the company's compiled financial statements were inadequate to provide lenders and Drexel the comfort that sufficient cash flow was there to support the proposed transaction. In addition, the two brothers were uncomfortable in divulging factual information on the company to alleviate lenders' concerns, for fear that they would have to refile former tax returns and pay penalties (and potentially face legal charges). One at a time, the wheels came off our vehicle and it became more difficult for SDGG to reasonably expect to acquire the company in a short period of time. The deal died a slow, painful death.

Perhaps, most telling for SDGG was that the efforts of the officers were being funded solely from personal savings. SDGG had been counseled many times to find an avuncular source of financing that would allow us to continue pursuing our goal over an extended period of time. At the time, the urgency of getting a company acquired and under management seemed more important than finding the financial resources to sustain our efforts over a longer period of time. By the start of 1990, although the leasing and consulting divisions were throwing off some cash, it was not enough to sustain the cash drain that the acquisition efforts had created. At this juncture, the team decided to maintain SDGG as a going concern, but also to pursue revenue generation individually until a satisfactory deal could be identified.

LET'S DO IT AGAIN

Since our days at SDGG, Eliot is now a successful equity manager for a large firm in New York. Jerry is a high-level executive for a multibillion-dollar corporation in Atlanta. I have since started a number of new businesses including The BiTH Group, Inc. and EntreTeach.com. But whenever the three of us get together in New York or Atlanta, we ponder the lessons learned from this experience. First of all, in spite of the difficulties, we all agree that a lot of things were done right. SDGG went out and found the right resources, and accounting, legal, and financial help, and established a company that had the right kind of goals, goals that were well received in the marketplace. SDGG kept costs low by leasing the necessary equipment where possible, working out of our homes and in confined office space, borrowing supplies from previous employers, using our cars as the major mode of transportation, and taking advantage of free consulting services from their enormous network of friends and associates. This strategy allowed us to operate for more than two full years on an erratic income stream.

Conversely, it's simple to find the mistakes that were made. The primary mistake was having poor capitalization of the company. As a corollary to having limited funds, SDGG had to put all of its hopes into the acquisition of one company and hope for the best. Near the end, the firm was left with very few options. Jerry and Eliot echo each other's comments when they admonish anyone who is seeking to do a similar type of transaction to put their funding in place before spending time chasing deals. By having the funding already committed, the buyer can often use this situation as leverage in negotiating more attractive pricing, terms, and conditions. Jerry is quick to add: "Remember, if you don't kill something, you don't eat!"

CASE STUDY

Mr. Gooden has built one of the most successful information technology firms in the country. By using government contracts as an initial base, he has used an acquisition strategy to solidify his competitive position. Mr. Gooden is an African American.

C. MICHAEL GOODEN

President and CEO, ISA, Inc.

"When I Was 12 Years Old, I Decided That My Vocation Was to Be a Business Person"

C. Michael Gooden is another highly successful entrepreneur. As President and CEO of Integrated Systems Analysts, Inc. (ISA), Michael used government, business, and personal relationships to develop a solid business. He extols the practice of using what you have and building from there.

As an entrepreneur, Michael is forthright and responsible with a keenly crafted business sense, honed through years of dedication and determination. Though many entrepreneurs view opening shop only in terms of one store, Michael took the same drive and catapulted himself into one of this country's most aggressive capitalists. His beginning is common. Far from spoon fed, Michael spent his early years with his family in Youngstown, Ohio. His father, a truck driver, his mother a homemaker, Michael seemed destined for life in a small town. He freely admits that his vision of being a man of business was bolstered only by his humble beginnings. "I worked a lot of jobs, everything from shining shoes to washing cars, carrying papers, bussing dishes . . . when I was growing up."

EARLY MENTORSHIP

However, Michael was not without his mentors. "I had a guy who took me under his wing. I managed a shoeshine parlor for him. He had several different businesses. I was attracted to that, but I knew I needed an education, experience, and so on."

He was also influenced by a chemistry instructor whose past naval experience intrigued him. "Mr. Smart had been a lieutenant commander. . . . he had received his undergraduate and graduate education while serving on active duty in the navy. I didn't have the money to go on to college, so I looked at the navy as an option to pursue educational opportunities." Too anxious to wait for graduation, Michael enlisted in the naval reserve while still a junior in high school.

ENTERING THE NAVY

With his direction set, he entered the navy a week after graduation where he remained for the next six years learning the most advanced technology involving tactical data systems. Still, his spirit grew restless for faster personal growth. "I felt stagnant. I learned about a program that the navy called Naval Enlisted Scientific Educational Program (NESEP), which accepted 400 of 2,500 candidates annually to major in math, science, or engineering."

Michael applied and was selected for the program. He chose to go to undergraduate school at Miami University in Oxford, Ohio, as it was one of two schools in the United States that offered a degree in systems analysis. Fortunately, the program allowed Michael to pursue his education without tethers holding him to some duty outside his academic requirements. In just three and a half years he graduated with a B.S. in Applied Science, and was commissioned a naval officer.

He was assigned to a guided missile cruiser and served in various positions, principally in the area of shipboard electronics systems. Michael used the experience to further his understanding and hone his mastery of these systems: "I opted to go ashore and pursued a position as an NROTC instructor at the [prestigious] University of Pennsylvania." While serving as an instructor, Michael completed a master's program, receiving a master's in engineering with a specialty in computer science. This strategically positioned him for selection as an engineering duty officer (ED). The ED Corps is a very small, specialized group of naval officers responsible for the design, maintenance, and acquisition of navy ships and ship systems. They are all master's degreed in an engineering discipline and require above average grades. "I agreed to accept a transfer to the ED Corps on the condition that I would be assigned in the Washington, D.C. area and allowed to manage an acquisition program."

Michael wanted to understand the business and contractual side of systems acquisitions. He came to the same crossroads as many entrepreneurs before him: to take the risk or see his vision fade. After learning that his plan to retire from the navy and then start a business was dashed by post-retirement restrictions against retired regular officers selling to the DOD, he opted to resign his regular commission after 17 years of service, but remained in the naval reserves (the restriction did not apply to retired reserve officers) until he could retire. Michael had to serve for 8 more years to be eligible for retirement.

BUILDING THE BUSINESS

Undaunted and with a vision before him, he took the initiative to begin planning, structuring, and building the business that he could see becoming a reality. One month after he resigned, Michael incorporated ISA. One day after his release from active duty, he opened the doors of the company. His discharge from the navy was a beginning rather than an ending. His training and experience with defense engineering systems provided access and ease of working in the computer integration technologies. He initially developed the company with a focus solely on defense systems. However, sharp downturns in defense spending through the 1990s prompted him to refocus the company in the information technology (IT) industry. ISA now pursues most of its business in the commercial IT market.

Michael explains that a Small Business Administration (SBA) program, section 8(a), helped his company during its early years. "When I first considered starting the company, I didn't know about 8(a), nor did I consider it important. I was just trying to build a systems engineering company that specialized in defense systems."

He obtained most of the company's early business working as a subcontractor to major defense companies.

> I had a fairly strong personal reputation in the defense systems engineering market, and I knew many of the large companies because I had done a lot of business with them while I was managing defense programs. When I started the company, I went to many of these companies and sought a subcontractor's role. It didn't hurt that I had customers who wanted my services, and they directed their prime contractors to subcontract to me. I was happy to be working and building the company as a subcontractor to the major defense companies. The first year that I started (actually half a year) the company did $200,000 in business. The next year we had revenue of more than $1 million. Then I saw a change in the way the government was doing business. . . . Customers would no longer be able to direct subcontracts.

Afraid of the potential impact on the development of the company, Michael used his fear to move the business to another level.

> I applied for and was certified in the 8(a) program not long after. At the time I was certified, a lot of changes were implemented in the program.

> Fixed program participation terms were imposed, which limited companies to seven years in the program. I put an aggressive plan in place that would have the company exceed the size standard in five years, after which ISA would leave the program. We left in 1987 having participated less than five years. By that time the company was doing more than $21 million in revenue, had more than 200 employees, and was positioned to compete in our primary DOD areas of contracting.

Michael explains that while many companies opt to retain the security of programs like 8(a), his goal was merely to use the program to assist in establishing his business.

> I had put together a strong talent base, had focused the talent in the defense systems industry, and had gained a respectable level of financial flexibility. Therefore, it was time to leave the program.

Though the 8(a) program has garnered considerable negative press, Michael strongly supports the program concept.

> Unfortunately, the program suffers because many of the regulations that control the program are made for political rather than business development reasons. The fixed program participation terms, the size standards, the net worth limitations, and contract size thresholds don't correlate with historical data on how businesses develop within an industry. Moreover, many of the limits versus the single standards inhibit the companies' ability to become self-sustaining and the net worth limits create an environment for the creation of front companies. The way this program is structured, it quite literally marches businesses to a cliff and pushes them off.

Michael places the majority of the responsibility for the success of the business on the entrepreneur, whom he believes should be knowledgeable of such issues as the fiscal health, market access, and building a sound management structure. Each in his opinion contributes to the health and sustainability of a business.

FOUNDATION FOR THE FUTURE

Finally, Michael and I discussed what he believes to be his foundation—the principles of success that have worked for him as an African American in the business arena. He refers to the philosophy of his company: Integrity, Pride, and Performance.

> I attribute much of the success that we've had as well as our sustainability to those philosophical beliefs. Integrity encompasses the entirety of business operations—how we interact with each other within the company, with our customers, with our business partners, and even with the agen-

> cies we're responsible to: IRS, Defense Contract Audit Agency, and so on. I believe that if you makes a commitment to someone, you must follow through, even if it is difficult to do so. If a manager makes a commitment to an employee, I expect the manager to follow through. If the bank or the auditors come in, I want my financial personnel to open the doors, open the drawers, and let them through.

Michael cites pride next.

> When I started the company, I had the option to take space in someone else's facility. I wanted first class office space so that customers, employees, and business partners would feel comfortable in our offices. I thought it was important for our employees to take pride in their work and in being part of ISA. I wanted customers and business partners to be proud to have ISA as a partner in the realization of their objectives.

Pride shows everywhere in ISA.

Performance is also extremely important and the last of the philosophical triad.

> I don't believe in a free lunch. In order to succeed you must perform well. I feel strongly about the quality of our services. I want to earn the dollars we are paid.
>
> I try to espouse and inculcate these philosophical beliefs within our organization. I remind people about them all the time.

Michael discusses his involvement with a major U.S. automobile manufacturer, which grew from a business venture into numerous opportunities based strictly on his company's ability to maintain integrity over the years. "If you build trust, you should work to preserve that trust over time."

Michael turns to what he believes are three important characteristics of successful businesspeople: focus, perseverance, and knowledge. By focus he means, "how you get people to buy into what you are doing. You have to have a well-defined message." Without a strong focus, he believes the business will surely fail. As for perseverance, Michael holds firmly that one should be made of stern stuff because "You are going to face rejection, but the more tenacious you are, the more persevering, the more doors will open for you." Finally, Michael believes that "the more you know about your products, your customers, and your markets, the higher the likelihood of success."

The example of C. Michael Gooden is like many who desired more for their lives. By securing his foundation educationally, organizationally, and philosophically, he has blazed a true and clear path for success.

8

Intrapreneurship: A Precursor to Becoming an Entrepreneur

GOING PUBLIC

I can recall growing up as a teenager in the hard-core projects of Baltimore City as if it was yesterday. My friends and I danced to the sounds of the Jackson 5, New Birth, the Delphonics, Blue Magic, 3 Dog Night, and British rocker David Bowie. I was surprised recently and a little intrigued when I read that David Bowie had decided to take himself public. The more I thought about it, the more I began to appreciate the genius of what he had done. Bowie was living out the concept of *intrapreneurship.*

The essence of David's ingenious plan was that after spending years increasing his value to fans, he decided to float a personal bond issue to finance the rest of his career as a musician and an entertainer. People who invested in the bonds would be entitled to a percentage of David Bowie's future income. To the surprise of many in the financial world, Prudential Insurance Company of America purchased the entire $55 million issue. The notes, which were rated single A-3 by Moody's Investors Service and have an interest rate of 7.9 percent, were all sold within an hour of being offered!

The new phenomenon illustrated by David Bowie's taking himself public has not stopped with the entertainment industry but is even evident in the professional sports industry. Back in the old days professional athletes were simply a small component of a massive organization. However, today the professional sporting world is comprised of an internetworking, loosely coupled array of free agents. These professionals work at increasing their value by perfecting and honing their skills and then selling these skills to the highest bidder. The more value a player can bring to his or her team (in the form of winning games and filling the seats in the arena), the higher their value to the organization. The higher their value to the organization, the greater compensation package she or he can command.

The concept of intrapreneurship is simply about learning how to increase one's value to the organization that she or he is a part of. By leveraging that value, one determines the compensation that can be commanded. In most organizations there is a direct correlation between the value that an individual adds and the earning potential. If we take this concept one step further, the idea of free agency can be likened to an individual taking himself or herself public. Like David Bowie, an individual who has proven his or her value consistently and persistently will build up a reservoir of real and perceived value. This perceived or future value is what investors bet on when they buy stock in a company. They bet on the potential of the firm (individual) which is often based upon the firm (individual's) past performance.

The first step toward increasing one's value in an organization and thus moving one step closer to practicing intrapreneurship on your job is shifting your paradigm about whom you work for. In consulting workshops that I conduct for corporations and government I often start the sessions with a lively discussion about whom they work for. I enjoy this discussion because I always get entertaining and thought-provoking answers. When asked, "Whom do you work for?" the answers include:

- "I work for my corporation."
- "I work for the government."
- "I work for the American people."
- "I work for the stockholders."
- "I work for the Internal Revenue Service."
- "I work for my children."
- "I work for my spouse."

Less than 5 percent of those polled will conclude that they actually work for themselves. In other words they are their own company and should be about the business of steadily increasing the value of the stock of their company. To do this they must first understand and appreciate the relationship between themselves, their suppliers, and their customers, as shown in Exhibit 8.1.

Suppliers are individuals or organizations that provide the intrapreneur with critical information necessary for him or her to perform the job. Without this information the intrapreneur is unable to perform or at best impaired in performing his or her function. Customers, conversely, are individuals or organizations that benefit from the work that the intrapreneur performs. The customers use the products or services produced by the intrapreneur to perform their job functions. Customers are unable to complete their functions without the input from the intrapreneur. Examples of the supplier-intrapreneur-customer linkage are illustrated in Exhibit 8.2.

Understanding the relationship between you and your customer/supplier linkages will make the conversion from employee to intrapreneurship easier.

WHAT IS INTRAPRENEURSHIP?

Becoming an intrapreneur requires an understanding of the concept of taking oneself public, so let's start with a definition of what intrapreneurship really is. Through research, I have defined intrapreneurship as *the process by which an individual uses skills normally attributed to entrepreneurs, to enhance and increase his or her individual value to an organization.* Furthermore, it is assumed that by increasing the value to the organization he or she is then able to command higher wages, enhance the standard of living, fulfill lifelong dreams, and as Abraham Maslow once articulated, reach the pinnacle of self-actualization.

Just as entrepreneurship was scarcely a household word in 1982 when I began my research at the Tuck School of Business at Dartmouth College, intrapreneurship is not a commonly used term. In fact, according to *Web-*

Exhibit 8.1 Supplier-Intrapreneur-Customer Linkage Diagram

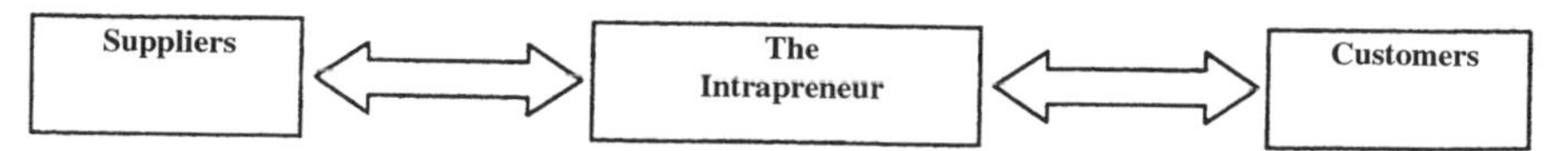

Exhibit 8.2 Supplier-Intrapreneur-Customer Linkage Examples

Supplier(s)	Intrapreneur	Customer(s)
Industry groups Corporate & government Insiders Trade organizations	Financial analyst	Private investors Institutional investors Financial publications
The end-user Other software engineers Technical publications	Software engineer	The end-user Immediate manager President of firm
Other teachers Universities and colleges Previous students	Teacher	Students Principal of school Parents of students Local legislators
The flight commander Navigators Radar technicians	Jet fighter pilot	Flight commander Co-pilot Nation Infantry located on ground

ster's Ninth Collegiate Dictionary, the word *intrapreneurship* is not even a recognized word. (Note: Keep in mind that there are approximately 500,000 words in the English language. The average person recognizes approximately 200,000 of these words. About 10,000 new words are created every year but only 1,000 of these words stick. I believe that *intrapreneurship* will stick.) Consequently, whenever I conduct intrapreneurship training, it is always necessary to spend time up front explaining what the term means.

Although I believe that I am one of the first researchers to study the area of intrapreneurship, the earliest work on this subject originated from Gifford and Elizabeth Pinchot in their book *Intrapreneuring*. In this earlier book and their subsequent book, *The End of Bureaucracy & The Rise of the Intelligent Organization*, the couple suggest that in today's complex and intelligence-intensive world economy, organizations can no longer rely exclusively on the intelligence of those at the top. Everyone in the organization must be able to think through tough and challenging problems—much like an entrepreneur is forced to do.

CONTRASTING ENTREPRENEURSHIP WITH INTRAPRENEURSHIP

The Pinchots made a significant contribution in understanding intrapreneurship but to put it in its proper perspective, this term may be easier to understand if it is contrasted and compared to entrepreneurship.

From a practical standpoint, I define intrapreneurship and entrepreneurship in a similar fashion. The differences in the two are simply in the degree and scope of each of the criteria used to define them. In both cases two conditions must be met to properly define entrepreneurship/intrapreneurship. The first condition specifies that an entrepreneur/intrapreneur is someone who recognizes an opportunity to obtain gain (for example, finance, power, prestige, market dominance, and so on) typically before the masses of people see it. The second condition is that the entrepreneur/intrapreneur then organizes his or her actions, executes a plan, and aggressively pursues the opportunity, with the expectation that he or she will realize profit.

The profit referred to above may not mean just monetary profit (although making money is very important). Specifically, profit realized can be broken into two general categories—tangible profit and intangible profit. Tangible profits are dollars, increased net worth, positive cash flow, and high return on assets. Conversely, intangible profit refers to those things that are often ignored but just as important. These items include value to society, pride in work, reputation among peers, ability to influence and contribute to the advancement of God's kingdom on earth, and the freedom to openly express oneself and to pursue personal fulfillment unhindered.

Understanding the differences and similarities between entrepreneurship and intrapreneurship can best be described by making comparisons as shown in Exhibit 8.3.

Another important contrast between entrepreneurship and intrapreneurship is the sequence in which the two occur. During my study of successful minority entrepreneurs, which was initiated during my graduate business studies at Dartmouth, I uncovered an interesting phenomenon. In the majority of the case studies analyzed, the subject entrepreneur had worked as an employee for another company or government agency before launching his or her business. There was a strong correlation between the industries that the individual worked in, the job function performed, and the nature of the business created. Put succinctly, most people start businesses and perform functions in industries that they had previous experience in before launching. The old adage that an apple does not fall too far from the tree certainly applies for individuals becoming entrepreneurs after having worked as an intrapreneur in their fields of business.

Christopher Williams, president and founder of The Williams Capital Group, L.P., worked for Shearson Lehman in their derivatives unit,

Exhibit 8.3 Contrast and Comparison between Entrepreneurship and Intrapreneurship

Criteria	Entrepreneurship	Intrapreneurship
Degree of risk	High. Most entrepreneurs put everything they own at risk to make their ventures successful. May lose their life earnings, their homes, automobiles, and all other tangible assets.	Low. An intrapreneur's largest risk is the loss of his or her job by the employer. Even if he or she loses a job at one company, as long as he or she has steadily increased the skill set and expanded the network, he or she can readily find new employment opportunities with a new employer.
Type of risk	1. Financial. Potential loss of all tangible assets in the pursuit of business opportunities. 2. Personal. Potential damage to one's reputation and credibility in the pursuit of business opportunities.	Similar to an entrepreneur, an intrapreneur also faces both financial and personal risks.
Wealth creation potential	High. Significant potential for wealth creation; directly attributed to the age-old correlation between risk and reward. The higher the risk, the higher the reward. The lower the risk, the lower the reward.	Medium. Medium potential to achieve wealth. As long as the intrapreneur works for someone else he or she will always be constrained by how much wealth can truly be accumulated.
Benefit	High. Actions and activities possess great potential to benefit the enrepreneur, his or her employees, the economy, and society as a whole.	High. Actions and activities also possess significant potential to benefit the intrapreneur, his or her organization, the economy, and society as a whole.
Span of control	Broad. To be successful, an entrepreneur does not necessarily have to have at his or her disposal an army of employees. Our economy has recently been flooded with a multitude of one-person companies that are profitable and that consistently add value to society. However, one of the important principles of true entrepreneurial success is the ability to use people as leverage in the production of products and the delivery of services. Therefore, the famous	Narrow. A successful intrapreneur does not require an army of individuals to achieve the objectives. In fact, most intrapreneurs simply labor within the confines of their assigned group, department, or division. In the course of their daily activities they directly impact a small number of people in pursuit of their business objectives. However, the art of leveraging other people's time and resources is just as important here as it is in entrepreneurship.

(Continued)

Exhibit 8.3 Continued

Criteria	Entrepreneurship	Intrapreneurship
	and notable entrepreneurs in our midst (e.g., Robert Johnson, Earl Graves, Bill Gates, and Michael Dell) all touch a broad group of people with their actions.	

selling and trading securities, before launching his own financial services company. Similarly, Wayne Armour, president and founder of OFO, Inc., perfected his engineering and Internet skills laboring for such technology giants as Bell Laboratories and IBM. These valuable experiences allowed Wayne to settle into a lucrative Internet business that specializes in providing Internet/intranet security for companies expanding into e-business and cyberspace. Of course, there are exceptions to this phenomenon but based on my research, the exceptions are few.

What is even more fascinating than the direct correlation between job, career, and type of entrepreneurial endeavors launched is the fact that many of these new entrepreneurs did in fact begin as intrapreneurs in their previous jobs. By performing his job at Shearson Lehman as if it was his own business, Chris Williams began uncovering new opportunities for achieving business growth and for providing his customers excellent service. His commitment to taking ownership of his career and his willingness to build long-term business relationships with clients served him well as he started The Williams Capital Group. Chris Williams and Wayne Armour both learned how to convert their intrapreneurial endeavors into entrepreneurial ones.

WHY IS INTRAPRENEURSHIP IMPORTANT?

As our nation and the world settle into the new millennium, the way that we do business is also shifting. The new way of doing business is shaped by numerous characteristics. These characteristics include high levels of uncertainty, diminished control of everyday matters and details of the job, increased accountability for one's actions and contributions, and the dying of the old economy and the emergence of the new economy.

The Old Economy

For the sake of this analysis of entrepreneurship, the old economy characterizes the period in our nation's business history from after World War II (1945) to the end of the Vietnam War (1973). The mode of operation during the old economy also led to changes in the American work force and their paradigms about their jobs, their positions within their companies, and the roles that they would ultimately play in the company's growth. The tenets of the old economy which proved to be true during this period included:

- America is a true meritocracy. If you are the best and brightest, you will get ahead the quickest.
- If you do your work, you'll keep your job.
- If you do your work well, you will be promoted.
- If you keep your job, you will get regular pay raises.
- If you get promoted, you will get a sizable pay raise.
- If you're loyal to your company, your company will be loyal to you.

My parents, who were born around the time of the Great Depression, lived by these tenets. My father, who worked in the steel mills of the large manufacturing plant in Baltimore, spent his life learning this system of operation. Dad used it, as much as a black man could back then, to survive and provide for his growing family. My old man lived and died by these supposedly unchanging rules.

The New Economy Emerges

Unfortunately, these old economy tenets did change and we have learned that they were not final or conclusive. America's and the world's way of doing business have been transformed. Anthony Patrick Carnevale in his book, *America and the New Economy,* suggests that globalization, new and advanced technologies, diversification, growing wealth of nations (particularly the emerging of third world economies), increasing value of time, and new competitive standards have all radically changed the way that we do business. The convergence of these trends has resulted in the emergence of a new economic order—the new economy. In the new economy there is a growing complexity in the pattern of standards that we must meet in order to win in economic competition. In the old economy, countries competed primarily on the basis of price, product, and productivity. Consequently, the nation that could produce higher volumes of goods and services using the same or fewer resources became the winner.

Carnevale further concludes that contrary to the old economy, in the new economy, our national competitiveness is based not only on productivity but also on timeliness, quality, variety, convenience, and customization. Consumers in this new economic order demand high quality, reasonable prices, variety, and flexibility, all at mass production prices. They know that if you can't meet these standards, then someone else will. Operating in such an environment requires the skills of an entrepreneur/intrapreneur.

Contrasted to the old economy, in the new economy it is understood that:

- America is not a true meritocracy. Your skills and talent alone may not move you ahead the quickest.
- The average tenure in a job in the new economy is three to five years.
- If you do your work, you might keep your job.
- If you perform excellently in your job, your reward may be that you keep your job. Promotions are not guaranteed.
- If you keep your job, you might get small or no regular pay raises.
- If you get promoted, you might get a pay raise. Even though the raise may come, it may take weeks or months before the rise is reflected in your paycheck.
- If you're loyal to your company, your company may be loyal to you. Unless of course they are forced to right-size!

THE PROBLEM EMPLOYEES HAVE THAT INTRAPRENEURS DON'T

Most people can look around and see the signs that we have transitioned from the old to the new economy. However, too many people are still operating under the rules of the old economy. This confusion has created an input/output disconnect in many of today's workers' minds.

Our lives as professionals and workers revolve around a system of inputs and outputs. We input things in life (i.e., work, study, learn) on a daily basis, that we hope will deliver the outcome (outputs) or results that we desire.

For example, it was mentioned earlier that my father worked in the old steel mills, which at that time was quite representative of the old economy ethos. In that environment you were expected to learn your specific job, put in your time, be obedient to your superiors, and stay out of trouble. If you happened to continue your education and added to your tenure, there would be certain outputs that you could expect to receive from that institution.

The type of outputs (outcomes) that you could expect, having provided all the above inputs, included things such as:

- Steady and predictable pay increases
- Steady and predictable advancement through the hierarchy
- Reasonable assurance of lifetime employment
- A sense of belonging to a large, powerful organization

Unfortunately for some, when our economy began its transformation from the old economy to the new, many people continued to operate and govern themselves according to the rules of the old economy. Consequently, we have large numbers of American workers who still focus on providing the same inputs as before but who become frustrated and disillusioned when they fail to see the outcomes they think they deserve. This frustration and disillusionment associated with this input/output disconnect will and does result in the burnout, frustration, high stress, underperformance, inefficiency, and disappointment that so many workers experience in today's work environment.

Intrapreneurship: Reconnecting the Inputs and the Outputs

For the American work force to survive and even prosper in the new economy, will require a complete change in our thinking about ourselves, our jobs, our companies, and the role that we play in our organization's growth and survival.

As corporations and government continue the process of downsizing and rightsizing, the people who make up these institutions must actively and aggressively start thinking outside the box. We must routinely challenge all business and professional paradigms that we maintain about what our value to the organization is, what our role is or should be, and how we fit in it. We must learn and understand the rules of engagement and commit to using them to our advantage.

The next important step in reconnecting the inputs and outputs of our lives is to aggressively leverage technology, especially information technology. One of the tenets of the new economy is that it will be driven and supported by technology. There is no profession today that is not directly impacted by technology. Technology, many experts have concluded, is the great equalizer of the new economy. Technology allows small businesses like my two companies, The BiTH Group, Inc. and EntreTeach.com, to effectively compete against giants like IBM, Arthur Andersen, Microsoft, and KPMG and win. Technology allows us to produce stunning proposals, conduct detailed and thorough research, market our company via the Internet, and leverage knowledge at a similar or even greater success rate than companies more than twice our size.

The third and last requirement for reconnecting the inputs and outputs in the new economy is to reengineer us into *virtual entrepreneurs.* A virtual entrepreneur takes the time and makes the effort to learn the critical skills of entrepreneurship and confidently applies these skills in whatever environment he or she finds himself or herself. The beauty of virtual entrepreneurship is that it benefits the professional whether he or she continues to work for someone else or decides to leave and launch his or her own business just as Christopher J. Williams, president and CEO of The Williams Capital Group, L.P., was able to do. For the remainder of this chapter, I use the terms *intrapreneur* and *virtual entrepreneur* interchangeably.

Let's discuss further the steps necessary to educate and develop intrapreneurs.

THE EXPANDING CIRCUMFERENCE INTRAPRENEURSHIP TRAINING MODEL

If we accept the argument that intrapreneurship will remain a key factor for achieving success in the new economy or the new economic order, the question must be asked: How do we become intrapreneurs? How do we take the skills and perspectives that are normally attributed to entrepreneurs and put them to use in our current jobs? Further, do we use these skills to add value to our organization and thus increase our value as free agents or as preparation for taking ourselves public?

The BiTH Group, Inc. is committed to training individuals and organizations to develop intrapreneurial skills and strategies. We have developed the expanding circumference intrapreneurship training model. The expanding circumference concept implies that the process of becoming an intrapreneur and the subsequent benefits to the individual and the organization are limitless and boundless. As you push yourself to embrace more and more of these qualities and tactics, you will see the universe of opportunities and realities explode before your very eyes!

As shown by the schematic in Exhibit 8.4, the model consists of a series of concentric circles that spill over into the surrounding larger circle. Circles are used to depict the critical phases of intrapreneurship because they tend to convey the feel of expansion, inclusiveness, and orderliness. The model also tries to illustrate that the process of becoming an intrapreneur first starts with self, which then spills over into understanding the rules of engagement or the principles of success in the specific environment that you're in. Having a clear understanding of the rules of engagement, the intrapreneur can then begin the process of planning the tactical steps necessary for his or her transition from employee to intrapreneur. Yet even a well-developed plan will go nowhere unless the individual has resources that are separate from himself or herself that he or she can call upon to assist in the implementation of the plan.

Let's explore the innermost circle, which is self.

SPHERE 1 (THE INNER SPHERE): THE ART OF KNOWING THY SELF

The inner circle—and some would add the most important circle—is self. One of the most important facts that I have learned from my 10-year research of successful minority and female entrepreneurs is that self is the starting point and catalyst for all human endeavors. Self is the cornerstone of all human triumphs and breakthroughs. Regardless of whether you look at Einstein and the theory of relativity, the Wright brothers and airplanes, Reginald Lewis and foods, or Earl Graves and publishing, self is always the starting point.

To prepare oneself for change and breakthrough, understanding yourself becomes that critical first step. For example, if you know yourself, then you will know if the job that you are currently performing is the right fit for you. If you know yourself, then you understand your strengths and your weaknesses. If you know yourself, you appreciate what it takes for you to be at your best most of the time.

The objective of knowing oneself is to maximize your ability and

Exhibit 8.4 The Intrapreneurship Training Model

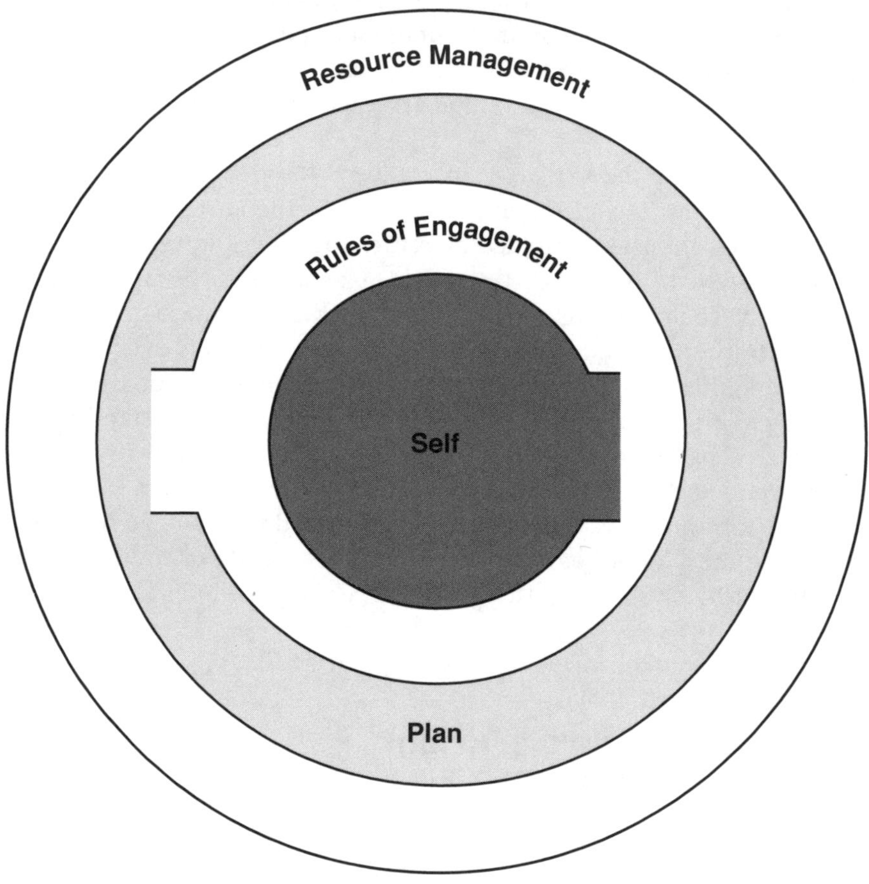

capacity to do work and to perform the essential tasks necessary for success in your field or profession. Maximizing your ability to do work suggests that you perfect the efficiency at which you routinely perform the functions essential to your organization. Likewise, maximizing your capacity to do work means that you're able to complete large volumes of tasks, often in a very short period of time, if necessary.

My studies have shown that in order for an intrapreneur to maximize his or her ability and capacity to do work and to perform tasks, she or he must recognize the interdependencies of the three selves—the physical self, the intellectual self, and the spiritual self. She or he must also commit to paying attention to and working on all three aspects of self every day of her or his life. These three selves make up what I call the *self triad of power.*

Know Thy Self Variations

The concept of self and its importance to us as human beings is not a new thing. It has been revealed to humankind since the beginning of time. Not only does the Bible speak of this concept but the ancient Kybalion (a book on hermetic philosophy) also speaks of this triad of self. Even recent scholars such as Stephen Covey have espoused the virtues of balance among the three selves of humankind.

Unfortunately, even with all the excellent guidance provided by the Holy Bible, the Kybalion, the Koran, and other authoritative sources, many people still end up with imbalance between their physical, intellectual, and spiritual selves.

In my analysis, there are three variations of the self-triad that are prevalent. I call these variations:

- The Jackie Robinson model
- The Wall Street model
- The Reverend Ike model

The Jackie Robinson model is the model of self that I recommend that people who are serious about gaining a breakthrough in their professions try to emulate. For those who may be too young to remember, Jackie Robinson was the first African American to be admitted into the all-white professional baseball league. Unwilling to settle for mediocrity on the field and refusing to succumb to the pettiness of racism off the field, Mr. Robinson excelled in his profession and became the best baseball player ever to play the game. He was an educated and intelligent man and he understood spiritually his role in life and his place in the hierarchy of the universe. He maintained a beautiful balance of physical self, intellectual self, and spiritual self.

The Wall Street model is a less flattering model. I called this the Wall Street model because it reminds me of some of my business school classmates who took jobs on the Street but lost themselves and their families in the process. People who fall into this variation of self are often very intelligent and highly educated. Because of their deep love of themselves they spend a significant amount of time working out at the health club and are often finicky eaters who are weight and appearance conscious. Unfortunately, their spiritual self is ignored and forgotten. They act like they are at the apex of the hierarchy of the universe and that everything else, including God, centers around them. These folks do fine as long as things are going their way. However, when difficult times come, as they surely will, these people, who have no spiritual base or connection, are devastated. Remember the professionals on Wall Street who attempted or contemplated committing suicide during the stock market crash of 1987? What a tragedy.

Like the Wall Street model, the Reverend Ike model is also less flattering due to the imbalance between the selves. At the risk of revealing my age here, Reverend Ike was a charismatic minister who practiced what some call a prosperity theology. He taught that you could gain prosperity through God and that Reverend Ike could help make it all happen for a small fee. I remember my father's sending money to Rev. Ike's ministry every week, even though sometimes we didn't have food on the table. People who fall into this self-model tend to pay attention spiritually. They understand what their position is in the hierarchy of the universe and appreciate the fact that they are here for a divine purpose. Unfortunately, they want God to do all the work while they do none. Although they want change and desire to improve themselves, they make no plans and take no initiative to make their dreams and desires a reality. In my opinion, they shame God and themselves.

Whatever model fits you, please understand what that means relative to you and then take steps to change it. Clearly, the first step in changing the model is to understand the physical, intellectual and spiritual selves.

Physical Self

The most obvious of selves that requires our daily attention is the physical self. Whatever we desire to do in life will require the use in some form or fashion of our physical bodies. To think of great ideas, we need our bodies. To produce outstanding proposals, we need our bodies. To meet with all the people necessary to put our great ideas into action and to bring them to fruition, we need our bodies. Whatever we do, we need our bodies. Yet, for too many people this part of self is often forgotten and neglected.

To maximize the returns on our investments in our physical selves we must pay close attention to what we eat, what we drink, what type of aerobic and anaerobic exercises we engage in, our chosen lifestyles, and how we live in general. There are many strategies and programs on the market today designed to help people maximize their physical potential—vegetarianism, tai chi, Dr. Samuel DeShay's Plus 15 program for reducing cholesterol and high blood pressure. It's important to find the one that works for you.

Furthermore, physical self is important because it provides the energy necessary for you to do what you do. The key is to maximize the amount of energy that you have and to concurrently increase the efficiency of its usage.

Once we've ascertained what energy levels we're working with we must now understand how the energy is used. What is our bodily priority for the use of our precious energy? The uses of energy listed in order of importance are as follows:

- Physical uses (to keep the vital human organs operating)
- Emotional uses (to handle the emotional stress and aggravation that we deal with every day)
- Intellectual uses (to fuel the thinking process)
- Supernatural uses (energy used to catapult the thinking process far beyond its normal or physical boundaries and constraints)

Our level of physical preparation will determine how much of our precious energy pool is consumed on the physical and emotional levels. Perfecting our physical selves means that less of our energy will be consumed responding to physical and emotional needs; thus more will be available for use in meeting our intellectual and supernatural needs. The objective of the intrapreneur is to increase the quantity of energy available for fueling the basic thinking process and then ultimately the higher level or psychic level thinking processes. Breakthrough ideas are always conceived when the intrapreneur is operating at the supernatural or psychic thinking level.

Intellectual Self

Just as important as an intrapreneur's physical self is his or her intellectual self. As is discussed in the previous section, it is important to operate at the psychic levels of the human intellect to obtain breakthrough. The intellectual self relates to the efficiency of our thinking process and the innate natural intellectual gifts that each of us possesses.

When we're thinking about the intellectual self it is a common mistake to assume that the intellectual self pertains only to one's intellect. From my observation of successful entrepreneurs and intrapreneurs I've observed an intellectual self-triad of intellectual forces that comprise the intellectual component of self. These intellectual forces are:

- Intelligence (innate and learned)
- Knowledge (the stuff of learning)
- Wisdom (experience + the internalization of experience)

Intelligence is defined as the ability to learn or understand or to deal with new or trying situations. Intelligence is further defined as the ability to apply knowledge to manipulate one's environment or to think abstractly as measured by objective criteria (as tests).

The issue of intelligence has been used throughout American history to drive a wedge between blacks and whites and between men and women. The institution of slavery was based upon the premise that Africans (blacks) were less than human and woefully intellectually inferior to whites. Even today many so-called scientists write and espouse the belief that blacks, Latinos, and other people of color are in fact genetically inferior and thus cannot learn as fast as whites.

Contrary to the race-based distribution of intelligence, my observation is that there are two pools of intelligence—the intelligence pool you're born with and the intelligence pool you acquire through making yourself smart via brain exercises. However, the pool you're born with is not a function of your race or your ethnicity. It simply is a function of your gene pool!

What works in conjunction with your intelligence is your knowledge level. Knowledge is simply defined as the stuff that you know. The more stuff you know, the more stuff you can put into your bucket. The more stuff you put into the bucket, the larger your bucket becomes.

An intrapreneur must understand that there are only three ways to get stuff into her or his knowledge bucket. The first way is to experience it personally. Another way is for someone to put it in for you by telling you. Finally, knowledge can be increased by reading and studying it. Consequently, you must perfect the skills of reading, studying, and listening for comprehension.

The integration of intelligence and knowledge leads to wisdom.

Wisdom is defined simply as the internalization of the experiences of life. This definition implies that wisdom is a function of tenure and age. While it is true that you have to live through many experiences to potentially gain from them, the key requirement is that you internalize these experiences. In other words you must remember them and understand the lessons that were learned. The learned lessons then act like videotapes that you can now play back when the need arises. The timing of the playback is very important. Wisdom tells the intrapreneur when to use her or his knowledge and when to apply her or his intelligence.

I mentioned previously that we are all born with some level of intelligence. God did not create us without some basis of starting our journey on earth. The fact is that we're actually given multiple gifts at birth that we can either choose to do something with or let waste away.

An intrapreneur needs to understand what intelligences (gifts) she or he has been endowed with. This information is important because the intrapreneur needs to align a career and professional aspirations with her or his God-given gifts in order to maximize the chances or probability of success.

To my amazement, when I ask people to share with me what intelligences (gifts) they have been blessed with, instead of answers, I often get blank stares from their faces. To assist you in ascertaining what your potential gifts might be, shown in Exhibit 8.5 are some examples of types of intelligence that we've observed in many of our clients and students.

Spiritual Self

Every student who has come through our training program on intrapreneurship has had little or no difficulty relating to or understanding the concept of physical self and intellectual self. But when we begin discussing the concept of spiritual self, people have a tendency to put up their defenses and disengage from the discussion.

No doubt, the concept of spirituality has been misused and abused for a long time. Some confuse spirituality with religiosity. In the context of this analysis, spiritual self simply means one's ability to connect with and leverage the unseen forces that guide and direct our universe. Some people may call this force God, Allah, karma, or the spiritual realm. Whatever you decide to call it, understand that these unseen forces are at work in our universe whether you know it or not. A wise intrapreneur learns how to use them to her or his advantage.

Exhibit 8.5 Potential Types of Human Intelligence

Types of Intelligence	Definition	Person(s) Who Exhibit This Intelligence
Analytical	Ability to think and reason	Wayne Armour
Spiritual	Ability to interpret the spiritual realm	Dr. Martin Luther King Jr.
Creative	Ability to connect the dots when most people don't even see the dots	Carolyn A. Wallace
Time Management	Ability to use time efficiently	Chris Williams
Organizational	Ability to arrange people in an efficient manner; ability to lead people in structured environment	John Robinson
Financial	Ability to manage money	Louis Hutt
Technological	Ability to understand and apply new technologies	C. Michael Gooden
Intuitive	Ability to have quick and ready insight, often without the benefit of direct knowledge or cognition	Eillen Dorsey
Qualitative	Ability to reduce from a general to a more specific form	Dr. Ben Carson
Quantitative	Ability to use and understand measurements of quantity	Egbert Perry
Physical	Ability to perform difficult physical acts exceptionally well	Michael Jordan
Perseverance	Ability to overcome seemingly insurmountable obstacles	African Americans and Jewish Americans
Leadership	Ability to lead people in structured and unstructured environments	Malcolm X
Interpersonal	Ability to win the trust and admiration of a myriad of people	Bill Cosby
Communicative	Ability to transfer and receive information from other people, quickly, effortlessly, and efficiently	Oprah Winfrey

SPHERE 2 (THE ENVIRONMENTAL SPHERE): BECOMING A STUDENT OF THE RULES OF ENGAGEMENT

Once an intrapreneur has established the self-component and clearly understands what it is that makes him or her special and unique, he or she must then progress to understanding the environment that he or she is in.

Understanding one's environment is important because unless he or she knows the rules of engagement (i.e., the hidden principles that govern how things get accomplished), an intrapreneur is doomed to fail.

I have worked for IBM as a systems engineer, for Procter & Gamble as a manufacturing engineer, for Westinghouse as a nuclear engineer, and DuPont as an environmental engineer. It is clear to me now how each culture and environment was so different and was governed by a set of rules of engagement or rules of success or principles of success that were unique to each firm.

For example, at IBM some of the rules of engagement, which were prevalent, included:

- Successful employees wore white shirts, power ties, dark blue suits, and black or burgundy wing tip shoes.
- Successful employees created the perception that they put the team first and themselves second. Being perceived as a team player was important.
- It was essential that you socialized not only with your first level superiors but your second and third level superiors as well.

For Westinghouse some of the observed rules of engagement included:

- An employee's technical competence was valued more than his or her managerial or business competence.
- Successful people had a reputation for working long hours and prided themselves on how many hours/week they worked.
- Academically astute research and careful due diligence were prized and respected. It was acceptable to make a mistake as long as you had completed and documented the proper level of research.

The Four Groups of Rules of Engagement

As an intrapreneur seeks to bring new products, services, and ideas to her or his environment, she or he should understand that there are four sets of rules in the environment that must be mastered, understood, and leveraged. The ability to initiate change and earn the respect of her or his peers is a function of how well she or he applies these rules to the intrapreneurship development strategy. These four sets of rules are:

- Rules of preparation
- Rules for building

- Rules of self-actualization
- Rules for maintaining

The rules of preparation are those rules that dictate how an intrapreneur should prepare himself or herself to complete the tasks that are necessary for creating new products, services, and ideas. In many environments the most critical requirement is for the intrapreneur first to build trust and credibility among his or her peers. For example, in IBM one of the rules of preparation was that as a young systems engineer, you had to team with a senior systems engineer who was well known and well respected. Young engineers, fresh from college, would commit strange and unnatural acts in order to be assigned to the right senior systems engineer. Conversely, it was an acknowledged reality that if you had the misfortune to be teamed with someone who was perceived to be a loser, you were automatically assumed to be outside the chosen ones mainstream. Not being one of the chosen ones meant that you would miss ever participating in the most lucrative and rewarding engineering opportunities.

Another example of the rules of preparation at a major information technology corporation was in the area of training and technical certification. In this company it was an unwritten rule that all successful software programmers were to attend at least 30 days of outside technical training per fiscal year. This rule never showed up in the corporate policy handbook, but it was an abiding rule that all the successful software programmers understood and followed. What was magical about 30 days I will never know. Nevertheless, to some degree, this obscure rule determined who was successful and who was not.

Rules of preparation such as the 30-day rule quickly lead (acquiesce) into rules concerning the building of one's skills and credibility. The rules for building are those that, when followed, allow the intrapreneur to add to his or her skill set and to sharpen the skills that he or she has already acquired. For example, one of the most sought-after engineering groups in the DuPont Company was an organization called the Field Engineering Group. Although there were numerous other engineering organizations within the DuPont Company, the Field Engineering Group was recognized as the place where all the rising star engineers tended to be assigned. Being in this engineering section meant that you were given multiple and varied engineering assignments in different divisions of the company. One year you might be assigned to the Chemical, Dyes, and Pigments Division. The next year you could get an assignment in Polymer Products, Photo Products, Human Resources, Research & Development Laboratories, or Public Relations. The entire domain of DuPont was yours for the taking.

Consequently, if you wanted to make a name for yourself in engineering within the DuPont Company, it was understood by some that you needed to have a stint in the Field Engineering Group at some point early in your career. Of course, there were successful engineers in the DuPont Company who did not come through the Field Group but it seemed to take them longer to reach the same level in the organization.

Having mastered the rules of preparing for your professional journey and the rules of building on your acquired skills and reputation, the intrapreneur must then understand the rules of self-actualization. These rules dictate what guidelines must be followed in order to set oneself apart from his or her peers. When I competed in track meets, we used to call the runner's ability to outrun his opponents as he was approaching the finish line, his kick. The rules of self-actualization determine the intrapreneur's ability to throw in his kick or afterburners in order to distance himself from the masses.

An example of what the rules for self-actualization looked like can be found in another major technology company. In this company there were numerous rules on how to self-actualize within that environment, but the two dominant ones exercised were being able to repeatedly save your group from disaster and second, being nominated for the Golden Circle.

Saving one's group from disaster basically meant that you had to take what seemed to be an impossible business situation and miraculously turn it around. This could have been as straightforward as making a gigantic sale on the last day of the fourth quarter and thus allowing the group to exceed its quota for the year. Or it could have been your ability to win back a major customer who had left your company to go with another vendor. Employees who formed a habit of rescuing the company in many different ways ultimately would end up in the Golden Circle. This was a special award that was given each year to the outstanding employees. People who achieved this honor were treated like they walked on water. They were sent away to exotic places for a week or more, were wined and dined, had access to the best amenities that money could buy, and were showered with first class entertainment and allowed to mingle with famous celebrities. When you got to the Golden Circle, you knew you were now in the club. Either way these two rules defined who would be set apart from the masses.

The Importance of Maintenance

Even if an intrapreneur understands and is able to apply the rules of preparation, building, and self-actualization, she or he will flounder and fail if she is unable to maintain what she has built. This set of rules echoes the words of pop singer Janet Jackson when she asks, in one of her hit songs, what you've done for her lately. Or to use a sports analogy, you can't win tomorrow's baseball games on yesterday's home runs. The rules of maintenance determine what an intrapreneur must do to maintain the benefits of his or her accomplishments to date. Benefits, once accrued, must then be protected from any subtle but persistent erosion. Protecting the benefits of one's labor requires work and great diligence.

The rules surrounding maintenance vary from organization to organization. In one financial services company a rule of maintenance was that in order to preserve your accomplishments you had to be promoted at least every two to three years. The assumption was that as you moved up the ladder you would automatically have a broader audience to which to play back your home runs. Another company had a set of maintenance rules that made it necessary for the rising stars to be able to recruit other rising stars and to build a pipeline of such recognized talent. By cloning yourself you in essence were reliving and reminding the organization of your past accomplishments and the value they created for the company.

Understanding all four sets of rules of engagement in your environment are necessary for all serious intrapreneurs to develop new opportunities for their companies. The better these rules are mastered, the quicker an intrapreneur is trusted and respected, and the easier it will be for him or her to usher in change, new ideas, new products, and new services. Yet a discussion like this one begs the question, "How do you determine what the rules of engagement are for your environment?"

How Do You Determine the Rules of Engagement for Your Environment?

Understanding that there are four sets of rules of engagement that an intrapreneur should be aware of and become successful at mastering is the first step to success. However, I have observed that many people have difficulty interpreting what the rules of engagement are for their respective organizations. Although there are no hard and fast rules for determining these principles, I do have some suggestions on how you might begin to construct what these rules are for your environment.

Believe it or not, there are some organizations that actually publish or document what the rules of engagement are for their particular organization. These rules are often not disguised as merely suggestions on how to get things done in a timely fashion. But make no mistake about it, if you can decipher or read between the lines of these recommendations, you will be able to discern the principles of success that govern your work environment.

The next best way to identify your company's rules of engagement is simply to observe the actions and tactics of those around you who are deemed to be successful. It has been said many times by numerous authors that success leaves a trail. Furthermore, success can be modeled and duplicated. Thus, determining the rules of success in your environment could be as simple as modeling the actions of the superstars within your organization. Of course you have to get close enough to these people to really understand how they operate and think. This leads to my next and final thought on how to determine what the rules of engagement are for your organization.

Probably the best way to uncover the rules of engagement for your organization is to secure yourself a mentor in the organization who is willing to *teach* you what the rules of engagement are. Discerning what the rules are from written documents and observing the actions of others are good approaches to use but are open to error of interpretation. Having a mentor who is successful in that environment and can teach you the rules of engagement is the most efficient approach.

Although I would recommend a hybrid approach that consists of studying all printed guidelines and rules that are published by your firm, observing the habits of key individuals in the organization, and seeking out a strong mentor, the important thing is to recognize that there are rules of engagement, which you must master, and the responsibility of identifying them is yours.

SPHERE 3 (THE PLANNING SPHERE): BREATHING LIFE INTO THOUGHTS

Once you have worked on an understanding of self and the rules of engagement for your environment, it becomes critical to develop the plan or bridge necessary to achieve the intrapreneurial results that you desire.

Sphere 3, the planning sphere, aggressively pulls from the other three spheres to develop the plan.

Sphere 3 of the intrapreneurship model focuses on helping the intrapreneur to bridge his or her present situation with the future objectives that have been defined as the desired outcome. Realizing that there is always tension between your present and your future, the wise intrapreneur is eager to spend large amounts of time planning and plotting to assure that the benefits of practicing intrapreneurship accrue to him or her and the organization.

The first task in developing the intrapreneur's plan to enhance his or her value to the organization and to develop new products and services is to conduct a key interpersonal exercise. This relates to what I call the principle of gratitude.

The principle of gratitude suggests that it is difficult and in some cases impossible to move to the next level of success until there is a sincere and respectful appreciation for the gifts and assets that an intrapreneur already possesses. Generally speaking these assets can be broken up into three major categories—time, talent, and treasures. We're all given twenty-four hours a day to live, seven days a week to strive, and fifty-two weeks a year to achieve. Likewise, we all have been given multiple talents and gifts with which we are to make a contribution to God, country, family, humanity, and yes self. Lastly, all of us have some measure of treasures. Treasures are the stuff that we own—houses, automobiles, cash, stocks, bonds, relationships, and so on.

The principle of gratitude says that an intrapreneur will never be able to leverage his or her three assets—time, talent, and treasures—until he or she first learns to appreciate them. It is impossible to leverage what you do not value. This principle introduces the concept of arduous striving, a concept that trains the intrapreneur to appreciate the assets that he or she does have, and work to improve them so he or she can achieve any desired outcomes.

The Planning Tools

After the intrapreneur has exercised the principle of gratitude, he or she can then begin to develop and engineer the plan—a plan for change. In planning for developing new tools, products, or services for his or her organization, I suggest two planning tools that can be utilized immediately in planning for intrapreneurial change. These are the 2 × 2 Rule and the five modules of intrapreneurial planning.

The 2 × 2 Rule

The 2 × 2 Rule is a visioning planning exercise that I developed in my work with entrepreneurs and intrapreneurs. The first step in using this tool is to envision the outcome that the intrapreneur desires. This may be the development of a new family of software for managing the mushrooming Internet traffic.

After spending time creating the vision for the future, the intrapreneur then begins to work backward from the vision to the present, as shown in Exhibit 8.6. At each level, the question is asked, "What must I do to achieve this outcome?" The intrapreneur must search for at least two answers to this question before he or she can then move to the next level. This same question and answer process continues through each level of the tree until he or she reaches a level where the tasks that are outlined are those that can be accomplished today. Once the intrapreneur is deep enough into the tree that he has isolated tasks which can be accomplished today, the intrapreneur then begins working his or her way back into the future in the direction of the vision. As you probably have ascertained by now, the nodes illustrated in the tree represent the components of the intrapreneur's business plan.

The 5 Steps of Intrapreneurial Planning

As for an entrepreneur, an intrapreneur must plan for change and breakthrough in his or her environment. Every opportunity that he or she

Exhibit 8.6 Extrapolating the Future Diagram

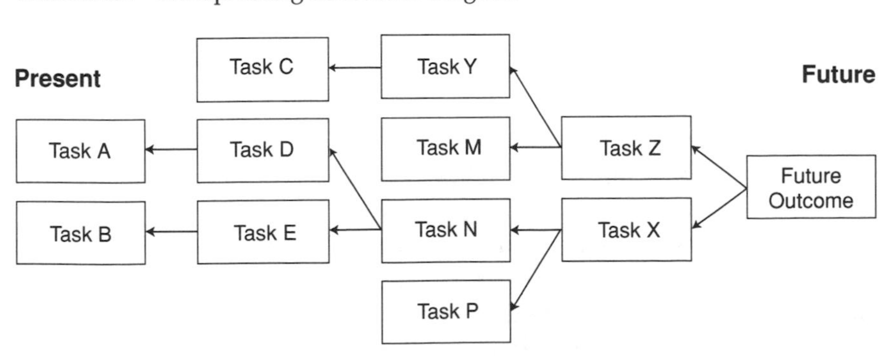

uncovers to add value to the organization and to set him or her apart from the masses must be explored as if it were his or her own private business deal. If I am a systems engineer for IBM and I want to consider providing my clients new and different services, I had better complete my due diligence on the matter to be able to convince IBM management that, by supporting my project, the company will benefit. If I am a marketing manager at Procter & Gamble's Cosmetics Division and I have decided that I want to expand my products more into the black and Hispanic markets, I'd better have done my market analysis, projected the potential cash flow and profits from this expansion, and thought through an implementation strategy to make it all happen in the time frame that I projected. Whatever the scenario, proper planning is the intrapreneur's best friend.

Proper planning does not have to be a mystery. All one has to do is simply put himself or herself in the shoes of an entrepreneur and ask the question If this project that I'm engaging in was the cornerstone of my own business, how would I proceed? The answer to that question is to always abide by the following planning steps:

- Identify product or service.
- Test the idea before making total commitment.
- Conduct the market analysis.
- Complete the financial analysis.
- Complete the business plan.

Step 1: Identify Product or Service

Intrapreneurs are adept at thinking of new products or services that will add value to their organizations. Maintaining a fresh supply of ideas for new products and services to meet your customer's needs requires that you allow your creative side to dominate. While there are no hard and fast rules on how this is to be done, here are some suggestions:

1. Remember that the job you're doing today will look quite different five years from now. Some business analysts predict, and my personal experience confirms, that 80 percent of the products that we will use five years from now do not exist today. This phenomenon of rapid change presents great opportunity for the wise intrapreneur.

2. Maintain a journal and keep a tape recorder with you at all times. All of us at one time or another have what I call flashes of brilliance. These flashes represent those times when we think of new and promising ideas on how to solve the world's problems. The challenge is that these flashes come at the most inopportune times. They may come in a dream while you're sleeping. They may come while you're working out at the health club. They may come while you're on the red eye flight from Los Angeles to New York. The key thing to remember is that you must capture these thoughts and ideas on paper or on tape before they get away. It is critical to keep your recording device with you or near you all the time.

3. Make it a habit to get out and be around people. This is the good way to spark your own thoughts and provide you some form of reality check. It is powerful how human beings feed off the ideas, successes, and failures of other human beings.

Step 2: Test the Idea before Making a Total Commitment

Carolyn Green, a successful manager at Procter & Gamble, has perfected the technique of testing her intrapreneurial ideas internally and externally, before making a total commitment to them. Carolyn recognizes that there is a tremendous payoff when you take the time to test your idea for a new product, service, or even business strategy. The first thing to do when testing your idea is to study the issue carefully by reviewing all publications that address the particular idea. This due diligence can consist of library and Internet searches. If you decide to use the library it is best to use the library of the graduate business school nearest your home. Even though I now live more than 500 miles from my alma mater The Tuck School of Business at Dartmouth College, I will often make the trip back to school when in the midst of some heavy-duty research (besides, it's nice to go back and see old professors and friends).

After studying the idea very carefully, it is prudent to then interview people, both internal to and outside your company. People on the inside can give you a corporate perspective on your idea and also provide some form of reality check. But be careful not to let insiders, who might be myopic in their thinking, discourage you from initiating a valuable breakthrough. Interviewing people on the outside also serves as a reality check but can also provide a new and refreshing look at an old problem. Last, throughout the whole process remember to assume a long-term time horizon in analyzing whether your new ideas make sense or not. Using a short-term time horizon to analyze the ideas may not provide enough time to allow them to take hold and provide a reasonable return.

Step 3: Conduct a Market Analysis

As we discuss at the beginning of this chapter on intrapreneurship, all intrapreneurs have both suppliers and customers. Having customers implies that you have or will have something to sell. Whatever intrapreneurial idea you come up with for a new product or service, for it to succeed it must have customers who will buy it. Marketing analysis and strategy must therefore become an integral component of every plan. In planning for this idea a marketing analysis must seek to answer the following questions:

1. Who is the customer you are trying to serve with this new product or service? How does he or she look? What defines him or her?
2. Where is your customer located? Internally? Externally? Nationally? Internationally?
3. How will you get the goods or services to him or her quickly and efficiently? Mail order? New service delivery staff?
4. What existing goods and services are in competition with the new idea that you're proposing? How is your new offering different? Better?
5. What convincing argument can you construct to convince a customer to switch from what they're using now to your product?

Step 4: Complete the Financial Analysis

If after completion of the market analysis you now feel that there is sufficient opportunity and rationale to proceed, the next step is to assess the total financial impact to the organization. The key point to remember in any intrapreneurial analysis or endeavor is that every action that you initiate must in the end add value to the organization. If it does not add value then it is safe to conclude that it is not worth doing.

Assessing what is considered adding value and what is not must be done carefully. I've learned that when doing the financial analysis the intrepreneur must look for both tangible and intangible financial value.

Tangible financial values are the items that are the most visible and obvious in most business transactions. These tangible items include increased revenues, reductions in operating costs, increased net worth of the company, enhanced retained earnings, mushrooming market value, and competitive earnings per share ratios. The intrepreneur often captures tangible financial value when she or he completes some form of profit and loss statement for the project. Depending on the needs of the company additional due diligence may require the development of cash flow statements, operational budgets, and market share growth projections.

Intangible financial considerations, while often ignored or discounted, are in some cases more valuable than the tangible ones. Intangible financial value tends to take a few years before the benefits are totally realized. For example, an intrapreneur may champion an initiative that actually costs the company more money in the beginning but in fact may reduce customer complaints and enhance customer satisfaction. The initiative may also make the customer more likely to become a repeat customer and maintain loyalty to the intrapreneur's brand. The loyalty exhibited by the customers and the new customers whom they bring in because of their loyalty to the brand have the resulting effect of increasing market share for the company and lifting profitability. This increased productivity then allows the company to increase the funding that it commits to research and development and the development of new and advanced products. The additional funding also allows the company to perfect its marketing strategy and positions the firm to consolidate existing markets and to enter new ones.

What is the financial value of the above scenario? You tell me. Yet it is clear that there would be a value-added proposition here simply because the intrapreneur took the initiative to enhance customer satisfaction. All would agree that the leveraging effect of this action would pay dividends to the company for years to come.

Step 5: Compose the Business Plan

The last step of the essential steps for completion of your intrapreneurial due diligence is to construct your business plan. Writing of the business plan may not necessarily be of the same detail that an entrepreneur might compose for an entrepreneurial endeavor. However, documentation of one's analysis is essential if your audience is to take you seriously. The reality is that the intrapreneurial idea does not become real until it finds its place on paper in a document.

Is It Worth It?

Determining if an intrapreneurial project is worth pursuing is simply in the eyes of the beholder. My experience and research indicate that it is always worth it to pursue these value-adding opportunities. While it is true that making the effort to forge new breakthroughs at your place of employment may not always pay off in recognition, increased earnings, and position, the *process* that you go through in evaluating new possibilities does and will pay great dividends. The more you go through the intrapreneurial process outlined previously the better you will get at it and the more opportunities you will realize as a result of going through the exercise. Yes, it is difficult to do and time consuming, but remember that opportunities in life will never be realized without putting in time and effort.

SPHERE 4 (THE RESOURCE MANAGEMENT SPHERE): LEVERAGING ALL AVAILABLE RESOURCES

The last sphere in the intrapreneurial model is the one that explains the importance of leveraging all resources available to help you be successful in your intrapreneurial endeavors. While a well-thought-out plan will begin to propel you in the direction of your dreams, it is safe to assume that you will not he able to achieve the outcomes you desire without the help of others around you. History has shown time and time again that great people are able to do great things partially because they have mastered the art of persuading people to help them. This phase of the model attempts to provide perspective on what resources are available to aid you in your intrapreneurial endeavors and how you must go about leveraging these resources.

Who and What Are Your Resources?

Webster's dictionary defines resources as something to which one has recourse in times of difficulty. Let's be clear. The shift from an employee to intrapreneur is rife with difficulty and uncertainty. It is rare that a person is able to make this transition on his or her own, without assistance and support from certain people in and outside the organization.

The three groupings of resources that I have observed in my research are self-based resources, internal resources, and external resources. Self-based resources are the obvious ones that include our ability to think creatively, to persevere, to build relationships, to garner trust, and to meet commitments. Internal resources are those resources internal to our organization that are usually stakeholders in our situation. These individuals include executive management, middle management, first line managers, peers and teammates. External resources are those resources that are outside your internal organization and may not necessarily be stakeholders in your intrapreneurial project but who can contribute to your success. These resources include individuals at other companies who have been successful at implementing intrapreneurial initiatives in their respective firms. This group could also include any publications written on the subject of intrapreneurship that could be found at the library or on the Internet. External resources could also include your spouse, family members, neighbors, and business associates.

How Do You Win Resource Commitment?

The art of winning resource commitment can be a challenging and often frightening endeavor. Although gaining commitment may seem a bit elusive, there is a process that has been proven to work time and time again. The suggested process is as follows:

Step 1: Take the first step and *ask* for help! It is amazing how many people need and desire help but never ask.

Step 2: Once you've gotten a few minutes alone with your resource, attempt to build rapport with him or her. Build on your responses to develop two-way communications.

Step 3: Identify a facet of your intrapreneurial idea that may interest or fascinate your resource. Provide transition to the business aspect of your meeting.

Step 4: Establish the linkage between your concept and the needs of the business. Use the funneling technique to sift out the specific needs that the resource has identified.

Step 5: Summarize the needs and verify your understanding of what those needs are.

Step 6: Using an assumptive statement, ask the resource for his or her help and support in initiating the intrapreneurial endeavor. It may be necessary to summarize the identified benefits and then do a second close.

Step 7: Present a plan of action for both you and the resource. Be clear on what you want him or her to do and what you will be responsible for doing. Make sure that you monitor performance of the assigned tasks.

Step 8: Show your gratitude to the person for the help he or she has provided. Send a note, card, or e-mail documenting your appreciation. Let others know that this person has helped you. Contrary to popular belief, good news also travels extremely fast.

EPILOGUE: AN INTRAPRENEUR'S LESSON FROM HANNIBAL'S MARCH TO ROME

Thank you for taking this journey from entrepreneurship to intrapreneurship with me. I pray that you have benefited from the investment of time in reading my book.

As I contemplate where we are economically as a community and where we need to move entrepreneurially and intrapreneurially, I'm reminded of the many lessons I learned from my professor of business strategy at the Tuck School of Business at Darmouth College, Dr. James Brian Quinn. Dr. Quinn, arguably one of the most brilliant minds around on business policy and entrepreneurship, was known to use military history and strategies to illustrate the key principles of successful business strategy. The most notable of all military strategists and probably the blackest, outside Colin Powell, was Hannibal. History books herald his cunning, bravery, intelligence, and will to fight against overwhelming odds.

Hannibal, an African, lived about 218 years before the birth of Jesus, in a North African city called Carthage. Like many other leaders of that era, Hannibal despised the Romans. Instead of accepting Rome's claim on his country, Hannibal decided that he would take action and do something about this situation. Unlike many of his counterparts, he refused to focus on the size and power of Rome. Instead of adopting a defensive strategy he embraced an offensive strategy and set out to conquer Rome.

With an estimated 90,000 foot soldiers, 12,000 horses, and 37 elephants, Hannibal set out in 218 B.C. to attack Rome. Hannibal brilliantly implemented his planned attack on Rome. First crossing the Pyrenees and then the Alps, he craftily descended on the startled Roman army. Even after losing more than 80 percent of his army during the actual march to Rome, Hannibal still was able to wage war on the Roman Empire for 15 years before he was ultimately beaten back by the Romans.

As you contemplate the effort that will be required to transition yourself from employee to intrapreneur, my mind conjures up images of Hannibal and his skirmishes with the mighty Romans. Understand, if your company has been operating under the old economy rules for a very long time, it will be difficult, but not impossible, for you to implement your new intrapreneurship strategy.

Yet like Hannibal, you must not allow yourself to focus on the enormity of the business and professional challenges that you face. Instead you must look for creative ways to seek breakthrough in your organization and outsmart the internal forces that resist change.

The first thing to do in order to accomplish this transition is not to focus on the obstacles preventing you from becoming an intrapreneur but to look beyond them. All of us have certain sets of paradigms that we use to manage our way through life. Unfortunately, some of our paradigms become psychological bars that tend to lock up our minds and disrupt our creative thinking. Focusing on the obstacles only serves to empower them, thus diverting valuable human energy from more productive intrapreneurship implementation tasks.

Second, diligently use the intrapreneurship training model discussed in this book. I have delivered this training to such firms as Procter & Gamble, Prudential Insurance Company, the U.S. Department of Health and Human Services, the Social Security Administration, and the U.S. Department of Agriculture and have collected enough data to know that the model works.

Third, you must assume full responsibility for your career and your success. Not assuming full responsibility means that you have given the responsibility to someone else. Whenever you disown a problem, you in effect relinquish all power to solve it. Take ownership and take no prisoners.

Last, take to heart the outer concentric circle (resource management) of the intrapreneurship training model. Remember, although you must lead and assume the risk of being a change master, you cannot and must not try to make this journey alone. Constantly seek out win-win propositions with the various stakeholders in your organization.

9

Where Do We Go from Here? 17 Strategies for Entrepreneurial Success

"We will either find a way or make one."
Hannibal

WHERE DO WE GO FROM HERE?

As the minority community contemplates where it should go from here in order to achieve economic justice in America, it should draw strength from the epic battles that Hannibal and other black soldiers have fought.

Like Hannibal, the minority community must not focus on the enormity of the economic empowerment problems facing it. It must instead look for new ways and strategies to outmaneuver and outsmart the forces in American society that seek to keep the community in a powerless position. This chapter attempts to construct a strategy to be used as a guideline in creating tactical responses to this economic dilemma.

When this research began a few years ago, it was determined that the success or failure of this project would depend upon the degree to which the following objectives were met:

- To bring the issue of economic empowerment of the African American community to the forefront of all the other issues that confront our community today and to keep it there.
- To underscore the critical role that African American entrepreneurs play in completing the power structure of the community,

thus broadening and deepening the power base of all African Americans.

- To stimulate the latent entrepreneurial spirit in some of us and motivate these would-be entrepreneurs to engage in the business development process, thus accelerating the formation and growth of businesses within the black community.

Can we achieve these objectives? Yes, we can. Although I do believe the problem we face is a serious one, I have never doubted the minority community's resolve and determination in solving the problem. Being an engineer by training, I've always been one to look at a problem logically, dissect the critical pieces of it, and then develop a set of alternatives that would provide viable solutions to the problem. Consequently, as a fitting conclusion to this work, I've included a strategic analysis of our community's economic position and some tactical and strategic suggestions that will allow us to capitalize on our strengths while acknowledging our weaknesses.

Based on strengths and weaknesses as shown in Exhibit 9.1 and a review of external factors that affect the community, Exhibit 9.2 lists both the opportunities that can be realized along with the threats that could easily derail any progress in pursuing these opportunities.

With a clear understanding of the black community's strengths and its current weaknesses, Exhibit 9.2 outlines some opportunities that capitalize on our strengths but takes into consideration our weaknesses. However, success is never guaranteed because there are always threats lurking on the periphery that serve to impede or destroy any attempt to capitalize on the opportunities. Based on this analysis, it is suggested that the African American community's strategy for the 2000s and beyond be conducted as follows.

W. E. Deming, one of the founding fathers of statistical process control and statistical quality control, once said, "A shared and commonly accepted philosophy of excellence helps provide constancy of purpose."

It is indeed constancy of purpose that will allow African Americans to rid themselves of economic lethargy and dependency and assume their rightful positions as leaders of commerce and business. The philosophy and strategy in Exhibits 9.3 and 9.4 summarize the author's views on what the African American community must do to achieve economic empowerment and maintain a constancy of purpose.

Exhibit 9.1 Strengths and Weaknesses of the African American Community

Strengths	Weaknesses
Strong and persevering people	Pervasive mental block concerning success and business development
Largest minority group in America	Failure of the system to educate and prepare our young people properly. Lack of training in technologies
Significant buying power (~$400–500 billion/yr.)	Continue to operate outside the old boy financial network
Cultural diversity within our own culture	Serious breakdown of values within the family unit
Changing work force demographics will make blacks, other nonwhites, and women the dominant groups in the new work force in the new millennium	Lack of clear and directed focus by young blacks Infatuation with drug culture and alcohol
Recipients of a proud and rich history dating back to ancient civilization	Failure to control or participate in the local economies within the black community
Overrepresentation in the areas of professional sports and entertainment. Collectively, this group represents a potentially significant source of investment capital.	Owns only 3.4% of the U.S. business firms and generates less than 1% of total business receipts
Growing and more astute African American middle class.	Make up a small percentage of the overall American population
Maintain pockets of political strength throughout the country, mostly in the major urban centers.	Overall, the black community finds itself in a weak economic position.
Maintain strong leading edge educational institutions to train and prepare our young people, which will help move the community forward.	High black-on-black crime in major cities. Potential for proliferation of weak family structure due to increasing teen pregnancies and fatherless homes.

Overall, the statements of purpose in Exhibit 9.3 underscore the point that the economic philosophy of black nationalism is simply for the black community to take control of its own economies. Furthermore, if blacks fail to gain at least this control, their power base will be eroded further, leading to the ultimate annihilation of the community.

To chart our course for the new millennium and to marshal our collective resources to achieve our economic objectives, the strategic vision in Exhibit 9.4 is offered.

To support this strategy and to deliver the stated mission and move toward our new vision, strategic choices will have to be made that channel our energies, enthusiasm, and initiatives. By concentrating on these

Exhibit 9.2 Opportunities and Threats

Opportunities	**Threats**
Actively participate in emerging technologies such as the Internet, health care, telecommunications, Web development, and distance learning	Escalating racism, bigotry, and indifference of white America. Class warfare.
Leverage political gain and strength effectively in the urban areas.	Weakened economy over the long term.
Regain control of the economic base within the black community	Deterioration of the family structure.
Develop mentor program between the African American entrepreneurs and promising young talent within the community	A lost generation of young blacks due to crime, drugs, violence, poverty, television, fratricide, and indifference.
Teach entrepreneurship to our young people at a very young age.	Failure of our community to engage in the economic development opportunities that abound.
Emphasize the private enterprise option to young professionals	
Actively engage in the economic mainstream of society.	Loss of desire to compete and to win.
Promote joint ventures between black-owned companies and white mainstream businesses.	Failure to take *full* ownership of our economic destiny.

Exhibit 9.3 African Americans' Economic Statement of Purpose

1. Provide services and products that are competitively priced, of superior quality and value, and best fill the needs of consumers within the black community, the overall American society, and ultimately the world.

2. Achieve that purpose through the rapid formation of business enterprises within the black community initially and later within the overall community. Provide a working environment where the best and brightest young talent are allowed to hone their business skills and assume prominent business leadership roles.

3. Through the successful pursuit of this commitment, expect the goods and services produced by members of the community to be second to none and to achieve leadership share and profit positions, and as a result of this commitment, black businesses and the black community will grow and prosper.

4. Become expert professionals in the fields of law, medicine, business, commerce, education, science, and the trades. Recognize the value of the proper education and training in developing young people to assume leadership roles in local and national economies.

5. Work effectively together to achieve common objectives; work individually and as a group to produce superior business results.

6. Value others' differences. It is these differences that produce a diverse and powerful community. Members of the community assume ownership of their individual and collective destinies and are committed to total excellence. The community recognizes that in order for it to grow, each individual must experience personal growth and be valued as an individual.

Exhibit 9.4 The Black Community's Strategic Vision

The Purpose

To accumulate wealth within the community by first meeting the consumers' needs as well as those of the residents and the aggregate community better than anyone else

The Mission

- Control the businesses in our local communities!
- Accumulate wealth!
- Engage in business opportunities nationally and internationally!

Strategies

The overall strategy should entail diverting sources of capital that exist within and outside the African American community in lucrative business ventures that regain control of our local economies. This will thrust us into leadership positions in the national and international business arena.

areas of strategic focus and working effectively together across all disciplines, we will achieve sustainable economic momentum. The suggested implementation strategies are as follows:

1. Leverage the black-based political muscle.
2. Aggressively engage in new and emerging technologies.
3. Regain control of local economies.
4. Develop mentor programs for potential young, black entrepreneurs.
5. Teach entrepreneurship to our children.
6. Actively engage in national and international mainstream.
7. Gain ownership of strategically positioned mainstream businesses.
8. Engage in joint ventures with mainstream companies.
9. Create and leverage business network among minority professional athletes, entertainers, and aspiring minority entrepreneurs.
10. Leverage the power and influence of the black clergy.
11. Promote sports transmutation.

12. Create business incubator sites within strategic locations.
13. Ensure that the talented 10 percent (of African Americans) assume their destiny.
14. Encourage one another to look between and beyond the bars and not at them.
15. Develop joint ventures with other minority companies.
16. Increase buying and selling among minority companies.
17. Keep your head to the sky.

STRATEGY 1: LEVERAGE THE BLACK-BASED POLITICAL MUSCLE

When Maynard Jackson was mayor of Atlanta, Georgia, the state was in the process of expanding its local airport. Initially, of all the money being spent to rebuild the airport, very little was going to minority firms. Using the weight of his office, Mayor Jackson postponed the completion of that multimillion dollar complex until minority businesses were provided an opportunity to participate. Mr. Jackson had leveraged his political muscle to fortify the position of minority businesses.

Minority political leaders need to learn from Mayor Jackson and become more aggressive in championing the cause of minority enterprises. Keep in mind that leveraging a community's political strength is not new to the American scene. European immigrants, the Irish, the Italians, the Jews, and others always used their newly won political muscle to help build up the small and burgeoning businesses within their communities. With the recent attempts by the right wing elements of our society to circumvent our hard-fought business gains, it has become increasingly difficult to legislate fairness into the business arena for minority businesses, but new and creative ways must be found to accomplish this objective.

STRATEGY 2: AGGRESSIVELY ENGAGE IN NEW AND EMERGING TECHNOLOGIES

Typically, all new products or industries move through a life cycle from the time of their inception to their replacement with new or substitute products or industries. This life cycle typically experiences three major phases as shown in Exhibit 9.5.

Exhibit 9.5 Product or Company Life Cycle

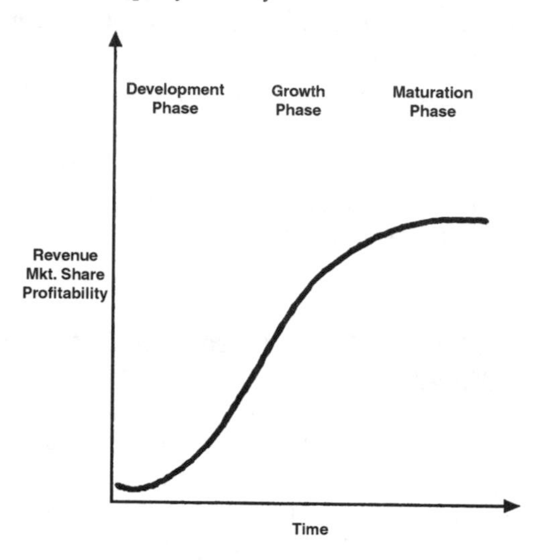

1. Development phase
2. Growth phase
3. Maturation phase

To take full advantage of this industry, you must first enter it as it moves into its growth phase or point of momentum. In this phase, you as an investor or player will experience explosive growth in a relatively short period of time. The maturation phase is the point at which the industry has shaken out; there remain a few competitors and the aggregate market size has peaked. In general, it would be unwise to enter a market or industry that has moved into the maturation phase.

There are, however, some industries that have moved into the maturation phase and still provide some opportunities for sharp and creative entrepreneurs. These industries are what I call the bread and butter industries, those that will continue to grow and thrive as long as there are people. These industries include food, clothing, and pharmaceuticals. Although the annual growth of such markets may not be very aggressive, they will typically experience positive growth over the long term, thus making them prime acquisition candidates.

One of the biggest mistakes we can make is to blindly embrace old and mature technologies and industries at the expense of participating in new and exciting ones. The bread and butter industries should be used as anchor industries to generate cash while we leverage these companies to capitalize on new markets. Some examples of these new industries or technologies might include:

- Systems integration
- Cellular communications
- Total quality management
- Microgravity research
- Small satellite technologies
- Internet technologies
- Web development
- LAN/WAN/MAN engineering
- Telecommunications
- Wireless communications
- Energy and environmental products
- Materials recycling
- Automation and advanced manufacturing
- Distance learning

Along with the preceding technologies, the National Center for Advanced Technologies has also identified the following technologies as critical to America's competitiveness and survival:

- Rocket propulsion
- Advanced sensors
- Ultra-reliable electronic systems
- Air-breathing propulsion
- Advanced composites
- Artificial intelligence
- Optical information processing
- Computational science
- Software development
- Superconductivity
- Advanced metallic structures

By penetrating these new technologies, or the industries that will support their development, we can position ourselves for future opportunities and growth.

STRATEGY 3: REGAIN CONTROL OF LOCAL ECONOMIES

With all due respect to Asian and Jewish people, there is no way that the local grocery, pharmacy, cleaners, and convenience food stores in an African American community should be owned and operated by anyone but members of that community. If these other groups are residents of the local community and participate in it there is no problem. People who serve only to drain resources away from the African American community and concurrently show disrespect to our people, must be replaced by African American business owners.

The beauty in these small, community-based bread and butter businesses is that you don't need a college education in order to own and operate them. Anyone with some basic smarts, energy, and drive can open a store and make it work. This must be the first action point in our strategy. The African American community must regain its local economy and then use this economic base to leverage into opportunities outside the local economy. Regaining our local businesses provides not only some economic muscle, but also serves to rebuild our confidence and help our people reverse the negative mind-set about our ability to perform in business.

STRATEGY 4: DEVELOP MENTOR PROGRAMS FOR POTENTIAL YOUNG, BLACK ENTREPRENEURS

The community's greatest asset is its young people. In spite of all the negative press that our young people receive, I'm still convinced that there exists a critical mass of young black men and women who are hardworking, trustworthy, talented, and energetic enough to become the next generation of business leaders. Unfortunately, they will never be allowed to blossom unless they're given the opportunity to polish their skills in a real business environment.

I look to those members of the entrepreneurial ranks to identify this talent, commit resources to them, and make it their mission to nurture them until they're ready to venture out on their own. Those business leaders may have sons or daughters to fill this role. Using your son or daughter is great, but entrepreneurs need to reach beyond familial boundaries to capture others who may not have the good fortune of having mothers and fathers in business.

STRATEGY 5: TEACH ENTREPRENEURSHIP TO OUR CHILDREN

Given the resources that they have and the problems they face, our public school systems do an excellent job of educating our young people. However, one area of weakness is that the system is not teaching our children about being entrepreneurs. As a child, I remember my teachers and parents admonishing me to go to school, get a good education, and find a nice job in some large corporation that would take care of me. At that time the big fatherly companies were Bethlehem Steel, Westinghouse, IBM, Procter & Gamble, and a few more. Not once did anyone explore with me the option of getting into business for myself.

If the cycle of economic dependence is ever to be reversed, we must stop encouraging our children to depend on large corporations for security and instead motivate them to develop enterprises of their own. This training must start as early as possible, preferably in the elementary schools. The emphasis, however, must remain throughout their formal training cycle. This includes teaching the rudiments of business formation in our high schools and community colleges.

It is unfair to place this burden solely on the shoulders of the school system. Parents have the ultimate responsibility to foster this type of thinking and growth among their own offspring as well. Not being in business is no excuse for not exposing your children to the entrepreneurship option. There are many ways in which parents can expose children to this option. Strategies that include putting them in contact with existing entrepreneurs, pointing out the importance of controlling your own destiny, and encouraging them to start child-oriented businesses, such as grass cutting, selling lemonade, selling papers, or shoveling snow, are easy to do. Use these experiences to highlight the nuances of actual business ownership. Teach them to take pride in whatever they create.

As a general rule, we need to de-emphasize the corporate option and emphasize the entrepreneurial option.

STRATEGY 6: ACTIVELY ENGAGE IN THE NATIONAL AND INTERNATIONAL ECONOMIC MAINSTREAM

When I went through IBM's marketing school, one of the things that I learned was that in order to drive the business and meet my quota, I had to engage the competition actively and ultimately create opportunities. The act of engaging simply means to become a part of the process—to become a player. As shown in Exhibit 9.6, engaging allows you to direct opportunities into the pipeline, such that you have sufficient qualified opportunities having gone through numerous personal filters that emerge from the other end.

Even with the various levels of filtering that go on as the opportunities are sifted through the process, it is reasonable to assume that the more you engage, the more qualified opportunities you'll be able to identify.

I am not suggesting that you engage in a reckless manner, but instead to use SWOT and value analysis to screen options and employ lim-

Exhibit 9.6 The Act of Engaging

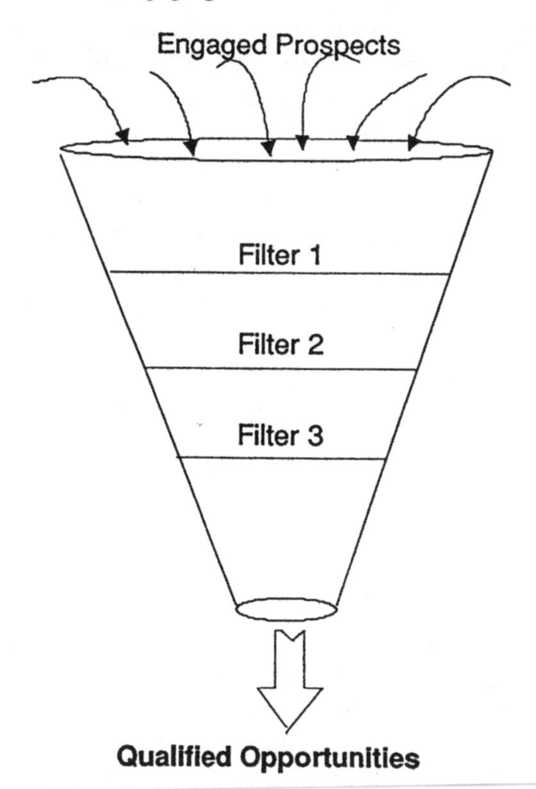

ited resources efficiently. But by all means remember these three lessons: Engage! Engage! Engage!

STRATEGY 7: GAIN OWNERSHIP OF STRATEGICALLY POSITIONED MAINSTREAM BUSINESSES

The 2000s will provide some unique business opportunities for those who dare to take charge. With Europe's and Japan's manufacturing complexes being either totally destroyed or severely damaged after World War II, the world turned to the United States to produce the goods necessary to rebuild these foreign, decimated economies. America's entrepreneurs rose to the challenge and responded by starting a flurry of businesses to respond to this national and international demand. On average, these companies started after World War II are about 50 years old, and the original owners are ready to retire. Those who have children interested in the businesses will likely pass the businesses on to them. However, those who don't have children or who have children uninterested in the businesses will be looking to cash out, and that's where we need to position ourselves to assume these established, viable businesses.

In certain instances, even if these businesses are in mature industries, a few changes here and there by an imaginative marketing and technology-driven management team could squeeze a few more years and profits out of the business. Caution needs to be exercised, though, when evaluating which of these enterprises is worth acquiring.

STRATEGY 8: ENGAGE IN JOINT VENTURES WITH MAINSTREAM COMPANIES

To the credit of our legislative body, in some instances mainstream firms are encouraged to initiate joint ventures with minority firms. The idea behind this strategy was to provide some knowledge transfer between an established mainstream company and an emerging minority firm. The partnership would also serve to get that minority entrepreneur through doors that would normally not be open to him or her.

The joint venture strategy is a potentially powerful one. With mainstream companies economically encouraged to assure the success of the minority firm, both organizations grow and benefit. Once the minority firm learns more details of the business and is given an opportunity to exercise what's learned, the next time around the firm can go out and pursue similar opportunities on its own. Visit our entrepreneurship training portal at www.EntreTeach.com to learn more on how to develop effective joint ventures.

STRATEGY 9: CREATE AND LEVERAGE BUSINESS NETWORKS AMONG MINORITY PROFESSIONAL ATHLETES, ENTERTAINERS, AND ASPIRING MINORITY ENTREPRENEURS

Although there hasn't been much analysis on this topic, I would bet that in general, the people who generate the highest level of income within the African American community are professional entertainers and athletes. Oprah Winfrey and Will Smith have the distinction of being two of the highest-paid entertainers in the industry today. Michael Jordan, Tiger Woods, and Grant Hill are three of the most marketable and visible professional athletes on the circuit. Just the income earned from endorsements usually far exceeds the millions they earn from playing ball. Michael Jordan still makes millions simply by allowing his name to be attached to a line of sneakers. Ironically, the new sneakers failed but Michael still made his millions.

One only needs to take a closer look at the incomes of African American entertainers to understand the enormous dollar potential that this special group of people controls. Consider the 1998 earnings estimates that *Forbes* magazine compiled. They ranked the incomes of the top 40 highest-paid entertainers in the industry today. The results of this analysis shown in Exhibit 9.7 may surprise you.

Exhibit 9.7 Highest Paid African American Entertainers

Entertainer	Ranking	Est. Total Income from 1997 and 1998 ($millions)
Oprah Winfrey	4	125.0
Master P	10	56.5
Sean (Puffy) Combs	15	53.5
Eddie Murphy	22	47.5
Will Smith	36	34.0

Source: Forbes magazine.

Surprisingly African Americans, who make up 12.8 percent of the American population, constitute 12.6 percent of the top 40 entertainers in America. The combined income of these performers is estimated to be close to one-third billion dollars ($316.5 million). This represents significant capital possibilities for the funding of business enterprises.

The income earned by African American professional athletes is equally impressive. A review of the incomes of the professional basketball athletes as shown in Exhibit 9.8 will underscore this point.

Boxing is another sport that is overwhelmingly dominated by African Americans. Although there are far fewer noteworthy boxers than basketball players, the salaries earned by the top boxers are just as impressive, as shown in Exhibit 9.9. There is no question that the African American professional athlete and entertainer generates significant income that could be a viable source of funding for business ventures.

Although the earnings picture for African American athletes skyrocketed in the 1980s, the earnings picture for this group looks even more astounding for the 1990s. *Forbes* magazine's annual list of the 40 top-paid athletes for 1998, Exhibit 9.10, reveals that 5 of the top 10 highest-paid athletes are African Americans whose combined income exceeds $150 million. Another interesting fact pointed out in the *Forbes* study was that a boxer has earned the top salary at the beginning of each decade since 1940, when Joe Lewis earned $250,000, a large sum for that time period.

Exhibit 9.8 Highest Paid African American NBA Players

Player	Team	1998 Salary ($millions)
Michael Jordan	Bulls	33.140
Patrick Ewing	Knicks	20.500
Horace Grant	Magic	14.280
Shaquille O'Neal	LA Lakers	12.850
David Robinson	Spurs	12.397
Alonzo Mourning	Heat	11.255
Juwan Howard	Bullets	11.250
Gary Payton	Super Sonics	10.514
Dikembe Mutombo	Rockets	9.610
Chris Webber	Bullets	9.000
Total Income ($millions)		144.800

Source: Forbes magazine.

Exhibit 9.9 Top African American Boxers

Professional Boxer	1998 Income ($millions)
Roy Jones Jr.	12.0
Lennox Lewis	11.4
Total Income ($millions)	23.4

Source: Forbes magazine.

Exhibit 9.10 is a ranking of black athletes pulled from the top 40 list, showing total income earned in 1998. As you can see this group continues to reap more than its fair share of earnings.

Not as wealthy as the professional athletes but just as promising, is a large group of well-educated, highly professional, highly motivated, young businesspeople who are rich on ideas and creativity but low on cash. There are even some black entrepreneurs who are run-

Exhibit 9.10 Top Earning African American Athletes

1998 Ranking (Top 40 in U.S.A.)	Athlete	Sport	Total Income ($millions)
1	Michael Jordan	Basketball	69.0
4	Tiger Woods	Golf	26.8
6	Grant Hill	Basketball	21.6
7	Patrick Ewing	Basketball	18.3
10	Gary Sheffield	Baseball	17.2
12	Dennis Rodman	Basketball	15.3
17	David Robinson	Basketball	12.9
19	Ken Griffey Jr.	Baseball	12.7
20	Gary Payton	Basketball	12.7
21	Shawn Kemp	Basketball	12.1
22	Alonzo Mourning	Basketball	12.1
23	Roy Jones	Boxing	12.0
25	Mo Vaughn	Baseball	11.9
28	Deion Sanders	Football	11.5
29	Lennox Lewis	Boxing	11.4
30	Hakeem Olajuwon	Basketball	11.0
33	Horace Grant	Basketball	10.6
34	Albert Belle	Baseball	10.3
39	Sammy Sosa	Baseball	10.0
40	Shaquille O'Neal	Basketball	9.8
Total Income ($millions)			329.2

Source: Forbes magazine.

ning stable and promising businesses but need only a major cash infusion to catapult their businesses from a Tier 2 business to a Tier 3 one. If we can successfully marry the deep pockets, market appeal, popularity, and charisma of our professional athletes and entertainers with the education, training, and drive of our young businesspeople, our community's ability to build large and profitable corporations could be significantly enhanced. A vehicle needs to be put in place to connect the two groups.

STRATEGY 10: LEVERAGE THE POWER AND INFLUENCE OF THE BLACK CLERGY

Ever since I've known Walter Thomas, he has impressed me as a spiritual, God-fearing man. Even when we were children growing up in the projects, there was always something about him that made me believe he would one day be a great worker for God and somehow play an important part in fulfilling God's will on earth. He was much older than I, but I often observed how he usually refrained from the abusive language, the violent outbursts, and drunkenness usually associated with the young males in my old neighborhood.

After I went away to college, I lost track of Walter for a couple of years until one day I happened to pick up a magazine in my doctor's office and came across an article about my friend Walter and the new, progressive church of which he had just become pastor. The article went on to pontificate about how he had taken over the church, increased the membership by 400 percent, introduced various programs to feed the hungry, protect the weak, clothe the naked, and provide housing for the homeless. He had indeed become somewhat of a celebrity in the city at a very young age.

When I returned home, I made a point to visit Walter at his new church—and what a church it was. Housed in a glorious cathedral, his congregation was energetic, young, educated, and proud of its blackness. It was amazing for me to see how easily he moved his audience with his silver tongue and strongly-articulated thoughts.

Then it hit me. What would happen if after Walter finished talking about God he then talked about economic empowerment and business formation within the African American community? With the influence and respect that this one man had with hundreds of people, he could easily transform the community's dormant entrepreneurial complacency into a bustling hub of commerce. What if all the Walters across this country, who are blessed with the same influence as he, started preaching economic empowerment and black entrepreneurship to their respective congregations? What if all the young people in those churches could hear the news and respond to it? What a difference that would make in the number of people within the community who engage in viable business opportunities!

We, as a community, need to leverage this special relationship that our men and women of God have with their communities. Although this special relationship is what helped blacks through the early days of the civil rights movement, I submit that this same relationship can be leveraged to aid in our climb to achieve economic parity through rapid and successful business formation within our community.

STRATEGY 11: PROMOTE SPORTS TRANSMUTATION

According to the 1999 census update, there are 34.8 million blacks living in this country (more if you believe that the census undercounts poor black folks). This fact implies that blacks make up 12.8 percent of the American population. Based on this group's percent of the population it would be logical to assume that blacks should make up approximately 12.8 percent of the players in professional sports. Although the more equipment- and facilities-intensive sports such as tennis, hockey, swimming, gymnastics, and others have very little minority participation, less cost-intensive sports like football, basketball, baseball, track and field, and boxing are often dominated by minority athletes.

Recently, it has been estimated that blacks alone make up more than 70 percent of all football players in the National Football League (NFL) and more than 90 percent of the players in the National Basketball Association (NBA). In the area of boxing, there has not been a serious non-black contender since the days of Rocky Marciano—even that was questionable. Even Tiger Woods is making inroads in the historically lily-white world of golf. Clearly, in the more visible sports, blacks are over-represented among these ranks.

Why do black men and black women make up such a large proportion of these professional athletes? Are blacks, as some would have us believe, natural athletes and outperform their white counterparts because of their innate physical superiority? I doubt it. Is it because white owners and coaches prefer the dark gladiators over the white ones, to carry out the owner's bidding on the fields and ultimately earn the franchise millions of dollars? There may be some truth in this hypothesis, albeit a small amount. I submit that the reason blacks, particularly black men, dominate these sports is because they are simply the best players. They are not the best simply because they are naturally better athletes. They are the best because they work at it the hardest.

The time our young men and women invest in playing sports from early childhood to adulthood is staggering. Many begin the training and indoctrination process before they reach the age of three.

For those of you still not convinced of this phenomenon, conduct the following test. If you have sons, how many times do well-meaning friends and family members tell your sons, "You're going to be a great football player one day [or a boxer or a basketball player]." Or you'll hear, "Look at the legs on that boy. He'll make a good tight end or lineman." Consequently, the boys grow up trying to fulfill this expectation and end up spending all of their spare time playing and practicing sports. Over time, the young man begins to equate his esteem and respect from peers as a function of his sports prowess. It becomes his badge of acceptability. Why do you think that so many young men engage in death threatening arguments over a game of basketball? Because too many equate how well they can play basketball with how much of a man they are or use it as a measure of their respectability. How frightening all of this is.

Sports transmutation suggests that the African American community needs to redirect some of the resources and energy that it channels into creating super athletes into avenues that will create super businessmen and businesswomen. Sports transmutation means the community should begin de-emphasizing the sports option and emphasizing more the entrepreneurial and business options. It means instead of always telling a young black male that he'll be a great football or basketball player, tell him instead that one day he'll be a great doctor, lawyer, inventor, or entrepreneur. Sports transmutation means that we encourage the young men to engage intellectually with their white peers on every front and teach them to believe they can excel in other areas as well as in sports.

Sports transmutation does not mean a young black male or female is denied the chance to participate in sports. Sports within the proper overall development strategy can be a powerful vehicle for teaching young people important lessons in life and for preparing them for the responsibilities of adulthood. Sports transmutation does suggest that the same qualities that help create a super athlete (endurance, leadership, mental and physical fortitude, and so on) are the exact same qualities that help build successful businesspeople. The only difference is the target end point. The African American community needs to reassess its end point for its young males and females and begin redirecting them.

STRATEGY 12: CREATE BUSINESS INCUBATOR SITES WITHIN STRATEGIC LOCATIONS

As a young pre-med student, one of the projects my wife, Carolyn, had to complete was to design, build, and operate an incubator system for young chicken eggs. This was a very demanding project because in order for the eggs to hatch into young healthy chickens, a number of critical environmental factors had to be created and monitored over some period of time. The temperature, pressure, humidity, air flow, and other critical factors had to be monitored and occasionally adjusted to maintain the proper incubating environment for producing healthy little chicks. If the environment was especially fertile, the little chicks would have a good probability of maturing into healthy, young adult chickens.

This same incubator concept that is taught in science classrooms could also be applied to small, fledgling minority businesses in our communities. This concept, although tried before, is seldom implemented correctly. For this strategy to work it requires that we:

1. Identify the appropriate businesses to participate in the programs. The businesses should be owned or managed by conscientious businesspeople who have the commitment and skills necessary to be successful.

2. Create successful businesses quickly. The public must see visible signs that the program is working. Success feeds on success. Consequently, early successes will motivate the other incubator businesses to strive for the same degree of accomplishment.

3. Choose candidates that are either in growth industries (e.g., systems integration, client/server systems development, telecommunications) or are in businesses that may not be high-growth areas but satisfy a long-term need within the community (e.g., food, fuel, auto repair).

4. Create a capital fund before the incubator is started, to fund the chosen businesses as necessary. Contributors might include the local government, local corporations, private donors, and insurance companies. Make sure that the financial commitment has been made before advancing the concept too far.

5. Use the local graduate schools of business administration to provide free consulting services to the incubator businesses. Work out a deal with the business school administrators where the students can earn credits based on the work that they complete for the small businesses. Where appropriate, invite certain students or the school to become equity partners in some of the ventures. Obtaining the buy-in of talented young people or the local college will provide a readily available source of funds and talent throughout the venture's existence.

6. Effectively leverage the WIFME (What's in It for ME?) concept. To win the full support of the local government, the incubator group must be successful at showing the government how it will benefit by supporting the incubator projects in their jurisdictions. Usually, the benefits will be blatantly obvious—boost for local economy, reduction in welfare rules, reduction in local unemployment, rejuvenation of subeconomies within the minority community, and reduction of the load on the social programs. Once the government buys into the concept, the next step is to gain their commitment to donate one of the vacant buildings (usually there will be plenty around) to be used to house the incubator businesses. The municipality will likely be amenable to some form of tax reduction for the businesses participating in the incubator program.

One successful entrepreneur who has been successfully applying the incubator concept throughout the Virginia, Washington, D.C., and Maryland region is C. Michael Gooden. Mr. Gooden, president of Integrated Systems Analysts, Inc., in Arlington, Virginia, is founder of one of the most successful systems integration firms in the country. Yet he has found time to mentor dozens of minority businesses in the federal government marketplace. Mr. Gooden's assistance to these small-fledgling firms includes advice on obtaining financing, guidance in developing business plans, help in setting up finance and accounting systems, assistance in understanding federal acquisition regulations, marketing, building strategic alliances, and the awarding of subcontracts.

Mike Gooden is unwavering in his belief that minority business is a critical link to mobilizing talent from within the minority communities. Mobilizing this talent to productive ends allows the minority community to fully contribute to America's economic well-being. Remember, the incubator concept can work as long as all the pieces are in place.

STRATEGY 13: ENSURE THAT THE TALENTED 10 PERCENT ASSUME THEIR DESTINY

In 1908 W. E. B. DuBois suggested in his work titled *Philadelphia Negro* that within the black community there existed a group of achievers who were capable of providing the creative leadership necessary to lead the community in solving its many problems. I believe the same holds true as it pertains to business leadership within the African American community.

I have never been able to convince myself that everyone has what it takes to start, develop, and manage a thriving business enterprise. On the contrary, it has been my observation that most people, regardless of race, ethnic, or religious persuasion, do not have what it takes to become successful in business. However, there exists a group within our midst who possess the skills necessary and who are destined to do great things.

The challenge remains: How do we get this talented 10 percent to recognize their talents and concurrently motivate them to resist wasting these talents working for someone else and making them rich when they should be enriching themselves and their communities? W. E. B. DuBois sounded the charge when he said:

> Above all, the better classes of the Negroes should recognize their duty toward the masses. They should not forget that the spirit of the twentieth century is to be the turning of the high toward the lowly, the bending of Humanity to all that is human, the recognition that in the slums of modern society lie the answers to most of our puzzling problems of organization and life, and that only as we solve those problems is our culture assured and our progress certain.

STRATEGY 14: ENCOURAGE ONE ANOTHER TO "LOOK BETWEEN AND BEYOND THE BARS" AND NOT AT THEM

My childhood friend Jimmy was not a bad kid; he just did bad things. Jimmy, who was intellectually keen and streetwise, always seemed to find himself in the middle of any trouble that erupted in the neighborhood. Whether it was gang fights, snatched purses, breaking into the freight trains that passed through our neighborhood, or burglarizing the local stores, you could bet that Jimmy was somehow involved. Unfortunately, because of Jimmy's propensity for injecting himself into the midst of controversy, he spent a great deal of time behind bars—locked in prison.

On one of my many visits to the penitentiary to see Jimmy, I found him in a very depressed mood, more depressed than normal. As we talked and I brought him up to date on all the latest gossip from the neighborhood, his eyes remained cast on the cement floor of the prison visiting room. No matter what I said his eyes continued to search the four corners of the floor as if he were waiting for a hole to open up and he could then flee the cold and treacherous environment that had become his life. Finally, after trying everything I knew to cheer him up, I asked him, "Jimmy, what the hell is wrong with you, man? I've been pouring my heart out to you for the last 30 minutes and all you've done is blankly stare at the floor of this damn room. What's wrong?"

Jimmy slowly raised his head from his hands and with tears streaming down his bearded cheeks his eyes met mine and I understood instantly what was happening. Jimmy confided in me, "Rob, this place, these bars are driving me crazy. During the day, I do nothing but fight my cell mate because he has on numerous occasions tried to rape me. I can't sleep at night because I'm afraid he'll either slit my throat or succeed in taking my manhood. Every morning that I wake up, I see these bars and when I lay down at night, I see these bars. Maybe this is the best I'll ever do. Maybe I should just give in and let him rape me. At least I'll be able to get some sleep and not worry about getting sliced to pieces in my bed at night."

Unable to find the right words to encourage and soothe him, I responded, "Jimmy, you've got to stop looking at these bars and try looking between and beyond them." Without knowing it, at that moment, I had given Jimmy enough encouragement to keep fighting, to survive the prison experience, and ultimately to turn his life around.

How many of us are like Jimmy and have bars that define our lives for us? These bars, if stared at too long, prevent us from reaching our potential and from going on to achieve great things. Our bars are anything that we use as an excuse for why we can't achieve and why we can't be great. Some of the bars that people use are:

1. Race
2. Economic status
3. Gender
4. Physical handicap
5. Education
6. Social status
7. Physical appearance
8. Weight
9. Speech or accent

What are your bars? Can you add to this list? The point here is that all of us need to encourage one another to accept the hand that life has dealt us and formulate a strategy that leverages the hand that we've been dealt into a winning hand. Anyone can make this contribution. By caring, communicating, and taking ownership of someone else's lack of confidence, we can help aspiring black entrepreneurs to not look at the bars created by the mere fact of their ethnicity, but instead look between and beyond those bars to the destiny that is truly theirs.

STRATEGY 15: DEVELOP JOINT VENTURES WITH OTHER MINORITY COMPANIES

It often appears that minority companies have a more difficult time entering joint ventures with other *minority* firms than they do with majority firms. Some minority entrepreneurs who could be categorized as Brown Bombers or Blood and Guts businesspeople are distrustful of people outside their respective companies and frequently fail to take advantage of larger opportunities.

Despite these fears, minority businesses have to begin identifying and leveraging joint venture opportunities among themselves. I wonder how much business has found its way back into the mainstream business channels because a minority firm did not have the resources to adequately do the job. This situation is even more tragic when you consider that the firm competing may have had 80 percent or more of the necessary skills and resources to complete the engagement, but was rejected because it didn't have the remaining 20 percent.

In developing potential joint venture partners, older, larger, more established minority firms should look not just to joint ventures with other large firms. There are many smaller, younger firms that have very talented young people working in them who could benefit greatly from the experience of an older firm and still provide some value to the partnership. An arrangement like this would also allow the more established firm to shape and mold an emerging minority firm into the larger firm's image and provide the groundwork for a long and profitable business relationship between the two firms. Remember, 1 percent of a big deal is a lot greater than 100 percent of a little deal. Think about it.

STRATEGY 16: INCREASE BUYING AND SELLING AMONG MINORITY BUSINESSES

Earlier in this book, I discussed the importance and impact of Africa Americans buying from and supporting African American businesses. However, the buck doesn't stop there. The corollary to this theory is that African American businesses must buy from other minority businesses as much as possible! The impact of the community realizing this strategy is phenomenal. Let's conduct a little exercise here to illustrate my point. Assume the following:

1. African American businesses currently generate approximately $20 billion in revenue each year (close enough).
2. On average, black firms spend 30 percent of their revenue stream on expense items such as rent, automobiles, energy, office supplies, travel, printing, accounting and legal expenses, and so forth.
3. African American businesses mirror the African American community and only 6 of every 100 dollars spent by the community is given to African American businesses.

Given the above assumptions, the total dollars available for black businesses is:

($20,000,000,000) × 30 percent = $6,000,000,000

The amount of money that is currently being spent by black firms with other black firms is:

$$(\$6{,}000{,}000{,}000) \times 6 \text{ percent} = \$360{,}000{,}000$$

$$\begin{array}{r} \$6{,}000{,}000{,}000 \\ -360{,}000{,}000 \\ \hline \$5{,}640{,}000{,}000 \end{array}$$

Whatever way you want to split the hairs, the result is the same. By just doing more business with ourselves, the black community can increase the annual receipts of its businesses by more than 25 percent (conservatively speaking). If we don't buy from ourselves, then who will? If not now, when?

STRATEGY 17: KEEP YOUR HEAD TO THE SKY

The African American's objective of realizing economic justice in the United States for the new millennium will be a tumultuous and difficult one to achieve. Not only does the community have some internal challenges that it needs to face but it also faces some formidable challenges from forces external to the community. It is unlikely that those who are already in control of America's economic engine will willingly relinquish even a portion of such power without a struggle. This is clearly evident from their overzealous attempts to dismantle any program or effort geared toward black economic empowerment.

Someone recently said, "Those in power do not concede power to the powerless unless the powerless first demand it and secondly show a determination to fight for it." Inevitably, there will be some casualties as a result of this struggle. Some talented, aspiring black entrepreneurs will never get their chances, and some black-owned businesses won't survive long enough to assume their rightful places in the journals of industry and commerce. However, if this is the price to pay for achieving economic justice for blacks and other minorities, then let the struggle begin. African Americans must continue to demand and fight for economic justice and achieve economic empowerment or the community's long-term survival will at best be questionable.

Despite these challenges and the difficulties that face the community, African Americans and other people of color must remain optimistic about the ultimate outcome of this fight. "Keep your head to the sky" means that you ultimately believe in the final morality of the universe and in the power of maintaining the moral high ground. This phrase, made famous by the music group Earth, Wind and Fire, conveys the thought that if you keep trying and never give up, ultimately you'll succeed. It means that no matter how dark and pessimistic the community's economic condition may seem, one must maintain faith. If a person continues to step to the plate and swing at the pitches, ultimately he or she will hit a home run and win the game. This is the faith that must carry us until economic justice is a reality. Remember, in the words of the apostle Paul: "Fight a good fight. Keep the faith and finish your course." Keep your head to the sky and always know that the God of the universe loves you!

Appendix: The Minority Business Executive Program at Dartmouth College

All the participants in this study are minorities and entrepreneurs, but there is one other common factor among them. The majority of them are alumni of the Minority Business Executive Program at the Amos Tuck School of Business Administration at Dartmouth College. This group of entrepreneurs was chosen because as a program facilitator at Tuck, I grew very close to some of them and was able to conduct thorough discussions with some on both their personal histories and business experiences. Since 1983 I have collected ideas, thoughts, concerns, and backgrounds of these individuals in preparation for writing this book. It seems appropriate that I provide a background on the very program from which it all started.

The Amos Tuck School of Business Administration at Dartmouth is the oldest graduate school of business in the world. Annually, the school conducts some of the most extensive executive training programs offered anywhere. One of those, which was the basis of this study, is the Minority Business Executive Program (MBEP). The Tuck School has conducted this program for senior executives of minority owned and operated businesses since the summer of 1980.

When the Tuck School unveiled its Minority Business Executive Program (MBEP) in 1980, its mission was to provide minority executives with the vision, skills, and ability to explore new opportunities to grow their companies. To date, more than fifteen hundred minority-owned U.S. firms have taken advantage of this training. This has meant growth and job development in minority communities across the country.

MBEP's growth and success could not have happened without help from resource organizations, government agencies, and major corporations. Among the earliest supporters were General Electric, which offered the first MBEP sponsorship in 1982; Aluminum Company of America; Boeing; Con Edison; FMC; Ford; Frito-Lay; General Motors; P&G; Philip Morris; Pfizer; Standard Oil of Ohio, now BP; and Wisconsin Bell, now Ameritech.

The National Minority Supplier Development Council (NMSDC) also has played an instrumental role in MBEP's growth. Early in MBEP's history, the Southern California Regional Purchasing Council awarded a full MBEP scholarship to its Minority Supplier of the Year winner. Other councils quickly followed. Today 19 councils provide scholarship support for their members to attend MBEP. Their participation has enabled MBEP to expand considerably in size and scope.

In recent years, scholarship funding from the Small Business Administration (SBA) has given more than 550 minority business executives the opportunity to attend MBEP and AMBEP.

These and other contributions have made it possible for Tuck's minority business programs to mushroom. In the early 1990s, Tuck developed Managing Success, a two-day workshop similar to MBEP. The pilot workshop in Los Angeles helped jump-start LA's minority communities after the riots in 1992. Subsequent corporate financing and support from NMSDC affiliates have underwritten similar workshops in Baltimore, Chicago, Cleveland, Dallas, Houston, and Washington, D.C.

The NMSDC and its affiliates, corporate sponsors, and various government agencies have been particularly valuable as partners by providing keynote speakers and workshop presenters, by serving as the subject of classroom case studies for MBEP, and by advising Tuck on new industry trends and their future supplier management education needs. The creation of a formal Visitors Program in 1996 has made it possible for sponsors to visit Tuck and observe firsthand the value of MBEP and their support.

Most recently, the Minority Business Development Agency, U.S. Department of Commerce, joined the ranks of MBEP supporters. The agency has provided more than 25 scholarships since 1997 for its national winners to attend the program.

Tuck is proud to have provided 20 years of the best management training available to minority business executives. It shares this achievement with the many corporations, nonprofit organizations, and government agencies that have supported its minority management programs and their mission almost from the beginning. And it looks forward to continuing these winning alliances dedicated to a prosperous future for minority business executives.

Although the qualifications for participating in the program have evolved since the summer of 1980, the basic requirements remain the same. Currently, minimum qualifications for inclusion in the program suggest that the participating chief executives have been in business at least three years and have minimum annual revenues of $300,000 and employ no less than three people. If a firm is fewer than three years old, the executive must then have management experience in a Fortune 500 or large, minority-owned company. Likewise, if a firm generates less than $300,000 per year but is an unusually successful venture or is unique in some way, exceptions can be made. Each summer the program attracts a diverse and dynamic group of African, Hispanic, Asian, and Native American entrepreneurs.

Participants of Tuck's minority business executive programs are immersed in an environment where they can focus on applying principles of management excellence to their own companies, learn from the best of their peers, and meet potential corporate partners. They become part of a nationwide network of alumni that actively promotes ongoing business opportunities. Currently, Tuck offers three minority business programs with plans for a fourth in the works.

The Minority Business Executive Program (MBEP) is a five-day, on-campus executive management program for minority business owners and key officers. In the 20 years since its debut, more than 1,500 graduates have improved their ability to make business decisions using financial data, create a market-focused strategy, improved performance management, enhance communications, explore ideas for growth, and utilize SWOT analyses. Workshops and speakers from business and the public-policy arena add to the learning experience.

The Advanced Minority Business Executive Program (AMBEP) is designed for graduates of MBEP. The focus of this five-day advanced program is strategic rowth for suppliers. Participants learn how to understand the value of their firm's core competency, manage supply-chain relations efficiently, address human resource issues effectively, and broaden their vision. AMBEP also offers a hands-on business simulation that provides competitive strategy experience without personal risk.

Managing Success: A Workshop for Growing Minority-Owned Businesses is offered twice a year in different cities across the U.S. The workshop, taught by Tuck faculty, focuses on key business concepts that improve management effectiveness and increase profitability in the areas of strategy, marketing, finance, and human resources management.

Strategies for Minority Business Growth is coming soon. Tuck currently is working on a program for minority business CEOs of large firms that will concentrate on strategies for expansion, business valuation and finance, and organizational effectiveness. It is offered in response to a growing trend by major corporations to focus on supply-chain relationships with high-revenue suppliers, effectively relegating many minority suppliers to second- and third-tier levels. Courses will be offered in three three-day modules on the Tuck campus.

THE EARLY DAYS

It was during the summer of 1980 that Paul Doscher, the director of conferences, negotiated a contract with the SBA to bring 48 presidents and owners of 8(a) companies to Hanover, New Hampshire, for a mini-M.B.A. seminar. The first MBEP faculty director, Willis Greer, and his Tuck colleagues offered a curriculum that included financial management, accounting, marketing, organizational behavior, and production. The participants also received a detailed briefing on recent legislation affecting minority business by speakers from both the government and the private sector. The program was administered through Tuck's conference office by Jan Bent until 1985, at which time Paula Graves took over as program manager. For many of the participants in the one-week residential program, it was the first opportunity to receive formal advanced management education, although most had several years of business experience.

In 1981 Tuck incorporated the MBEP fully into its annual executive education programs. The school reached beyond the original 8(a) participants to admit a national group of participants along with minority alumni of Tuck's full-time M.B.A. program. The alumni of MBEP 1980 were encouraged to provide continuity as the program began the transition from year to year. Guest speaker Wallace L. Ford II (D '70), then Assistant Secretary of Commerce for New York State, summed up the mood of the class saying:

> It is important to point out that what the Tuck School is doing is extremely significant in serving as a model for what other business schools have to do and certainly what the private sector has to do in this country if we are to see some real progress and some substantive economic development in the American minority community.

If you'd like to attend this program or desire more information about the curriculum, you should contact:

Ms. Paula Graves
Minority Business Executive Program
Amos Tuck School of Business Administration
Dartmouth College, Hanover, NH 03755

You may also contact the author:

Robert L. Wallace, President
EntreTeach.com
P.O. Box 1311
Ellicott City, MD 21042
e-mail: rwallace@Bithgroup.com
www.Bithgroup.com
www.EntreTeach.com
Phone: (410) 730-0077 Fax: (410) 730-2410

Bith Technologies, Inc.
and EntreTeach.com
9151 Rumsey Road
Suite 150
Columbia, MD 21045
e-mail: rwallace@Bithgroup.com
websites: www.Bithgroup.com
www.EntreTeach.com

Glossary of Business Terms

Affirmative action Business actions undertaken by government and corporations in the hiring and employment of minorities, women, and other disadvantaged groups to remedy past abuses and discriminatory practices.

Aggregate The whole group of people somewhat loosely associated with one another.

Asset Something owned by a corporation or individual. Balance sheet classifications include:

> **Current assets** Assets that can be converted to cash within one year.
>
> **Long-term assets** Machinery, real estate, furniture, equipment, and so on.
>
> **Prepaid assets** Assets that represent expenditures to be used over a certain period of time before being reversed or amortized.
>
> **Intangible assets** Assets whose value is placed on the books without a corresponding cash transaction.

Asset base The combination of assets that are owned by a company or individual and that serve to add value or can be used to generate wealth.

Book value The value of stock that is not based on market value but instead is based on actual tangible net worth of business. The book value is usually calculated by netting out intangible assets from net worth and dividing this result by the number of outstanding shares of common stock.

Break-even analysis A calculation involving comparisons between fixed and variable costs to determine the volume of sales required to cover expenses, usually on a monthly or annual basis.

Budget A summary of the anticipated costs and expenses a company or individual expects to expend over some predetermined period of time.

Business cycle A term that describes recession or inflationary trends in the national economy.

Business planning The process of predicting future events that could have an impact on a business and concurrently mapping out a business plan of action to use the events to the company's advantage or minimize any possible negative impact from such events.

Collateral Property pledged by a borrower to protect the lender in case the borrower defaults on a transaction.

Current assets Assets that can be converted to cash within one year.

Debt service The total of principal and interest payments on a debt over some specified period of time.

Economic empowerment The process of making it easier, practical, and possible for a person or group to produce, market, and distribute goods and services to the marketplace.

Economic injustice The act of systematically preventing a person or group from freely and practically producing, marketing, and distributing goods and services to the marketplace. Group's economic progress is usually hindered through overt and subtle discriminatory practices.

Economic life The time period in which a capital asset is expected to remain in practical use. After this period, the asset is considered to be obsolete and has no economic value.

Economic value The current market value of an asset.

Equity capital Capital contribution made by equity participant in business start-up or expansion, which allows him or her to retain partial ownership of business.

Factoring A financing strategy used to raise capital that involves utilizing accounts receivable as collateral.

Financial accounting Type of accounting that emphasizes the historical reporting of the operations and financial position of a business to external users on a periodic basis. It encompasses accounting for the company's revenues, assets, equities, and expenses.

Financial statements Set of financial reports that serve to summarize a business's financial condition. These reports include the balance sheet, income statement, statement of retained earnings, statement of changes in financial position, statement of changes in owners' equity accounts, and other notes.

Fiscal year The twelve-month period recognized by a company for tax purposes. The fiscal year does not have to follow the calendar year and can vary for different companies.

Fortune 500 The 500 largest corporations in America.

General Services Administration (GSA) Arm of federal government that coordinates service provision to the other arms of the federal government.

Gramm-Rudman Bill passed by the Congress to reduce the federal deficit systematically.

Hierarchy of needs A widely adopted theory of human motivation developed by Abraham H. Maslow that stresses two fundamental premises:

1. Humans are wanting animals whose needs depend on what they already have. Only needs not yet satisfied can influence behavior.

2. Human needs are arranged in a hierarchy of importance. These five levels of need are physiological, safety, social, esteem, and self-actualization. Once one need is satisfied, the next level of need becomes primary and demands satisfaction.

Intangible assets Assets whose value is placed on the books without a corresponding cash transaction.

Leverage The use of borrowed capital to gain control over the most investments and property as is possible. Using someone else's money to acquire businesses.

Leveraged buy-out (LBO) The takeover of another company by using borrowed funds or someone else's capital. The assets of the acquired company are usually used as collateral for the loan, and theoretically the loan is repaid from the operating capital of the target company.

Long-term assets Machinery, real estate, furniture, equipment, and so on.

Management accounting Reporting of accounting information for the sole purpose of enhancing management's ability to maintain control of the operation.

Mean income The average income of a specified group. The number is calculated by adding the incomes of all members of the group and dividing by the number of members.

Median household income The middle value of household income, such that one-half of incomes are below this number and one-half are above. The median may be a more accurate measurement than mean when the data group under consideration has exceptionally high values at both ends of the distribution.

Net worth An entrepreneur's ownership in the business. Value is derived by subtracting all liabilities from all assets.

Per capita income Income by or for each person.

Prepaid assets Assets that represent expenditures to be used over a certain period of time before being reversed or amortized.

Private sector That part of the national economy that invests in the production of new capital equipment, such as factories, warehouses, equipment, machinery, automobiles, or nongovernmental services. These goods and services are usually sold in a market.

Public sector That segment of the national economy in which services are supplied by government and are not sold in a market. Consequently, in this sector, there is no price that can be used to value the productive activities of government. Therefore, government services are valued at the cost of providing them. The three levels of the public sector are federal, state, and local. This sector includes services such as national defense, health care services, police, education, and fire services.

SWOT Strengths, Weaknesses, Opportunities, and Threats. A strategic analysis tool used in the development of short-term and long-term strategic planning.

Total capitalization The combination of all debt capitalization and all equity capitalization. Debt capitalization includes all contracts, bonds, and notes. Equity capitalization includes all retained earnings, shareholders' equity, and paid-in capital.

Unemployment rate The number of persons without jobs who are actively looking for work divided by the total size of the labor force. Labor force here includes both the fully employed, the underemployed, and the unemployed.

Working capital The funds available to pay for current operating expenses such as labor and materials.

Bibliography

Anderson, Dan Robert. *Minority Enterprise Development Program.* MadiA-son, Wisconsin: Bureau of Business Research and Service, Graduate School of Business Administration, University of Wisconsin, 1973.

Ambry, K. Margaret. *1990–1991 Almanac of Consumer Markets: A Guide to Today's More Complex and Harder to Find Customers.* New York: American Demographics Press.

Bates, Timothy Mason. *Government Promotion of Minority Group Entrepreneurship.* Madison, Wisconsin: University of Wisconsin, 1974.

Blackman, Courtney, and Newlands McLaurin. *Black Capitalism in Economic Perspective.* New York: Irving Trust Company Economic Research Department, 1973.

Blagrove, Luanna C. *Strategy for Minority Businesses.* Stamford, Connecticut: Blagrove Publications, 1980.

Bradford, Ernie. *Hannibal.* New York: McGraw-Hill, 1981.

Brarda, Roger H. *Personal Traits and Values Contributing to the Success of Spanish-Surname Entrepreneurs in the United States.* Los Angeles, 1979.

Connolly, Peter. *Hannibal and the Enemies of Rome.* Silver Burdett, 1978.

Davis, Lenwood G. *Black Businesses, Employment, Economics, and Finance in Urban America.* Chicago: Council of Planning Librarians, 1974.

———. *Black Capitalism in Urban America.* Chicago: Council of Planning Librarians, 1974.

Dickens, Floyd, Jr., and Jacqueline B. Dickens. *The Black Manager—Making It in the Corporate World.* New York: Amacom Publishers, 1982.

Donnelly, James H., Jr., *Fundamentals of Management: Functions, Behavior, Models.* Dallas: Business Publications, Inc., 1975.

Dupuy, Trevor N., Jr., *The Military Life of Hannibal, Father of Strategy.* Los Angeles: F. Watts Publishing, 1969.

Ewing, Samuel D. *Minority Capital Resource Handbook.* 2d ed. Washington, D.C.: Securities Industry Minority Capital Foundation, 1980.

Farr, Walter G. *Minority Economic Development.* New York: New York University School of Law, 1971.

Feingold, Norman, and Dr. Leonard G. Perlman. *Making It On Your Own.* Acropolis, 1971.

Fierce, Hughlyn F. *Improving Minorities Share of Aggregate Income.* New York: New York University, Institute of Afro-American Affairs, 1979.

Fromm, Erich. *The Art of Loving.* New York: HarperCollins, 1989.

Gilbreath, Larry Kent. *Economic Diversification on the Navajo Indian Reservation,* 1971.

Goldman, Peter. *The Death and Life of Malcolm X.* Champaign: University of Illinois Press, 1979.

Holliday, Thelma Y. *Minorities in the Field of Business.* 3d ed. Washington, D.C.: Institute for Minority Business Education, Howard University, 1975.

Johnson, Ruth Ellen. *The Development of a Unit on the Afro-American Entrepreneur in the United States Before 1866.* Philadelphia, 1979.

Lamb, Harold. *Hannibal, One Man Against Rome.* New York: Doubleday, 1958.

Light, Ivan Hubert. *Ethnic Enterprise in America.* San Francisco: University of California Press, 1972.

Perry, Bruce. *Malcolm X: The Last Speeches.* New York: Pathfinder Press, 1989.

Rummel, Jack. *Malcolm X: Militant Black Leader.* New York: Chelsea House Publishers, 1990.

Scott, William C. *Key Business Ratios of Minority Owned Businesses.* Dallas: Center for Studies in Business, Economics, and Human Resources, University of Texas, 1981.

Sheffrin, M. Steven. *Macro-economics: Theory and Policy.* Ohio: Southwestern Publishing Company, 1988.

Sowell, Thomas. *Race and Economics.* New York: Longman, Inc., 1975.

Stickney, Clyde P. *Financial Accounting: An Introduction to Concepts, Methods, and Uses.* New York: The Dryden Press, 1982.

Tideman, T. Nicolaus. *Efficiency in Minority Enterprise Programs.* Cambridge, Massachusetts: Harvard University, 1972.

Trower-Subira, George. *Black Folks Guide to Making Big Money in America.* East Orange, New Jersey: Very Serious Business Enterprises, 1980.

Venable, Abraham S. *Building Black Businesses.* New York: Earl G. Graves Publishing Company, 1972.

Yancy, Robert J. *Federal Government Policy and Black Business Enterprise.* Massachusetts: Ballinger Publishing Company, 1974.

Other Sources

An Analysis of How Eligibility Criteria Are Applied for Participation in the 8(a) Program. Washington, D.C.: U.S. General Accounting Office, 1978.

Business in the Ghetto. Chicago, Illinois: Section on Corporation, Banking and Business Law, 1969.

California Utilities Utilization of Minority/Women Business. Sacramento: California Legislature, Committee on Utilities and Commerce, 1985.

Directory of Marketing Assistance for Minority Businesses. Washington, D.C.: American Marketing Association, Department of Commerce, Office of Minority Business Enterprise, 1976.

Effects of Government Regulation on Small Business and the Problems of Women and Minorities in Small Business in the Southwestern United States. Washington, D.C.: U.S. Congress, Senate Select Committee on Small Business, 1977.

Franchise Opportunities Handbook. Washington, D.C.: U.S. Department of Commerce International Trade Administration, U.S. Government Printing Office, 1984.

Guide to Doing Business with the Department of State, revised ed. Washington, D.C.: U.S. Bureau of Management, Office of Small and Disadvantaged Business Utilization, 1985.

Guide to Minority Business Directories, 10th ed. Minneapolis: Minority Business Campaign, 1975.

Helping Small Businesses to Respond to Consumers' Needs. Washington, D.C.: U.S. Department of Commerce, 1982.

How the Law to Prevent Railroad Discrimination and Encourage Minority Participation in Railroad Activities Is Being Implemented. Washington, D.C.: U.S. General Accounting Office, 1980.

Key Indicators of County Growth 1970–2010. Washington, D.C.: NPA Data Services, Inc.

Minority Business and Its Contributions to the U.S. Economy. Washington, D.C.: U.S. Congress, Senate Committee on Small Business, U.S. Government Printing Office, 1982.

Money Income and Poverty Status in the United States. Washington, D.C.: U.S. Department of Commerce, Bureau of the Census, 1989.

Office of Minority Business Enterprise Could Do More to Start and Maintain Minority Businesses. Washington, D.C.: U.S. General Accounting Office, 1977.

Small and Minority Business Ownership in the Cable Television Industry. Washington, D.C.: United States House Committee on Small Business, U.S. Government Printing Office, 1982.

Source Book of Marketing Demographics. 5th ed. Washington, D.C.: CACI Marketing Systems, 1990.

Source Book of Zip Code Demographics. 7th ed. Washington, D.C.: CACI Marketing Systems, 1990.

The State of Black America. Washington, D.C.: National Urban League, 1988, 1989, 1990, 1991.

Statistical Abstract of the United States. Washington, D.C.: U.S. Department of Commerce, Bureau of the Census, 1991.

Whatever Happened to Minority Economic Development? Chicago: Dryden Press, 1974.

Acknowledgments

As I look back over my life and ponder my future, it becomes quite obvious to me that I am who I am because of my God, my ancestors, my parents, my wife, my children, my brothers, my community, my professors, my friends, my enemies, and my lofty dreams.

The writing of *Black Wealth* is indeed the fulfillment of a childhood dream and a combination of the influences of those who are dear to me. Let me make a fragile attempt at acknowledging those who have made the writing of this book possible.

Above all, I'd like to thank God for giving me life and for teaching me how to dream even after I had lost the desire to do so. Especially during my dry seasons I take solace in the fact that I will spend eternity in the presence of my Father, conversing with Christ, and mingling with the angels.

To my adorable bride Carolyn, thank you for believing in my dreams even when so many others did not. Even when I feel down, I never feel alone, because of her. When I feel like quitting, I never give up, because of her. When I'm fearful, I never let them see me sweat, because of her. Thank you, Carolyn, for giving me the honor and privilege of being your husband. I love you.

To my mother, Irene, and my deceased father, Daniel, thank you for keeping the family together through some of the toughest times one could imagine. Thank you for introducing me to God, for loving me, for teaching me the value of a good education, and for not walking away when it would have been easy to do so.

A tremendous debt is due to my grandfather, Elzie Curry. For more than one-half a century, my grandfather worked as a porter on the B&O Railroad. Thank you, Grandfather Curry, for sharing all your stories with me about working on the railroad and how you and your peers from the Brotherhood of Sleeping Car Porters courageously confronted the racism that was strangling America during that time. Your battles against bigotry helped make my skirmishes that much more successful.

To my five children, Bobby Jr., Joshua, Collin, Jordan, and Taylor Irene, you have made my life so enjoyable. Thank you for loving and supporting me during the writing of this book. A special thanks to my sons Bobby and Joshua for assisting in the exhaustive research required to complete this project. All of you represent my legacy and I'm comfortable that the future is secure.

My brothers Richard, Ronald, Randy, and Raymond also helped shape the outcome of *Black Wealth.* Thank you for shielding me from the cruel realities of being raised poor and black in the Cherry Hill housing projects of South Baltimore. Although we struggled as a family, we stayed united, remained focused, and resisted the temptations to succumb to the evils of drugs and alcohol abuse, fratricide, and hopelessness. A special thanks to Randy for finding a way to feed us on a $10 per week food budget and to my brother Raymond for being a faithful friend.

A special thank-you goes to Mr. Harry W. Holt Jr., Vice President of Training and Professional Development at the BiTH Group, Inc., Ms. Josephine Blake, my Administrative Assistant, Ms. Vesta Jackson-Crute, my Public Relations Manager, and to all employees.

To my extended family, the Greens, and the "Home Boys in the Hood"—Kenny, Big Wayne, Lil' Wayne, Elroy, Lee Bone, Johnny "Qui Qui," Kai Kai, Leonard, "Sweet Baby" Bruce, "Mad Max" Dalton, Butterball, David, and the rest of the gang. While it is tough being black in America, always remember that God is on our side.

A warm thank-you to Carolyn Green, Cheryl Williams, and George Blake for their research on the case studies. All of you deserve some credit for helping to bring my ideas to life.

My sincere appreciation is also extended to my very talented agent, Ms. Andrea Pedolsky, and my editors at John Wiley & Sons,

Ruth Mills and Airié Dekidjiev, who have proved to be invaluable in advising me.

Even with all the support I received, none of this would have happened had it not been for the Amos Tuck School of Business at Dartmouth College and the Minority Business Executive Program (MBEP) sponsored by the school. Thank you to the many MBEP graduates who took the time to work with me on researching the topic of minority entrepreneurship and economic empowerment, particularly the graduates whose case studies I use in this book. A heartfelt thank-you goes to Paula Graves and the staff at the Tuck School of Business. I am especially indebted to my mentors, Doctors Hector Guerrero, Kenneth Baker, James Brian Quinn, Len Greenhalgh, and Dean Kropp.

I have also benefited greatly by counsel from former Congressman Parren J. Mitchell. Mr. Mitchell, a lifelong advocate for minority business rights, reviewed my manuscript in its very early stages and encouraged me to complete the project because he saw value in what I was saying. His encouragement brought new life into this very ambitious project.

A special thank-you to my lifetime instructors, Ms. Gwendolyn Brown of Cherry Hill Junior High School, Mr. Greg Sanford at Polytechnic Institute, and the deceased Dr. Jacob Abel at the University of Pennsylvania Towne School of Engineering. I promise that I will never let you down.

Index